LOVE
AND
OTHER
INFECTIOUS
DISEASES

ALSO BY MOLLY HASKELL

From Reverence to Rape:
  The Treatment of Women in the Movies

LOVE AND OTHER INFECTIOUS DISEASES

A MEMOIR

Molly Haskell

William Morrow and Company, Inc.
New York

This is a true story. Only some of the names have been changed.

Library of Congress Cataloging-in-Publication Data

Haskell, Molly.
    Love and other infectious diseases : a memoir / Molly Haskell.
       p.   cm.
    ISBN 0-688-07006-X
    1. Haskell, Molly.   2. Sarris, Andrew.   3. Cytomegalovirus
infections—Patients—United States—Biography.   4. Marriage.
I. Title.
RC136.8.S27H37   1990
306.81—dc20   89-28554
                                                                   CIP

Printed in the United States of America

First Edition

1 2 3 4 5 6 7 8 9 10

BOOK DESIGN BY MARSHA COHEN

For Andrew, of course

ACKNOWLEDGMENTS

Among the many kind individuals who helped me in the writing of this book, I would like to mention the following:

My editors, Ann Bramson and Laurie Orseck, for their unfailing enthusiasm, good judgment, and patience;

Georges Borchardt and Anne Borchardt, my agents and good friends;

The doctors who provided counsel and information beyond the call of medical duty: Jeffrey Laurence, Robert Ascheim, Barry Hartman, Samuel Rapoport. And Richard Hannay;

My mother, Mary Haskell, whose first commandment to her infant daughter was to tell the truth;

And all the friends—some of whom appear in the story and others who do not—who sustained me during the difficult period described in the book and afterward.

Also, I would like to thank the Rockefeller Foundation for providing me with a writing residency at the Villa Serbelloni at Bellagio, Italy, in 1987.

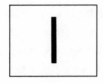

It should have been a dark and stormy night, with rumblings of mortality, when Andrew announced he had a headache and fever. Instead, it was a balmy night in late June, daylight stretching to its sweet, languorous limits, the sort of night when New York is a thing of beauty, a joy to return to. We'd been back for a week or so from the Cannes Film Festival, with brief stopovers in Paris and Italy, and summer had come in our absence. The fruit blossoms in the corner of Central Park we could see from our window had been replaced by green leaves, and the runners, bare-legged and sleeveless, were out in force, having been joined by fair-weather joggers. I'd once done some jogging myself, but no longer.

We were tired, exhausted, but then Cannes was an endurance test in itself, and being tired was a condition we'd come to accept as normal, the price we paid for our supposedly glamorous and exciting lives as married movie reviewers. The sort of schedule that friends and colleagues seemed to manage routinely—going to screenings, completing deadlines, overcoming jet lag—had us panting by the end of the day. We were Nick and Nora Charles, Tracy and Hepburn, the screwball couple dwindling into middle age when the screws start to loosen and life to unwind.

If there was anything obviously wrong, it was chronic: this business of *mutual* fatigue, and our inability or unwillingness to distinguish where it came from and to whom it belonged. We shared it as part of the mysterious and exacting bond of sympathy that united us: it would have been impolite, a betrayal, for one of us to be tired and not the other. Perhaps it was because we were falling at the same speed—like the person and the object falling from the roof in Einstein's famous Principle of Equivalence—that we didn't recognize that we were falling at all. It was the rest of the world that was furiously in motion; we were at stasis.

The difference was that Andrew seemed to accept this as the natural order of things. He lived closer to the ground, and was content to be supine—his Mediterranean background, he said. If he was tired, he guiltlessly and happily took a nap. He lived in his head (it was the theater of his life, the place where the show always went on), and he treated his body the way you're supposed to treat plants, with benign neglect. It obliged by taking him pretty much where he wanted to go, which was never very far. He was like those box turtles, recently discovered in North Carolina, whose entire lifespan (of 125 years!) had been lived within a 100-yard radius of where they were born. Andrew's locomotion was the human equivalent of a yard a year, and a sort of mystique had developed around it. His ability to get to things without moving had made him something of a legend in tennis hacker circles, where he managed to win games, matches, and tournaments by standing stolidly in one spot while his opponent scurried from corner to corner.

I was the manic one, driven, restless, furious at my tiredness even as I rushed from one activity, one stimulus, to another, from screening to tennis game, from writing to friends, like a surfer catching waves, then crashing. I always looked and felt harried, and I could tell from our friend Billy's expression when he arrived for dinner that night that if he'd had to bet on one of us becoming seriously ill, it would have been me.

A pal from pre–New York days, Billy was a patrician good ole boy, deceptively genial in the style of the transplanted Southerner. Deceptive, because if they were as easygoing as they appear to be, these refugees would never have left easygoing Anniston, Alabama, or Lubbock, Texas, or Richmond, Virginia, for the prickly, restless, neurotic anonymity of New York. I knew Billy in the way one knows relatives—with a companionable sense of familiarity, yet not well at all. He was a lawyer involved in environmental issues, and his radicalism had a way of getting under Andrew's skin, so I felt something was amiss when Andrew failed to get into an argument with him. We had invited him over for dinner and what commiseration we could offer. His wife, Ellen, had died of cancer, in a particularly horrible and haunting death, earlier in the spring. During the nine months following her discovery of a breast tumor the summer before, it had ravaged her body like a forest fire. Ellen, a smart and scrappy woman who worked as a lawyer for Planned Parenthood, had had no intention of taking it lying down, and if positive thinking were the solution, she would be alive today. Cancer had made her furious and she had gone into overdrive, seeing friends round the clock, playing tennis, working like a demon, taking the offensive like a tigress protecting her young, and one by one her "young"—her bones, her lymph glands, her liver, and her nervous system—went down before the enemy. When I saw her at Columbia Presbyterian Hospital about a week and a half before she died, she was blind, she couldn't eat, and she weighed about sixty-five pounds. She was still making plans for the future.

We talked politics. Then, "I'm going to write about this as soon as I get my sight back," she said. And "Do you think I'll be able to play tennis?" I was floored. How could she even imagine . . . ? I said yes, of course, grateful at least that she couldn't see the astonishment in my face. I couldn't get the sight of her out of my mind. I was looking at death, and death was laughing at me.

We hadn't seen Billy since the funeral, and we wanted to touch base, talk about Ellen if he wanted to, laugh, weep, get drunk, reminisce. Or argue. Death and bereavement wouldn't have gotten in the way of a good argument. Andrew had a low boiling point in those days, and Billy always seemed to know how to increase the heat to just the right notch. Politically, Andrew was both passionately polemical and a man without a country, a sort of reverse Will Rogers: he had never met a man with whom he could agree. A Stevensonian liberal, yet conservative by temperament (a holdover from his parents' monarchist views), he was alienated from radicals on the one hand—many of our friends and all of his colleagues at The Village Voice—and, on the other, from the dyed-in-the-wool Republicans we occasionally met. Strangely enough, we had arrived via different routes at the same ideological resting place so that in essence, if not in formation, our politics were identical. The big difference was that Andrew would force a confrontation while I would do anything to avoid one. In a new group of people, Andrew had a way of recognizing a potential adversary, then luring him onto controversial ground, forcing him to make just the remark that would set Andrew off. Billy had only to raise the subject of Cuba or the Hollywood Ten for Andrew to sniff out the subtext and respond as to the red flag of Stalinism. But on this particular night, he failed even to bristle.

The next day and the next, as his fever fluctuated between 102 and 104, he was testy and querulous with me, resisting when I tried to make him drink liquids, irritated if I left him, yet unresponsive when I was there. This, given the intensity of our relationship, and his sweetness and solicitude where I was concerned, was odd behavior.

Normally, Andrew was the sort of person who rarely got sick, but when he did, it was grand opera. If he got a stomachache during the night, he would wake me up, writhe in agony, moan and groan, nervously smack his lips (if I threatened to doze off), call in the police and the fire department, and leave messages every five minutes with the doctor's answering service. I, on the other hand, when stricken, would lie in clenched-teeth silence the whole night. He was no less histrionic about *my* ailments. He made heavy weather of my least complaint, while I made light of his. It was accepted between us that Andrew, who had inherited none of his Greek mother's Spartanism, was the melodramatic Mediterranean, I the stoical WASP; he was the one who would fly off the handle at any moment, while I would do anything to preserve decorum. As so often happens in marriage, roles that had begun almost playfully, to give line and shape to our lives, had hardened like suits of armor and taken us prisoner. They weren't exactly false, just too narrow and ill-fitting for the ways in which we had expanded, changed each other over the course of fifteen years. We were a long-running comedy routine—Laurel and Hardy, Jack and Ms. Sprat—who didn't dare play against type or risk losing our audience (ourselves; our friends).

If we were a combination that no right-thinking biologist or horsebreeder would have brought together, nevertheless we seemed to mesh symbiotically, like one of those ocean hybrids, the clam and algae.

Only in tennis, our mutual battleground, did we give full play to the tensions that lay submerged in the rest of our lives. Tennis was the guilty secret of our marriage, an addiction masquerading as an "activity," and I mention it here because I secretly suspected that Andrew's illness might have been brought on by a humiliating loss the previous Sunday in a mixed-doubles tournament.

One fateful day in Cape Cod, my mother had persuaded Andrew to pick up a tennis racket so that we might enjoy together the sport she so loved. Thanks to this seemingly innocent gesture on the part of my mother, a talented and keenly competitive sportswoman herself, our marriage had never been the same since. Other couples choose sports and hobbies that will bring them together; we chose one that would tear us apart. Like bridge, it would express what the social scientists call "the latent pathology of the partnership," and if there was ever a sport designed to bring out the vulnerability of our marriage, it was tennis.

There was a Jekyll and Hyde quality to the thing. Off the court we were to all appearances a well-matched partnership of "equals," moderately successful and functioning. Andrew was a full-time professor at Columbia, author of ten books, and the weekly film critic for *The Village Voice*. I had written on theater, film, and women's issues since 1969, had published a book, and was currently film reviewer for *Vogue*. We had a host of friends, mostly writers and academics, the usual manic-depressive New Yorkers compared to whose tics and neuroses ours seemed minor. We lived in a harmony of mutual interests and tastes, with surprisingly little friction considering our differences in background and temperament. Perhaps too little friction, hence tennis, the Dorian Gray portrait of our otherwise happy marriage, the demonic arena in which our pasts caught up with us and punished us for thinking we could escape.

The very qualities that attracted me to Andrew—his unworldliness, his lack of concern about how he looked—became a liability when he appeared on the court, a walking affront to the genteel Country Club tradition. In mismatching shirt and shorts, socks with different color stripes, ostentatiously disheveled, he was a spectacle that only his mother could have loved . . . and of course, only a man so loved, only a man with unshakable inner confidence, could appear in public, walk onto the court, in such disarray. Whereas I was determined to maintain decorum at all times, he was an exasperating compendium of form-shattering mannerisms. He would walk at a snail's pace to the back court to pick up balls, move lethargically into place for his serve, and then bounce balls ritualistically for this none-too-awesome feature of his game. During play, while everyone moved swiftly and silently around the court, he heaved and exhaled like a sick rhinoceros, the result of a tennis pro having once told him to breathe deeply during tense moments. This attempt to quiet his nerves merely got on everyone else's.

His game was crafty and inelegant: he would hit soft, bloopy balls, designed to exact a maximum expenditure of energy from his opponent and a minimum from himself—a sign of his indifference to form and his primitive belief that the point of the game was to get the ball over the net as many times as possible. Also, a sure way of getting ostracized. "Oh, he gets everything back" was the kiss of death in macho circles. It meant you played a sissy, defensive game, which in turn meant that Andrew was constantly being blackballed by the Big Boys, the hard-hitters.

There seemed to be a collusion between Pam, the games mistress, and the A players, to keep Andrew out of the good games. He would storm away from the club, declaring he would never return. A half hour later, he would cool down.

"It's horrible, like being back in school all over again," he would say, trying desperately to regain his dignity. And he would tell me about the awful day when he had been rejected by the fifth-grade softball team, a childhood trauma that had taken on mythic overtones and that he seemed destined to relive at every club in Westhampton. It was a heartrending story: his classmates had persuaded the fifth-grade teacher to keep him after school so that he'd arrive too late to get on the team. My eyes would well with tears, I would shake my fist at the thought of the treacherous teacher. Yet part of me—oh, faithless wife!—would identify with Andrew's torturers. There was something about him—his disposition rather than his athletic ability, which was considerable—that made one want to choose almost anyone else for one's team. He wasn't a "happy warrior." He brought a spirit of gloom and foreboding onto the playing field. One look at Andrew on the tennis court and I knew I'd have been one of the ringleaders of the fifth-grade mob.

"Keep him in the classroom," you'd want to plead with the teacher, with Pam. "Don't let him rain on our parade." But Andrew was compelled to create and re-create the scene of shame, as the rest of us—Pam, myself, others—were sucked into the role of tormentors.

Then, time—minutes—would pass. Andrew would be awash in contrition, I in forgiveness. We would laugh. It would never happen again.

"The difference between the Freudians and the rest of the world," he'd say, allying himself implicitly with the former, "is that the Freudians know we never grow up." Andrew had ridden in, a knight in the shining armor of insight, to rescue the buffoon he'd just been.

How could you not love a man who says that? And in laughing and forgiving, in our wisdom and awareness, it seemed we had exorcised our demons, but in fact we had merely wiped the slate clean, prepared ourselves for a repeat performance the next day.

I was neurotic in a less obvious way. Unlike Andrew, I was determinedly cheerful, my good sport's smile stretched across my taut face, my shoulders hunched up to my ears as high as a camel's humps, tense with a competitiveness I didn't dare admit, much less show. The temperamental differences that gave zest to the rest of our lives rose up to haunt us on the tennis court, yet we couldn't give up.

As with bridge players, neurotic behavior among tennis-playing couples is legion—which is why we never quite saw how grotesque we were—but we were in a class by ourselves. We ran through clubs the way other people run through tennis balls. In five years, we'd belonged to four in the Westhampton area, storming off at the end of each year in high dudgeon, joining a new one the following year, sure the problem was not us but always the "cliques" (definition of "clique": three or four people who won't play with you). Play with Andrew, that is, since it was his role to play the troublemaker, mine to trundle along behind like a martyr, mending fences.

Yet the virtue of his defect emerged in tournament competition, where all that tenacity and stubbornness and imperviousness came to his aid. In the summer of 1982, Andrew entered the Men's B Tournament, and winning week after week, beating superior players (his quarterfinalist opponent quit tennis for good and took up pottery), he won the trophy, was crowned King of the Bs.

Together, however, we were a disaster. We detracted from each other as a doubles team, and we couldn't even warm up without fuming and sulking. We fought constantly, endured terrible post-game re-criminations, yet continued, year after year, to force the issue, believing that any two people who were as compatible as we were off the court—and who loved tennis as much as we did—should be able to translate these qualities and our relative competence into a successful doubles partnership.

All of this is by way of saying that like most addictions, tennis played a major if misunderstood role in our lives, and because of this, I had a strange feeling that Andrew's illness had been brought on by the blow to his tennis ego—the most vulnerable part of a fairly sturdy sense of self—from a tennis defeat we'd suffered in the annual husband-wife tournament.

"That's it, and I mean it," Andrew said. "I'm never playing tennis again." I had heard the renunciation speech often, but never delivered quite so mournfully or with such conviction.

That was on Sunday, June 24. On Tuesday, Andrew apparently renounced his renunciation, for he met his friend and *Voice* colleague Ross Wetzsteon, another tennis junkie, for their weekly game at the Murray Hill Racket Club, and Ross remarked afterward that he'd never seen Andrew so down-at-the-mouth and so dog tired.

It was that night, when Billy came, that Andrew announced his headache and fever, and on Wednesday it oscillated between 103 and 104. As alarming as any of his symptoms was Andrew's failure to take an interest in Wimbledon, which was being broadcast every afternoon on HBO. Inveterate fans, we usually spent these two weeks holed up every evening from five to eight, avoiding calls, postponing engage-ments or taping the day's sessions when some unavoidable duty pried us away. I was becoming more and more uneasy as Andrew would drift into the living room, glance at the television, and return listlessly to bed, where he would lie with glazed eyes, radiating heat like a furnace, utterly indifferent to my presence.

I knew what every ordinary person knows—that fever itself isn't harmful and that, on the contrary, it's a sign of the body's struggle with infectious agents. But Andrew's moods seemed to go beyond the normal lassitude and irritability of the flu patient.

That afternoon, I called Sam Gessner, our internist. "What's wrong with him?" I wailed. Sam was our doctor and a friend of some fifteen years.

Asked to describe Andrew's condition, I said, "He's . . . out of it. Not delirious, but not really . . . responding."

"You're not being very clear, Molly," said Sam. That's the kind of thing he always said to me, to nip in the bud any pretensions I might have as a lay diagnostician.

Sam was cool, an anti-alarmist. We had a genial but needling relationship that both expressed and concealed certain unarticulated feelings: his suspicion that I didn't think him the most driven and dedicated of doctors; mine that he wasn't. Of course, my concept of an appropriate degree of dedication was somewhat beyond the normal expectation, even in the days when doctors were thought to be members of a calling: twenty-four-hour service to the Hippocratic Oath, a willingness to forgo pleasure, forsake family, devote oneself unflaggingly to one's patients (especially me), and with any time left over, keep abreast of the latest developments through the medical journals. Sam was on vacation whenever anything went wrong, never mind that whenever anything went wrong it was August, Christmas, Thanksgiving. . . . I also felt that doctors, like ministers, should work more or less for nothing. (After all, isn't the adulation of a grateful flock remuneration enough?) And Sam thought doctors should work for a great deal more than nothing and enjoy the fruits of their labor in various earthly paradises sprinkled through the Caribbean.

At Sam's suggestion, I took Andrew by his office the following day for a blood test: if bacteria were the source of the fever, he could be treated with antibiotics. Trying to convince myself he was actually getting better, I left him in the waiting room and fled to a screening. I told myself that it was our policy to carry on when the other was sick (a policy that Andrew had had more occasion to implement than I for reasons that will become apparent), and that my presence was required—it was a special screening for members of the New York

Film Festival Selection Committee—but in fact it was a relief just to get away from his scorching un-Andrew-like presence for a few hours.

Sam told me on Friday that the blood tests were negative, but not to worry—it was probably just a virus that would run its course. This was an altogether reasonable assumption, but I was already dreading the weekend. Weekends, I knew from experience, were when emergencies were most likely to happen, and weekends (particularly summer weekends) were when New York doctors went away, especially New York Hospital doctors and especially Sam. There were always covering doctors, of course; but what kind of doctor would be working on a summer weekend when the superstars were out gardening or golfing or drinking or driving around in their Porsches? (A wallflower! An understudy! A doctor nobody wanted!)

That night, Andrew was still feverish and agitated. In order to get some uninterrupted sleep, so I could care for him the next day, I moved into the adjacent room, the office that doubled as guest room, for the night. Early Saturday morning, I was startled by a clatter, which I dimly recognized, as I came to, as the sound of water glasses crashing from the night table to the floor. I rushed in, only to meet Andrew stumbling toward the bathroom. He got himself in and out, but when he emerged, his eyes were darting furiously. "I'm better, I'm better," he said incongruously, in a kind of breathless babble. "I think I'm getting better."

I felt a chill of apprehension. I knew I had to take his temperature, yet, sensing some escalation of the disease, I could hardly bring myself to do so. With good reason: the unmistakably clear numbers on the digital thermometer read 105.9. (Was that enough to die from? To fry the brain? I didn't want to know.) I called Sam's number, left a message for the covering doctor, and waited for a period that was surely no more than fifteen minutes but seemed endless. Time is relative. Summer is the blink of an eye, but minutes stretch to infinity when you are alone and responsible for someone else's life. I would have called a friend, the operator, even Dial-a-Prayer, anything just to hear the sound of a sane human voice if I hadn't been afraid of tying up the phone.

At last the phone rang; a doctor whose name I didn't get—Gribovsky, Gabriski, Kandinsky?—said to bring Andrew in and he would meet us at the Emergency Room.

That proved no easy task. Getting Andrew dressed was minor compared to my effort to convince Lionel, one of our doormen, to call a taxi. Lionel was a "character," an awkward behemoth who had real affection for his tenants, especially Andrew and me (he was a film buff, and lay awake nights thinking of the *minutest* of trivia questions ["Mr. Sarris, Mr. Sarris, whatever happened to Darren McGavín?"] with which to trap Andrew when he was late and scurrying to or from the elevator), but who was conscientious to a fault when it came to the rule that doormen should stick to their post. More than any of our other doormen, Lionel was draconian in his observance of this rule: he would raise his hands in mock helplessness (his red face secretly pleased), as some tenant struggled with packages, or an elderly man stumbled getting out of a taxi that was a foot beyond the radius Lionel had ascribed to himself. As I yelled at him over the intercom, I thought fleetingly and enviously of other people's chronicles of sick husbands and Good Samaritan doormen rushing to the scene of the crisis, running blocks to find taxis and racing wheelchairs as far as the hospital.

"Lionel," I screamed, "Andrew is critically ill. You *have* to get me a taxi," but it was no use. I went back, struggled to get Andrew dressed and down and through the downpour to the corner, where we somehow managed to get a cab. Within minutes we were pulling in to the familiar cobblestone courtyard of New York Hospital's Emergency Room entrance.

Yes, familiar. If Andrew had had his wits about him, we would have looked at each other with yet another forlorn expression of *déjà vu*. This was June of 1984 and the beginning of what what would come to look like a grotesque game of medical one-upmanship. I had arrived in February 1982 at this same entrance with pains for what proved to be an obstruction of the intestine, requiring emergency surgery.

It was the evil work of scar tissue, or adhesions, from an earlier surgery. Never having been really sick in my life, in August of 1981 I collapsed on a tennis court in Westhampton, got through a weekend of pain and nausea, and found myself in Southampton Hospital the following week being prepared for emergency surgery. The problem was diagnosed as a ruptured ectopic pregnancy. This strange out-of-the-blue occurrence was the first sign of mortality in our married life, after which nothing that ever happened to us, not my subsequent two hospitalizations, nor even Andrew's calamity now, would ever seem so startling.

Though fairly ordinary in medical terms, my illnesses had changed the way we lived and behaved with each other, subtly altering the roles we played and contributing to the overall weariness that had settled down between us like a fog.

My battle scars, one across my pelvis, the other a major highway down my abdomen running into it, were no longer an angry vermilion, only a pale pink, and I was rather proud of them. The terrible depression that had overwhelmed me after the first operation was an experience I didn't want to repeat, and I had gratefully accepted the verdict that adhesions and obstructions are a purely mechanical problem (as opposed to such stress-related gastrointestinal problems as colitis and ulcers, for example); therefore they weren't "telling me something" about my life—that, as my mother would have said, and did, that I was "overdoing it." Overdoing it: who didn't? Wasn't that what New York life was all about? What life was all about?

And now here we were, less than two years later, in this grim basement antechamber where it is always four in the morning.

The Emergency Room is actually a sadly lackluster affair in contrast to the bustling battle zone pictured in television melodramas and medical soap operas, where support teams stand by, oxygen masks and IVs at the ready, while bleeding and inert bodies on stretchers, jostling with each other like bumper cars, come and go, and wounded barroom pugilists stagger in. Actually, there's a grimy pall, more like a small-town Greyhound bus station early on a Sunday morning. Past the admitting desk, there's a "visitor's section," outfitted with cheap hard-back chairs, bright orange for Optimism, where those who've accompanied the sick and wounded (it always seems to be the same people) sit slumped, trying to ignore the huge television suspended high up in a corner, the on-off knob out of reach, relentlessly beaming newscasts and soap operas and game shows on the unattending.

Yet I'd been rescued from disaster here, healed and soldered, and

I felt a sense of homecoming. I even recognized the woman on the admitting desk, a beacon of humanity and intelligence who had surprised me the first time around when she had known our by-lines and was familiar with our work. It is never a small thing for a writer to be recognized but it was especially gratifying here, in this Dantesque Limbo where you are stripped of clothes, personality, identity, suspended in a state that is neither grace nor damnation, a slab of flesh upon a table waiting to be assigned your circle of inferno. This kindly Cerberus was as interested in our names as our insurer's, and she was medically savvy as well.

"You're lucky he hasn't had a seizure," she said. "They often do with a fever that high." Actually the comment was hardly reassuring since I hadn't thought of this possibility before, but at least she was on my side.

I thought back to the low point of my hospital life, a humiliating examination at the hands of a woman gynecologist when I came into the Emergency Room in February of 1982. She was the resident on duty, a tough, no-nonsense prison-warden type, who'd been called in because of suspected endometriosis. I'd been having severe pains for some months, but this woman, who'd modeled herself on Louise Fletcher's performance in *One Flew over the Cuckoo's Nest*, quite obviously thought I was faking.

Long, detailed questions about my sex life, followed by repeated questions about what I'd had to eat and drink for dinner. When I protested I hadn't eaten or drunk for two days, she eyed me skeptically, and fairly gloated when she pronounced I didn't have endometriosis. She was ready to send me home with what she obviously thought was nothing more serious than indigestion when a series of tests revealed I had the obstruction at a dangerously advanced stage.

"Hoo-ray," I wanted to cry, perversely. "There *is* something wrong with me! Look at this, you bitch. Give me death but don't call me a hysterical woman!"

Yes, oh yes, we've made great strides in the last twenty years in getting ourselves taken seriously by the medical profession; depression is a real illness, not an imaginary one. Likewise PMS. Yet beneath our apparent truce lurks the woman who is still more afraid of being thought hysterical than of being seriously ill. Marching through our collective unconscious are cultural stereotypes: those forties doctor movies when the young intern, at the crossroads of his career, is asked by the mentor-doctor: "Well, do you want to be a *real* doctor and cure yellow fever or [eyes narrowing, voice sardonic] do you want to be a *society* doctor and take care of hysterical rich women and listen to their imaginary ailments?"

About an hour or so after we got there, the doctor—Dr. Howard Kempinski was his name—arrived.

"I've been talking to your husband," he said, "and that doesn't sound like the man who writes those insightful columns for *The Village Voice.*"

Now I grew wary. A little flattery is a welcome thing but too much recognition arouses suspicion. I couldn't imagine Dr. Kempinski reading the *Voice.* His rebel son, perhaps, but not this middle-aged man with a moustache and kindly Jewish-mother eyes. Was this a subterfuge? A ploy designed to divert me from what he knew and didn't want to divulge or, alternately, from the ignorance he didn't want to admit?

He might have been suppressing dark imaginings of his own, or he might have been utterly baffled, but in either case I felt and gratefully accepted the unspoken rule of silence governing our relationship. He wasn't my *real* doctor and was not to be held accountable. I wasn't to press him, and in any case I didn't want to know. There are times when third parties enter our lives, during a crisis, and their detachment allows us breathing space. I remembered, as vividly as if it were yesterday, the long silent trip home when, the day after my father died, a business associate came to pick me up from college. What had finally killed my father after a three-year battle was ALS (amyotrophic lateral sclerosis), the degenerative illness known as Lou Gehrig's disease, but the acquaintance said only that he had taken a turn for the worse. A neurological disorder characterized by a deterioration of the muscles, ALS is a death sentence without a reprieve and is one of the most harrowing illnesses there is. The victim loses the use of his arms and legs, is finally unable to talk or swallow, while the brain remains cruelly clear. My father had been near death for three months, but he'd managed to hang on until I packed my trunk and left home for the first time.

As this virtual stranger and I drove through the low mountains of western Virginia, radiant with the beginnings of fall color, neither of us spoke of my father or named the event that lay between us. For two hours we sat in silence, two hours during which, thanks to this man to whom I was obliged to say nothing, I could keep my father alive. More than that: in these two hours in which the rules of intercourse were suspended, life itself was suspended, and I could bring him back to the way he was, tall and handsome, before the disease had begun its ravaging course, turning a bright-eyed god into a withered wraith of a man.

And now Dr. Kempinski, this doctor who was standing in for Sam, allowed us both to remain in limbo a while longer, prisoners on whom no sentence has yet been passed. The next order of business was getting Andrew admitted. When he reported that Andrew had requested a private room, my eyes rolled upward. Thanks to our recent experiences, Andrew knew full well the prohibitive cost of a private room—$190.00 a day over and above what Blue Cross/Blue Shield would pay. We had no source of income other than our writing and teaching jobs, though as Kempinski had no way of knowing that, I gave him to understand the situation as delicately as I could. This was so like the Andrew of the money's-no-object-in-a-crisis philosophy, and if a real crisis didn't arise, he would invent one, and then find ingenious and expensive ways to solve it. The current situation would no doubt qualify for "only the best treatment"; and in asking for a private room, what Andrew no doubt had in mind, to the extent that his mind was in the picture at all, were the river-view privates and semi-privates in "the Tower," i.e., Baker 12, 13, or 14. These rooms, luxurious by the standards of the rest of the hospital (about which more later), were occupied by an assortment of VIPs—the stretch-limo crowd of plutocrats, celebrities, gangsters who had escaped the fatal intentions of a hit man, public officials, and even ordinary people whose doctors got them in or who lucked into them.

The three Tower floors had wide halls, were bright and cheerful, and best of all had access to terraces and a separate kitchen that prepared almost-edible food, but they were not known as the best nursing floors and for acute cases other floors were preferable.

On these grounds alone, I vetoed Andrew's request, but by that time he had been categorized as possibly contagious and therefore requiring a private room (which would therefore be wholly reimbursable). This turned out to be not one of the Baker rooms, but a rather large, grim room on one of the neurology floors.

It was still raining hard, and the room's meager light, from one small, northern window, added a sense of gloom. Andrew was placed on a cooling blanket to bring the fever down, and then came the battery of social and medical-history interviews that are the patient's rite of initiation into a teaching hospital and that seem to be conducted with exhausting redundancy. Name, age (Caucasian male, 55). Where were you . . . ? What did you eat, drink . . . ? Past illnesses, hospitalizations, vaccinations, etc. Over and over again, with each new shift or resident or doctor, like a police investigation. "But, Officer," says the weary witness, "I already told the police everything." You know the checking and double-checking are for your benefit, and for the information of each battery of physicians, but why does it just seem as if nobody's listening, as if the accumulation of data is not a way of understanding, of zeroing in on the ailment, but a way of covering the bases to avoid slip-ups and mis-diagnoses (no small thing, to be sure).

By 8:00 P.M. the fever was down to 103.5.

After he had been pancultured and treated "symptomatically" (Tylenol, ice, applied to symptoms rather than deeper causes), he was, to our astonishment, given a third degree about drugs and sex.

An intern told me that Andrew had "presented" like someone who'd had "bad drugs on the street." If I'd been in a different frame of mind, I'd have found some amusement trying to imagine how the image of Andrew scoring a deal on Forty-second Street would have struck our friends. This was a man whose one encounter with grass, among a group of superannuated hippies in the mid-seventies, had been a social disaster (he'd "toked," held onto the joint instead of passing it on, and thus marked himself as a hopeless neophyte) and whose idea of the illicit was softcore porn movies and fantasies of Margaret Sullavan and Vivien Leigh.

This was 1984, remember, an age of relative innocence regarding AIDS. We both knew of the disease, and possibly even HIV (then called HTLV-III), the actual virus producing the disease, but only dimly, and thought of it as something affecting a minute and exclusively gay portion of the population. For instance, across the hall from Andrew was an angelic-looking and very sick young man who was being walked up and down the corridor by a male friend. When I was told he had leukemia, I saw no reason to doubt it. The medical community and hospital staff were, of course, far more aware of the spread of the disease, and would have automatically considered the possibility, though there was no specific AIDS test at the time. From what I could gather, I didn't think they seriously considered Andrew as a possible carrier, but who knew . . . ? The idea was ludicrous, of course . . . Andrew and a same-sex love affair! Andrew and an opposite-sex love affair! Andrew and I were not quite as chaste as Abélard and Héloïse, but we were not dues-paying members of the liberated generation. As we had grown closer, more "familial," we had lost that separation, the need to overcome distance and strangeness that is the aphrodisiac to desire. In its hothouse intensity, the modern marriage unconsciously seeks to re-create the cocoon of the original family, inheriting its Oedipal taboos: we seek affection, closeness, intimacy, togetherness, a buffer against chaos, then wonder why we no longer experience the frisson of sexual longing.

Leaving Andrew to the tender mercies of the staff, I went home to pack a few of his things, gather my thoughts, and face the most important problem: whether or not to call my mother. Under normal emergency conditions, I would have called and she would have come, but we were in a cold-war period and relations were strained. Put simply, the three of us couldn't be together under the same roof for more than twenty-four hours without some sort of explosion occurring, and the last time Andrew and I had visited Mother in Florida we had had to cut short our stay and make a hurried and ignominious exit.

It was a tragedy for me that the two people I loved most couldn't get along, yet it was a situation that I, in my own dividedness, had created. Only children, someone wrote, expect those they love to love each other, and the child in me persisted long after the adult should have taken over and accepted the inevitable. And yet, beloved of triangles, creators of triangles by our very birth, how is it possible not to keep re-creating them, and reinserting our mediating and troublemaking selves into their midst?

Things would begin cordially enough, since on the surface we all wanted this to work, or so we thought. We would find ourselves playing tennis, that grand game that Mother had found to bring us all together, and a seeping cloud of ill will would envelop us. Mother was getting on now, and not up to strenuous play, but she was determined to hang in there. Andrew, unorthodox in style as I've indicated earlier, was not a sight to gladden the heart of his mother-in-law. When they played partners, Mother simply pretended he wasn't there, dashing around in front of him, while he would call out, "Mary!" and throw down his racket in exasperation.

Basically their pained looks and noises would pass each other by and hit me, like magnetized arrows, and settle in my stomach.

The cocktail hour was our Armageddon, the moment when the demons that had been suppressed by sobriety and the presence of outsiders came to the surface. The first drink would pass in a strained facsimile of civilized decorum, but then Andrew, who was partially deaf anyway and whose voice had a tendency to rise with the least emotion, would unwittingly interrupt Mother. Mother would wince; I would feel her wince and cringe; I would be angry with her for her fastidiousness, angry with Andrew for his boorishness as we turned into a Tennessee Williams parody of ourselves: Andrew the elemental brute, Mother the impossibly refined hostess, and me, rigid with the sense of my two halves breaking apart, feeling vaguely responsible.

Tensions between in-laws are nothing new, are the stuff of jokes and cartoons, but the ferocity of ours had to do with the fact that Mother hadn't ever really accepted my marriage as a *fait accompli*. It wasn't just what Andrew was, but what he represented: my other life, a me that was far out of range, even antithetical to the me Mother had brought me up to be. Or what she'd *thought* and *intended* she'd brought me up to be: a ladylike daughter of the Old Confederacy who would marry appropriately, join the Garden Club, and settle down and raise a family nearby. Andrew was my rejection of that dream staring her in the face.

After this last visit, Mother and I had determined to have no more three-way reunions. We had arrived via our own methods at the practices of the aborigines described by Freud in *Totem and Taboo*, in which all communication between mothers and sons-in-law is prohibited. Hinting that we of the civilized world might do worse than adopt such an arrangement, Freud, in one of his brilliant if overingenious feats of interpretation, translates tribal practices into modern psychological terms: the son's incestuous wish for his own mother, whose place the mother-in-law takes; the mother's possessiveness regarding her daughter and resistance to surrendering her dominant position in the household; the husband's jealousy of the person his wife loved first; and his unwillingness to face this older version of what his idealized wife will become. There may have been bits and pieces of these factors in the tensions that arose when we were together, particularly an unwillingness on Mother's part to relinquish control of the daughter—in a traditional society, keeping a daughter within her sphere of influence is one of a woman's major powers; it may be the one real power she has. But mainly, Mother was a sensible, rational woman. In her eyes, Andrew and I simply didn't make sense, we couldn't *work*.

Still, didn't a disaster of this magnitude mean that all bets were off, that the avoidance taboo could be lifted temporarily and hostilities suspended? I simply couldn't imagine getting through this without Mother. Anyway, if Andrew remained in the hospital, Mother and I would be home alone. But that only made me more apprehensive. Mightn't she not want to come precisely because she sensed she might have me all to herself? The question wasn't even whether Mother would come—I was sure she would, for me. But if I suspected there might be, in the depths of her unconscious, some small note of satisfaction, some hope for Andrew's death, I couldn't have borne it.

I made the call, my ears pricked for the slightest note of ambivalence. Her reaction was slow—it always is. She doesn't take in bad news right away, but absorbs it in increments, sometimes taking twenty-four hours or more. It's a habit she got into when my father was ill, when, she once told me, she began to shut down to the increasingly bad news that the doctors, optimistic or lying at first, had given. She felt that her mind was like a row of mailboxes, and each time my father came in with another piece of bad news she would ask him to wait while she composed herself, then she would place the latest tidings in an empty slot and shut the door on it. As we talked, I realized she hadn't quite taken it all in, but I also felt, with overwhelming relief, the sympathy in her voice, uncomplicated distress as she promised to fly up the next day. There are times when only a mother will do, when differences go by the board and that powerful link that is the oldest and earliest human bond reasserts itself in its purest and most unambivalent form. In distress, Mother's comforting presence would be essential, unequivocal. What's more, she would be useful, rising to the occasion with the dazzling strength of a Southern woman in crisis. If her concern was primarily for me, it was for a me that she knew would be shattered if anything happened to Andrew.

When I returned to the hospital, I was greeted in the hallway by the woman resident—a Gloria Steinem look-alike, with large spectacles, a curtain of blond hair, a supreme air of competence— and told that Andrew had had a "bed-shaking seizure." Fortunately he hadn't gone into a coma, but his CPK count had gone up to 801, indicating a possible heart attack.

CPK is an enzyme inside the muscle cells that is released when the cells are broken—by a car accident, a stroke, or a heart attack, even by marathon running. The normal count is 50 to 120. Although marathoners often register as high as 3,000, there's a difference between CPKs in the striated (skeletal) muscles in the legs, where a count of 10,000 to 15,000 is not considered dangerous, and those in the smooth heart muscles, where a much smaller rise can signal a stroke or a massive heart attack. There's a special machine that differentiates between the two kinds of muscles, separating them into bands, but it wasn't in use on weekends, so we wouldn't know until Monday what had caused the rise, but meanwhile Andrew was hooked up to an EKG to monitor the heart.

One of the doctors reported that Andrew had begun acting out movie plots (verbally, I presume, since he was hardly mobile!), and he tested positive on what they call mental-status changes. He fared poorly, for example, on such basic tests as name, date, location, and spelling a word backward, on the somewhat more difficult serial numbers (count backward from 100 by 7s), and on memory—he was given three unrelated nouns which he had to repeat in two or three minutes; but he performed remarkably well on proverbs: in other words, in the area of metaphor (a patient is given a proverb suitable to his cultural or intellectual IQ—say, "People in glass houses shouldn't throw stones"—and asked to explain it).

Of the doctors who examined him, all but one reported normal motor skills and sensations. The exception, Dr. Manuel Ramir, a neurologist I hadn't met yet, noted a Babinski sign on Andrew's chart: when pressure is applied to the ball of the foot the toes should curl around in a grasping motion; instead, Andrew's toes had shot up.

I was ravenous for information, and although most of what I was being given was baffling, I was so flattered at being treated like an intelligent human being that I never asked for amplification or explanation, and simply jotted down words and phrases with the intention of looking them up later. I was afraid that if they realized how dumb or panicked I was, the lines of communication would close. It didn't occur to me that perhaps they'd simply forgotten how to translate information into lay terms, or that there was safety in jargon, and they were breathing a sigh of relief that they'd gotten off so easily.

The problem is that with doctors we begin, like children with their parents, on an unequal basis: we need them more than they need us, and so for the rest of our shared life, while they attend to "important" things, we brood and maneuver, devising whatever tactics we can to get more than our share of their attention. We'll charm, whine, flatter, flirt, grovel, cajole, abase ourselves shamelessly and in whatever way necessary. Like children, we compensate for our powerlessness by being shrewd manipulators. Instinctively, we try to ferret out and play on a doctor's vulnerability, present ourselves in a manner calculated to endear or, failing that, intimidate. My husband, far from being the strong and silent type, was, as we discovered during my hospitalization, the weak and noisy type on my behalf. He made scenes. He had one huge advantage over me and over most of the rest of the world: he didn't care what anyone thought of him. He was uninhibited by that most enslaving need, the need to be loved. If he were in my position now, he would buttonhole the doctors, scream at them, create a major disturbance, and they would respond, if only to shut him up.

I alternated between being the beneficiary of Andrew's explosions or their most embarrassed witness. Sometimes both. Once, at Orly airport, coming back from Cannes, seven of us raced miles from the domestic terminal to connect with an Air France flight to New York just as the plane was pulling out. The nose of the plane was gliding backward as we arrived at the gate, and, seeing us, the faces of the French officials lit up with that smirk of ecstasy that French officialdom assumes when it is enforcing a particularly sadistic regulation. But Andrew, after years of experience with the security people at Cannes, was equal to them. He just let loose a barrage of noise, Mediterranean sound effects, free-floating vituperation—unintelligible but all the more terrifying for that—that had the officials stunned and the plane back at the gate within minutes. It was a heroic moment, in its way, with verbal brute force vanquishing them when mere words wouldn't have had a chance.

We were quickly boarded, and of course Andrew, instead of being given a wide berth as an ugly American, was applauded as a hero by his fellow passengers.

As you may have gathered, taking the offensive was not my style. My feeling (or rationalization) was that aggressiveness might drive them off. Yet passivity was the other side of the equation: if you held back, they would ignore you altogether and, to boot, you would despise yourself for cravenness.

As I was trying to resolve these dilemmas, someone mentioned "brain scan" in the same breath with "Mr. Sarris," and, knowing Andrew's terror of anything to do with the brain, I rushed to his room. As an inured and battle-scarred moviegoer, he could sit through the bloodiest and most depraved horror or gangster movies without flinching, but if anyone mentioned brain scan he would close his eyes, and if sinister medical machinery appeared on the screen he would walk out.

From an early age, Andrew had felt that his head was his destiny, but it had been something of a pawn in the war games between his mother and father.

"Don't hit him on the head! Don't hit him on the head!" his mother would scream in Greek at his father, who was bashing him for some act of stupidity. As she saw it, it was this head that was going to make the family fortune. His father saw it differently.

"*Kaname voythee*," he would say in disgust, meaning "We created a *voythee* [slang for horned animal like a bull, a stupid animal that bashes his head against the wall]."

In a sense, both were true: his brain was his prize possession but what made it so was an unusual combination of refinement and obstinacy, a laserlike incisiveness and a snorting, grunting determination to go its own way.

As writers, we lived in a world in which our brains were always being evaluated, scanned, and tested—metaphorically, at least. I expected his fear of a brain scan would have penetrated the delirium, and sure enough, they had gotten him as far as the door, where he lay on a gurney refusing to be taken an inch farther. After I'd explained in detail the painlessness of the procedure (I'd sat through the movie scenes he'd missed), he agreed to go through with it, but when we finally got down to the X-ray room and put his head in the doughnut hole, he was trembling so much that the procedure took hours instead of minutes.

In the late afternoon, he was returned to his room, and after an orderly returned him to his bed, I left while he was given a spinal tap. Later, as I stood beside him, we talked in a desultory way. Andrew was bemused by the interrogation, particularly the questions regarding his sex life. "They asked me if I'd ever had a homosexual experience," he said, looking quizzically at me, almost laughing.

The atmosphere had become oddly surreal: periods of frantic activity, during which one or more or whole groups of doctors clustered around, getting cultures, asking questions, and nurses came and went, then long stretches of time in which we were left completely alone, to all appearances forgotten. Surely he was just as sick then as before . . . sicker. I was nervous (Would they ever come back? It was Saturday, had they all gone home?). Yet between the moments of acute fear would come dull patches of peace.

He was in the middle of a sentence, when all of a sudden I couldn't understand what he was saying. One minute, he made sense, the next, he didn't. I froze, my hand flew to my throat in a reflex gesture. He was slurring his words. Until now, nothing had really gotten to me—the fever, the seizure, the CPKs, the possible heart attack. But now . . .

"Andrew, Andrew." I stared at him, pleaded with him to talk, connect. But no, the words had begun to slur and fade, the sentences to become garbled. In that split second between sense and nonsense,

past and present came together: it was as if I were standing by my
father's bed, a teenager, watching while he tried to make himself
understood, mentally urging him on, trying to pull the words out of
him as the speech muscles failed. My father's was a neurological disease
that came on slowly and I knew that Andrew didn't have ALS, yet the
likeness was overwhelming: the two men I loved most in the world,
the two men to whom I was bound, heart and soul, by talk, ceasing
to talk!

My father was a prince, a pal, a god, a hero, the incarnation of
a little Southern girl's dream of a daddy, a man who having died when
he did had become three times as heroic in death as he had been in
life. I had done what adolescents do—suppressed the rage, the ambivalence, discounted the tensions that had already developed between
us as I spread my wings—and enshrined him in my memory as a
saintly figure who hovered over my life, eternally young, my "secret
love." He was, in fact, a casually dashing father, sweet and honorable
and funny. But he was a bit of a snob and a dyed-in-the-wool conservative as well, an oak-tree male of the old school who believed that
men should protect and pamper their women—a philosophy that
might well have irritated my independent-minded mother, but not
me. He was a businessman, and like most American businessmen, he
had little interest in literature or the arts—a blindness that might also
have irritated my mother. But what did these failings matter to a child?
If anything, they brought us closer together: we were better matched
mentally and culturally. I was a miniature grown-up desperate to be
treated like an equal, and he was a man-child full of talk, teasing,
blather, rambunctiousness. Before he got sick, we lived in the country,
and he would drive me the ten miles in to school in the morning, go
to his office, then pick me up in the late afternoon. A half hour each
way. On these intimate journeys, we would sit in the front seat of his
Chevrolet, joke, laugh, call each other names, play the radio—"our
songs" like "On Blueberry Hill" or admittedly stupid songs like "How
Much Is That Doggy in the Window?"—discussing his work at the
office and mine at school with the same utter seriousness, as if they
were on the same level.

The farm that we lived on during those seven idyllic years was
the green paradise, in Baudelaire's phrase, of my childhood loves—

loves that centered around animals, books, sweet-smelling fields of alfalfa, and my father, in his old clothes on his John Deere tractor, riding those fields as if he were a captain at sea: memories that were to become warped and blighted by his illness. But our daily trips along River Road have merged into one long-playing memory with which I have continued to redeem his illness and dying. In those drives, talk became the leitmotif of my life, conversation the sacramental bond between a male and female. And of all the horrors of my father's illness, his ceasing to be able to communicate with me was the most painful. No wonder that when it happened to Andrew, it seemed as if night were closing in and a giant shadow from the past falling on me now.

It was different, I kept telling myself that. I could tell by his expression. Andrew looked dazed, didn't know he wasn't making sense, whereas my father had been excruciatingly aware of everything; his eyes, once as bright as stars, recorded the frustration and humiliation of a man who couldn't make himself understood, was too ashamed to want to see anyone but his family. He lost weight, his body shriveled, he could hardly move, but you could see and feel the mind still working perfectly, blazing forth in anguish, like a man trapped in a caved-in mine, his headlamp burning to alert rescuers who can't reach him. He was being buried alive.

Andrew at least felt no such frustration, but the dissimilarity of the diseases didn't lift my spirits. For me, it was as simple and monstrous as a divine judgment, lightning striking in the same place twice. The two men, virtually the same age, struck down through words, words the magical essence of our lives, the umbilical cord between us; it bordered on the uncanny.

Like my father and me, Andrew and I overlapped: we finished each other's sentences until sometimes I thought we were the same person. Sometimes my father would grope for words and grow angry. When no one else could understand him, I would be called in as interpreter. I could somehow intuit what he was saying, put the slurs and gasps and silences into sentences, usually simple requests—for water, to be turned over, to watch the huge television that his brothers and sisters had given him. And now the boat was pulling out for the second time without me. The only cheering thought was that it was too coincidental: I wasn't important enough to be dealt retribution on such a scale.

I ran from the room and found myself sobbing in the arms of a young psychiatric intern who had come to my rescue earlier in the day. Daniel was an aspiring analyst and a wellspring of empathy. Unlike the other doctors, who were focused entirely on Andrew, Daniel intuitively took my part, worried about my state of mind. Where they were cryptic and clinical, he was all compassionate concern. How, I wondered, would he acquire the necessary "abstinence" to become an analyst, to achieve that poised and disinterested state where he could say, as Beatrice must to Virgil, "La vostra miseria non me tange," "Your wretchedness does not touch me." His warm eyes looked into mine and I felt a rush of gratitude. Then I wrung myself out. Though one is never reluctant to have the magnitude of one's suffering confirmed, I was now more famished for information than for fellowship.

Where was everybody? Who was in charge here? By now it was about 6:30 on Saturday evening and no one had told me what was *wrong* with Andrew. There were no chiefs; there weren't even any Indians. But of course! How could I have forgotten? Play was suspended until Monday. Hospitals, like airports and supermarkets, only pretend to be open nights and weekends. Their minimal staffs are invisible; the bedside buzzers chime unavailingly; people apparently stop having heart attacks . . . or die of them, since the PA system grows silent, and the appeals for cardiac emergency teams mysteriously cease.

Frantic with the need to talk to someone, I began making phone calls to anyone I could think of. Dr. Kempinski (for whom I left a message), friends, then—with a sudden inspiration—I thought of Jeffrey, my cousin Annie's friend, a young doctor-researcher at New York Hospital–Cornell Medical Center. I had met him only once but seemed to remember he specialized in strange viruses. I managed to find Annie, my charming will-o'-the-wisp cousin who flitted back and forth between New York and Richmond, where her father lived. She got hold of Jeffrey, who called me, and within less than an hour he was in the room examining Andrew.

Jeffrey Laurence was to become my mainstay and savior. Tall and bespectacled, and a bit gawky back then, Jeffrey looked like the classic brain in the high-school movie who gets his revenge by zapping the opposition with his ferocious IQ. A virologist who early on realized the seriousness of AIDS and got into AIDS research, he became the first medical member of the Gay Men's Health Crisis and has since, as head of AIDS research for New York Hospital–Cornell Medical Center, been a major figure in developing public awareness. He's "on the map" where he belongs and where he always wanted to be: his picture's frequently in the paper, and he's interviewed on television. He has a beautiful and savvy Southern wife named Linda, but at the time, fortunately for me, he was neither married nor famous, and therefore could devote a generous amount of time to our case.

To me he became that ideal ally, the friend who's also a doctor. Since he wasn't involved professionally, he could report on what the other doctors were saying among themselves, and as a world-class explainer, he proved to be one of those people who can take a complex technical problem and, without sacrificing its nuances, sum it up in a way that is perfectly understandable. Moreover, as a young, smart, skeptical doctor without undue reverence for either New York Hospital or the medical profession, and no need to bask in its reflected glory, he could be free with his comments on both.

Along with Dr. Kempinski, who appeared moments after Jeffrey's arrival, he agreed that Andrew had a viral meningoencephalitis, i.e., a brain virus that had reached the meninges, the sheath surrounding the nerves. It would be a long illness with a difficult recovery, Jeffrey warned me after Dr. Kempinski left, but not a fatal one. Jeffrey had to go and check out some test results, but he promised to come back for me in half an hour and take me out for a drink (I had declined dinner), and left me feeling encouraged for the first time. With the awkward, swooping grace of a crane, he moved down the hall—he had this way of skipping backward and coming toward you at the same time, a person always in flight—calling after, "He's not going to die, Molly. I promise you, he's not going to die."

This was an intuitive stab on Jeffrey's part, but it entered my brain and coated it with a layer of hope. It kept me going for a good portion of the next twenty-four hours, and became a touchstone to which I would refer when things got grim.

It was now about eight o'clock, still Saturday, June 30, the day of Andrew's arrival. While Jeffrey made his rounds I called Andrew's mother in Queens and gave her the news in as reassuring a tone as I could. Themis seemed to take it in stride. I assumed it was because she'd seen Andrew through major and minor illnesses and was a female Zorba, one of those towers of strength whose frames of reference don't include frailty. She had come to this country as a young girl brimming with her own energy and talents and expecting great things.

"Nobody could tell me a thing, Molly," she once told me, "but then I learned." The Depression came, her husband lost all his money—or more accurately, made it, lost it, made it, lost it—in real estate. He would have been happy to remain in Brooklyn, scrounging enough money for cigarettes, newspapers, movies. But Themis, who had the idea of starting a boat-rental business, insisted they move to Howard Beach, which they did. All one winter, in a tiny house on waterfront property, the family—Themis, George, and their two boys—had built their boats with their own hands, sawed away in the living room, hammered and nailed, until the spring came and a fleet of forty rowboats emerged. Thus did Andrew go to college and fulfill the dream of an education his mother had always had for him.

She'd taught herself English and even now, alone in her Queens apartment, she subscribed to *The New York Times*, read it through, wrote down the unfamiliar words and looked them up. She'd lived alone some twenty years now, having survived her husband's death (of leukemia in 1943), her younger son's death (George had died at twenty-eight in a skydiving accident), and the belated departure of Andrew himself, who finally left the nest and got an apartment in Manhattan when he met a girl from Virginia who looked askance at a thirty-seven-year-old man still living with his mother in Queens.

Andrew was the unquestionable center of her life. Most women make a choice, conscious or unconscious, between their children (normally, their sons) and their husbands. Themis had made hers and never pretended otherwise.

"When I came home from the hospital with Andrew," she told me, "I couldn't believe it. I looked down and I knew this was the greatest thing in my life. My husband knew it, too. He looked at me and saw the way I looked at Andrew, and it was never the same afterward. He was always jealous of Andrew."

She spent her days cheerfully alone, sustained by her thoughts of (and calls from) Andrew and me. She was in perfect health except for one thing: her legs were mysteriously giving out, she had occasional falls, and some days she could barely walk at all.

"I'm indestructible, Molly," she would say, in her accented English, after she had taken a tumble, bruised her head, and emerged (so she said) unscathed, betrayed once again by the legs that were wearing out faster than the rest of her.

Themis wanted to visit Andrew the next day, so I gave her instructions on how to do so and hung up. By now, all I could think of was that drink, and when Jeffrey arrived, we made our way across the courtyard to the Rockefeller University Faculty Club. New York Hospital-Cornell Medical Center, and Payne-Whitney Psychiatric Clinic, comprise one of the most impressive medical complexes in the world, not least because of its twenty-block command of the East River it practically turns its back on. In the center of Rockefeller's vast, Arcadian grounds on York Avenue is a tennis court that from a real-estate point of view must be the most expensive tennis facility in the world.

It was still raining lightly and smelled of the lush, fresh beginnings of summer as we walked under the arbor, up the vine-covered path, and entered the bar, and I found myself in one of those huge, dark-paneled rooms, reeking of male privilege, that manage to bring out my most passionately mixed feelings. It may be that even as I sat here, this one was becoming a dinosaur. Women were entering the medical profession in record numbers, and although their influence couldn't yet be felt in this leathery sanctuary, gradually the atmosphere would become genderless. I ordinarily spent as little time as possible thinking about men's clubs—so lacking in irony, so weighty with self-importance, the last bastion of a besieged, but not really threatened, male power base—and was embarrassed by the efforts of my fellow feminists to gain admittance. And yet at this moment, all my deep-rooted yearning for male authority and omniscience rose to the fore, my need to *believe*. Oh, these shrines whose attraction is constituted precisely on their exclusion of women—do we want to worship at them, or to tear them down and pillage them? Do we want to dilute them with our presence? Or do we want to cuddle up and disappear amidst the overstuffed leather chairs, the Chivas Regal, the brandy and cigars, while the ancestral portraits of founding fathers stare down without irony?

We want to sneak in, immerse ourselves in the heady atmosphere of old books and silence, newspapers and dry martinis, and watch while our "sisters" batter vainly at the door. The issue becomes infinitely more loaded when the founding fathers who look down, in whose hands we have placed our care, are not mere men but doctors.

One regresses in emergencies. I found myself ordering a Scotch and soda, a "highball," nectar of earlier days, of a safer order—and sinking into the armchair, letting Jeffrey and the aura of doctors surround me like a down comforter. I completely abandoned myself to fantasies of rescue, to shameless idolatry.

The need to believe in a superior virtue outside oneself is enormous and at times—like this one—overpowering. I needed to believe in the omnipotence of the medical profession as I needed to worship Andrew, the man in me and outside of me. And doctors were an extension of that power. I know there are women, modern, brave and businesslike no-nonsense women, who challenge doctors, pester them, ask questions, demand service, question their officiating, treat them as equals or even servants, and go into hospitals and offices in full battle dress. I envied such women, admired them as models. I read about them enthralled. I was, however, not one of them. If men in general and doctors in particular weren't superior, what hope had I for the recovery of the man whom I considered superior to myself?

Nietszche was at least half right when he wrote that it is women who create religion and keep it going. Because it is women's disposition to nurture, worship, and sacrifice, he argued, we need a strength outside ourselves to which to apply these qualities; whereupon we invent that strength, call it God, and lean on it as if it were really there.

What has happened now, though, is that in a secular age we have invested doctors and scientists with Godlike powers. It is hardly surprising that in a society that has discouraged women from living for themselves and in their own names, the supplicant's position is the natural one. Nietzsche's famous girlfriend and intellectual turn-of-the-century pinup, the free-spirited Lou Andreas-Salomé, maintained that women are capable of a less self-interested love than men because they worship a Platonic ideal of beauty and truth beyond themselves and find individuals to impersonate it. Thinking to counter Nietzsche's claim, she became its ironic embodiment. Known to us now not for her own writings but for those glittering "gods" she chose as lovers or companions (Rilke and Freud among them), her concept of "selflessness" becomes yet another rationale for the annexation of a strong female mind to an even more brillant male one.

A good female mind is a straw in the wind if the love habit is strong within her. Ortega y Gasset speaks of love as being not a happenstance or an instinct but a spiritual invention. A work of art. Certainly loving Andrew had turned out to be one of the things I did best, and my idealization and romanticization of him was part of that love and part of my identity, feelings and an attitude I couldn't imagine myself without.

Furthermore, in annexing myself to him, I had gained the advantages of maleness by the association. To have believed less in his superiority would have diminished me. How complex the whole thing was, a "special relationship" that empowered me, gave me "independence" in the world at large while allowing me to remain feminine and in some degree childlike. I had loved men in my time, shamelessly played ball with the patriarchy, and I was not going to relinquish my special relationship now. In my guilty lust for that delicious bargain with the devil, I was like Augustine, both wretched and happy in his disease of concupiscence. He knows he must give up the path of the swinger for the bond with his Lord, but in one last grasp at earthly pleasures, he cries to God, "Give me chastity and continence, only not yet." I looked at the future, recognized my need to be a freestanding agent, but what I called out was "Give me independence and autonomy, God, but not yet!" Far from wanting to do battle with the gods and ghosts that haunted the place in the name of equality and feminism, I worshiped at Olympus, and in the Hippocratic pantheon, Jeffrey took his place as an intermediary. He was one of the immortals, but mortal, too, and skeptic: not the all-powerful and unapproachable Zeus but Hermes, the go-between.

His words, part gossip, part talk of Andrew, were reassuring. Andrew would live. I went home in a strange mood of euphoria. There was a satisfaction in simply having faced down the horrors of that day and gotten through. "The first day's night had come," begins one of Emily Dickinson's most beautiful and harrowing poems ". . . and grateful that a thing/So terrible—had been endured/I told my heart to sing."

And so my heart sang—Andrew would live, Jeffrey's promises and the Scotch did their work—and I slept.

2

When I woke up, I reached instinctively for Andrew, only to feel his absence everywhere: in the smell of his neck on the pillow, in the rumpled depression on the sheet where his body had been, as if he had been there all night and just gotten up. I rose quickly, fixed myself breakfast, and propelled by fear and adrenaline toward the practical, whirled into action, making phone calls, questioning friends on Long Island.

What did Andrew have and where had he gotten it? Viral meningoencephalitis was merely a description: a virus in the head and meninges. What virus? Of necessity, we live in a do-it-yourself medical world, with a network of friends our principal source of information. Doctors, our first line of defense, are not always up to the task, either forgetting to tell us what they know, or simply not knowing, fighting what increasingly seems to be a rearguard action against a fourth-world army of viruses and bacteria.

In questioning us the day before, the doctors had seemed less interested in our trip to Italy and France, the perils of unknown African and European viruses and unpasteurized foods, than in our recent weekend in Long Island. I described rich meals in Tuscany, a touch of indigestion relieved by Fernet Branca; a twenty-four-hour bug in Cannes—especially Cannes, the U.N. of disease, the site where flus from all over the world gather and intermingle—but they bore down on what Andrew might have contracted in Quogue, on the South

Shore of Long Island. Cases of Lyme disease, which would double and quadruple in the following summers, were trickling in. One of the New York Hospital doctors had contracted a case of it in Shelter Island the previous weekend. Less common but possible were other tick-borne viruses that migrated to Long Island from various parts of the country, such as Rocky Mountain spotted fever and equine encephalitis.

I told the doctors that Andrew, a thoroughgoing urbanite, wasn't likely to pick up anything that came by way of grass, water, trees, or animals. He had grown up in the shadow of trees in Brooklyn and on the water in Howard Beach in Queens, a provincial outerborough life that was neither urban nor rural. He wandered along the beaches, never going in the water (inflammation of the mastoids and an over-protective mother had seen to that), his sights attuned to the anonymous sidewalks and tall skyscrapers of the city while he listened to (his then favorite music) Gordon Jenkins's "Manhattan Towers."

Manhattan represented choice and anonymity. For him, as it had been for so many others, as it would be for me, coming to New York was a way of breaking away from family while upholding the family tradition of breaking away.

Andrew's father, a gambler by nature, had been the real adventurer in the family, a young man who took to sea at the age of fifteen when, in a Hamlet-like drama, his mother remarried and a jealous stepfather forced him out of his home. He had told Andrew of the moment when he and his best friend, a fellow sailor, had landed in Marseilles and were trying to decide what to do next.

"Egypt," said his companion, looking south from the port, "is the place to go."

Andrew's father thought a minute, then shook his head. "No, America," he said, and with no more than that shake of the head, his die was cast.

Andrew had inherited little of his father's wanderlust—or perhaps wanderlust is just another name for displacement, for what drives a man when he has lost first place in his mother's heart. Andrew lived, inviolable and safe, within the enchanted sphere, which may have been why he felt no need to venture forth into the plant and animal world.

In any case, he had felt his lack of knowledge sufficiently that, as a would-be writer, hoping to write the great American novel, he enrolled in a course in botany at Columbia in order to learn the names of flowers and trees.

"I wanted to be able to write lyrical nature descriptions," he once told me, "like having a heroine walk through a field of zinnias." Instead, like all of us who took botany for the same reason, he had learned Latin names and the Linnaean system of classification and never learned that zinnias do not grow in fields like corn. We loved Thurber's all-time classic account in *My Life and Hard Times* of signing up for a botany course: every time he looked into the microscope, he saw only water bubbles or blackness. Finally one day he looked into the microscope and began drawing furiously. The teacher, pleased to see some sign of activity, came over to inspect and reacted in horror. "That's your eye!" the teacher shouted. "You've fixed the lens so that it reflects! You've drawn your eye."

I called Joan, a neighbor at Quogue, an environmentalist, also a watchdog and unofficial housemother, a zealot of helpfulness who not only knew the names of plants, trees, and birds but would also know of anyone who might be suspected of circulating with a virus similar to Andrew's. Round Dunes was an oceanfront complex where my mother had bought a studio apartment in the late sixties with the idea of the three of us spending weekends together. It hadn't worked out; it was too far for her to drive up from Richmond, and actually too small for three, so she had handed it over to us.

The complex had a number of disadvantages, most prominently the size (they were tiny studio apartments, too small for us both to work in); close proximity with seventy other tenants; the cost of maintenance all year round when it was only open for five months; and the fact that it was a long way from our friends farther out on the island.

Every year, starting in December, we began debating whether or not to get rid of the apartment. But all we had to do was drive out in May, walk in, open the blinds, look at the ocean, and fall into a trance of cosmic rapture.

It was ideal for unworldly and impractical people, domestic incompetents like us who could never have managed a house. At

Quogue, we had that built-in parent figure, a superintendent, and a built-in community of "adults"—couples a little older than we were, who could give us advice and with whom we were friendly without being intimate. When I had been suddenly hospitalized in the summer of '81, our Round Dunes neighbors, most of them veterans of medical wars or skirmishes, gathered around Andrew like a collective nurse-maid. I was sure they would do the same now: all I had to do was plug in to Joan. In fact, she did know of a man, a fellow nature lover, who had contracted a weird virus, but the more she described it, the less it sounded like Andrew's. She promised to check with everyone she knew—and that would cover not only Round Dunes but the environmentalists and ornithologists in the area—as to whether there was anything new circulating in our woods and marshland and call me back. And in fact, everyone seemed to know of someone who'd been hit by one strange virus or another. But it wasn't until I called Pam at our tennis club that I hit pay dirt. Pam arranged games from the desk, another nerve center, and thus would be familiar with every symptom, true and false, being bandied around the club. She knew of no one currently suffering from anything serious, she said, but then remembered that only last year, a member had collapsed with a high fever, had been diagnosed as having Rocky Mountain spotted fever and, after a great deal of weight loss and a long recovery, had come back, was even playing tennis again. Of course! It was then I remem-bered: Andrew, against his better judgment, actually *had* walked through marsh grass at the Singers' on Saturday night. Mike, our host, had invited Andrew to walk down to the inlet behind their house—a mere twenty yards—to see his brand-new boat, and Andrew had some-what gracelessly complied. It was in that swampland, I was convinced, that nature had finally taken its revenge. At least, this seemed a good working theory.

When I got to the hospital at midmorning, Themis was in a chair beside the bed, beaming.

"Look, Molly," she said, "I think he's getting better."

Andrew was sitting up over a breakfast tray, a definite improve-ment over the night before, but I could tell from his glowering expres-sion that he wasn't in a cheerful mood.

"Where have you been?" he demanded with an irritation uttlerly unlike him.

"I've been making calls," I said, too excited to be put off, "and I've found out what's wrong with you. It's Rocky Mountain spotted fever, I'm sure of it." I supplied the details of my detective work. Andrew struggled with his breakfast, unimpressed.

"This food is vile," he said. A startling phrase, the first sign the demons were in him. "Vile" simply wasn't a word he ever used . . . too coarse, too obvious. What's more, the badness of New York Hospital food was—as we both had cause to know—of a banality more deserving of irony than vehemence.

I now began buttonholing doctors with my theory. Was it possible, I wanted to know, for Andrew to have gotten one of the tick encephalitides without displaying a bite or rash? Possible, the consensus seemed to be, but not likely.

I was standing in the hall outside Andrew's door waiting for some procedure to be completed, when I looked up to see this neat little person in a traveling suit coming toward me and realized it was Mother. She looked particularly tiny and fragile. She was five feet six to my five nine, but the gap seemed to have widened in recent years, and worry always shriveled her. She had come straight from the airport. We embraced daintily, the way we always did, as if afraid we might bruise each other.

My mother, radiantly lovely yet firm of character, was one of those steel-spined flowers that flourish in Southern soil and that have recently become the stuff of myth and dramaturgy. Yet that type didn't begin to describe her. She was a Tarheel born (Fayetteville, North Carolina, in fact), but not a Tarheel bred, and a certain cosmopolitanism was in her blood. Her father, a chemical engineer, half Yankee and half French Huguenot, had developed and patented a device for extracting rosin from tree stumps, and before the Depression, the five of them—the parents, Mother, and her brother and sister, Frank and Dorothy—crossed and recrossed the world. There were exotic decals on her trunks, ashtrays from great hotels in Cairo and Constantinople. Had she really wanted to "settle down"? I sometimes wondered. She was complicated in the way of people who are torn in many directions.

She'd been a belle—a strenuous profession in those days—and a painter, played golf and tennis, and then, postponing marriage as long as possible, she'd gone to New York in her twenties and studied painting at the Art Students League by day, partying at night, finally succumbing to marriage at twenty-nine. I was seen as having broken away from Richmond and abandoned the "place" my mother and father had made for me, yet I was only continuing the quest my mother had begun, pursuing to its conclusion the path on which she had set out, waiting to marry until I, too, was twenty-nine.

Mother was, I think, a mystery even to herself, and to me she was sometimes as opaque as the people in her paintings—women ironing or cleaning fish, fishermen, fruit pickers, all rendered featureless, abstracted into figures in a sort of human still life whose emphasis was color and composition.

She'd had youth, beauty, and love. And character. For her, character came first. With character you could survive the loss of everything else.

Beauty of the seductive kind my mother possessed was not officially recognized in the culture in which I grew up. Perhaps the very concept was toxic, divisive. For better or worse, in the cataloguing of virtues, females were rated and accepted the way you would livestock: all varieties of attractiveness were lumped under "good looks," which took their place alongside, and beneath, other assets of bloodlines and breeding: manners, personality, comportment, moral fiber.

Did I resist the idea of my mother's beauty (she had little vanity) or did I just not see it? In any case, it wasn't until I grew up that I came to appreciate the impact she had had on men. I would occasionally meet one of the old beaux for whom she was still the Mary Clark of Fayetteville who had danced her way from one end of North Carolina to the other. It would be at some cocktail party or another, some watering hole up or down the Eastern Seaboard. They were retired tobacco executives, lawyers, industrialists, ex-college football players, with wives who looked like what they were—gracefully aging grandmothers. Emboldened by the second drink, the watery eyes in the still-handsome pink faces would mist a little or the whiskey voice would catch a notch and confess that they had known Mother "when." And there Mother would be across the room, slim, almost girlish, a long cigarette in one hand, a Scotch in the other, with someone in thrall.

"She wasn't like anybody else," the one-time beau would say, and then he would look quickly, guiltily over at the woman who had shared his life, and I would know what the lady with the matronly figure didn't know: that she had been second choice.

Yet the really astonishing thing about my mother was that she had lived almost half her life alone, in the South, in a world that was social above all else, one that revolved around couples and in which widows were as welcome as Dutch elm disease. And it was one about which she had no illusions.

"We might as well be in India," she would say, "where widows throw themselves on the pyre when their husbands die." Or she would tell a horror story of three widows, herself and two friends, left alone at a large table at a dinner dance, while couples flocked together, filling all the other tables. Of rising, finally, and leaving, like pariahs, erasing their embarrassing presence from the eyes of the other guests.

What enabled her to survive as an unattached woman in a couples world was a fierce sense of independence. She didn't really want to be obligated to any man, never had, and she seemed to prefer loneliness to the opportunities for matrimony, which became grotesque as she pictured them.

"Widows just run after the widowers," she would say. "Snap them up before the wife's cold in the grave." Or "I don't want to get saddled with some man who's going to get heart disease or arthritis or become bedridden . . . [the possibilities were endless] and I'll spend my last years as nursemaid." Of course her hidden aversion to marriage was implicit in the very terms she used. Like so many women who complain about the shortage of men, yet rarely put themselves in the way of possibility, some substantial part of her really didn't want to give up her independence, but she needed to convince herself—and her friends—that she really did want a man and would have allowed herself to be persuaded if a plausible one had presented himself.

As we waited outside Andrew's room, his neurologist, Dr. Ramir, approached, wearing a face mask and appearing even more sinister than usual. Ramir was a dramatic-looking, swarthy man with Mediterranean good looks and the slightly furtive air of an Arab sheik. Now, with his face half covered, the effect was emphasized: he looked like a charging chieftain who might pull out a saber at any moment.

In fact the saber he unsheathed was the warning that there was now some fear that Andrew might have one of the extremely contagious herpes viruses and we were to wear masks. The masks seemed to me a belated precaution, since everyone had gone without them for twenty-four hours. Nevertheless Mother and I dutifully put them on, as did the nurses. Only Themis, not about to permit anything so trivial as the risk of infection and death to come between her and her son, refused. When we walked in, Andrew looked at us in horror.

"Am I dying?" he asked. Realizing for the first time how we must have struck his none-too-stable mind, and feeling like Judas Iscariot, I yanked off my mask. But it was too late: I had failed the test, clung to life while Themis had leaped into the breach with her mother love. Oh, the monumental unselfishness of the ethnic mother! Standing on the shore, I felt awe, shame . . . and jealousy. Her morality was monolithic: she lived *for* Andrew, and she would die with him. Didn't I love Andrew as much as a woman can love a man? And yet when I was presented with the split-second opportunity to follow him over the divide, I had chosen life. Would it have been different if he had been my child instead of my husband? Or were Themis and I made of different stuff? How ridiculous these great moments are!

It was a relief when both mothers had departed, Themis to Queens, Mother to my apartment, and I could be alone with Andrew. He still had a fever of 104, was agitated and making sense only inter-mittently, and was now hooked up to a cardiac monitor—a matter of routine, I assumed. I'd never seen one up close, and I watched it as compulsively as an adolescent with a video game, anxious over the minutest variation in the pattern of peaks and planes. Andrew's heart signals plodded along with what I took to be reassuring monotony: like a slightly bumpy country road, with an occasional sharp hill. It was only later that I discovered that even as I watched, the coronary care unit had been alerted to the possibility of malignant hyperthermia and that the lack of distinctness in the mounds indicated an abnormal rather than a normal condition.

To get my mind off that screen, I turned on the television,

switched channels until I stumbled on—of all things—*The Searchers*, John Ford's great western starring John Wayne that was the American movie we both loved and admired above all others. Once a cult favorite, the movie had taken its place as a generally acknowledged masterpiece, thanks largely to Andrew's influence as the auteurist critic and rediscoverer of the American cinema in the mid-sixties. But it had become "our" movie, consolidating our sense of ourselves as a couple when we saw it in Paris in 1969 shortly after we were married. By contrast, our actual wedding and reception had only underscored our differences. The service, traditional and Episcopalian, passed with only a few hitches: Andrew and his best man, Vincent Canby, were pinned into morning coats and the pins showed; and my mother, in unconscious protest, was seized by an uncontrollable coughing fit that lasted throughout the service.

But the reception will always be remembered by those who were there—New Yorkers hardened to the strange and the incongruous— as one of the most bizarre events they ever attended. This phantasmagoria of colliding worlds took place on the ground floor of 1A East Seventy-seventh Street, a handsome turn-of-the-century mansion that rented itself out for such occasions. It was divided into three large rooms, each opening onto the next, and no set designer or director could have created a more brilliant objective correlative for the tensions within our relationship. The crowd had apportioned itself thus: in the first room, where the orchestra played, were the Greek guests. They had all given lavish wedding presents, expecting a five-course ethnic wedding feast, and were dancing their hunger away with Zorba-esque abandon; around the corner, in the room with the bar, the Southerners gathered for serious imbibing; and in the middle room, our New York friends, who thought they had seen everything, looked from one room to the other in amazement, while waiters came round with finger sandwiches.

I had nightmares for six months afterward, dreams in which distorted images of Greeks, Southerners, and New Yorkers jumped deliriously in my head like the flaming dancers in *Dance of the Red Death*. In them, the threat of disintegration and the terror of marriage mingled.

Thus it was that as a couple we were still feeling a bit ragged-edged when we found ourselves "at home"—in a Left Bank movie theater watching *The Searchers*, experiencing, in our love of Ford's great drama of loss and redemption, that identity of taste that would become our most solid bond as a couple and that is itself a sanctification and a redemption.

This is the movie in which John Wayne, in an uncharacteristically morbid role, becomes an instrument of revenge in pursuit of the Comanches who have wiped out his brother's family. Wayne's wrath in pursuit of retribution turns into a malignant obsession, as he drags his raggle-taggle posse on a trek that Ford invests with cosmic meaning, an awesome landscape of snowstorms and burning heat, winter turning into spring, spring into summer. A juggernaut propelled by hate, Wayne ignores time, reason, the turning of the seasons, and arrives finally at the Comanche hideout to find that his niece, the child who was stolen by the Indians, has grown into a beautiful woman (Natalie Wood) who is, for all intents and purposes, a Comanche. He looks at her, this creature of his blood who has become the hated Other, and one fears the worst—an explosion of fury, a final wrathful act of vengeance.

He seizes her in his arms with the obvious intention of killing her, and then, in what is surely the greatest reconciliation scene in all of cinema, he takes her in his arms and embraces her.

In this union of opposites, father and daughter, man and woman, are reconciled, but also the dividedness of Wayne himself, and madness, the madness of solitude, are overcome. It's an ending that no one I know has ever been able to resist, even those who oppose Ford's traditional, community-minded world view on political grounds, or find the theme of the movie—Wayne's paternalistic Indian-hating, however critically viewed—disturbing. Andrew and I not only shared a certain temperamental conservatism, but the theme of loss, and the claim of the dead over the living, had particular meaning for us.

I had lost my father in 1957, Andrew had lost his in 1943, then George, his brother, in 1960; we had been conducting dialogues with the dead for years. These losses were the central facts of our lives, the wounds around which our adult personalities had formed their scars and defenses. In some ways, until we met each other, our ties were, as Andrew wrote of the bonds between Ford's characters, "more securely fastened beyond the grave than ever they were on earth." Perhaps it was this very sense of incompleteness, of amputation, that we recognized and responded to in each other, some symmetry of matching sorrows. Two loners joined by a central ache.

One of the great attractions of movies, of course, is that they allow us to experience vicariously, through artistically distanced forms and fables, those feelings that are too overwhelming for us to confront directly. The "primal screen," as Andrew called one of his collections, serves up surrogates for our long-gone love objects, provides a catharsis for feelings and memories that have been lost, distorted, repressed by time. We are able to transfer onto those monumental figures on the screen some of the intensity of our original relationships, losses we have never come to grips with, longings and desires that have been wrested in terror and shame from their original object. Movies, our collective unconscious, give us back our pasts, plunge us into the wellspring of feeling with images as vivid and artfully disguised as dreams.

What could have been further from our own childhoods and urban lives than cowboys and Indians in a post–Civil War western setting? What could be further from my own ideas of modern womanhood than an Irish-Catholic director's loving portraits of sacrificially maternal figures? Yet the family feelings that Ford evokes, and the tension between the solitary adventurer Wayne represents and the community he is bound to serve, speak to the continuing conflicts in all of us, poised as we are between a past—community-minded and obedient to an order that transcends man—and a Godless present in which man/woman is the measure of all things, and there is no context, no healing environment, for the divided and fragmented self.

When I looked over at Andrew, barely watching, I felt an added frisson as I watched that ending. Heretofore, I had always identified with Wayne, the aggressor-hero, but this time I felt, like the Natalie Wood character, that unconscious pull toward surrender and annexation. In this duet, I was suddenly the reclaimed daughter, embraced and forgiven by a father whom she had "dishonored." Andrew and I had long defended Wayne against the derisive oversimplifications of the Left: he was a quintessential movie actor, his career full of subtleties and tensions, quiet brushstrokes, that contradicted the flag-waving jingoistic image ascribed to him, but I know too that on the instinctual level, I was drawn to him because of his resemblance to my father, with whom he shared that mix, not as contradictory as we would like it to be, of masculine arch-conservatism and an almost feminine gentleness.

As Natalie Wood's "defection" had enraged Wayne, so mine would have horrified my tradition-bound father. His heart might have turned murderous; certainly it would have hardened against me, at the idea of my coming to live among the New York heathens, marry an alien, adopt their values. Yet it was the sudden disillusionment prompted by his death and the disorder that ensued—the realization that my previously harmonious world wasn't governed by a benevolent God, by any God at all that I could imagine—and the rupture of the sacred dialogue that had "freed" me, set me to wandering on a road where I would have to seek out my destiny rather than have it handed to me with the family silver.

Andrew's eyes showed no sign of recognition—what would *he* have made of the remarkable coincidence of this particular movie materializing now?—yet I nevertheless had the feeling that he knew intuitively what was going on.

"When does this take place? Right after the Civil War?" I asked him.

"Yes," he answered, then paused. "There's a scene where Ward Bond says to Wayne, 'I haven't seen you since the surrender.' And then he pauses and says, 'As a matter of fact, I didn't see you *at* the surrender.'" Andrew smiled; I smiled. On some level, he was still in communion with John Ford.

I watched the ending. I knew that its power for me lay in something even more subterranean than the idea of reconciliation, the fantasy of rescue. Thus the source of contradictory emotions: I could fantasize my father's arms around me in forgiveness, yet it was Andrew who was my rescuer, who had saved me from the Enemy. And the enemy wasn't Comanche but "Old Richmond." In an ironic transposition of the usual mythical coordinates, my "Indians"—i.e., those from whom I had to escape—weren't the "savages," but the paleface respectables native to my world. I had come to New York, to Andrew, to "de-assimilate." But hadn't I exchanged one rescuer for another?

One loving and beloved idol who had died for one who now lay in a precarious state.

The fever was still high and, as the evening wore on, it increased and Andrew's "mentation" deteriorated. The Babinski sign that Ramir had noted earlier—the toes curving up instead of curling over when the ball of the foot is pressed—was definitely observable now.

Encephalitis, a word I had heard the day before for the first time, is more a descriptive than a diagnostic term, referring to a derangement of brain function (literally, inflammation of the brain). It is known primarily by fever, then by any or all of a number of accompanying symptoms such as convulsions, delirium, confusion, stupor or coma, loss of speech or muscle control.

Andrew was proceeding along the checklist. He hadn't had convulsions, but it looked as if he might slip into a coma. He was having difficulty moving his right arm and leg, which meant that the left hemisphere of the brain, the part that controls speaking, was affected. The virus was picking off the cranial nerves along the base of the brain, beginning with the pair involving speech and the tongue. Eyesight would be next and then the diaphragm.

The prognosis for viral encephalitis—or viral meningoencephalitis, meaning the meninges are involved, which they almost invariably are—was by no means as optimistic as Jeffrey had indicated. As I was to learn, there's a 5 to 20 percent chance of death with acute viral encephalitis and in another 20 percent of the cases there's a good chance of residual effects—mental deterioration, amnesia, personality change, and/or partial paralysis.

The causes are varied. Measles, mumps, or even tumors can produce encephalitis, but the thinking was that Andrew's would eventually turn out to be one of the six forms of encephalitis caused by insects that have been isolated and identified by the Centers for Disease Control as common to North America. *Eventually*, because it would take weeks to grow out viral cultures. These cultures are used to grow the virus itself, which is then detected in the cultures by foreign antibodies. Eastern, Western, California, and Venezuelan encephalitis, equine encephalitis, and sleeping sickness were possibilities. (The latter, transmitted by the tsetse fly, is still a potentially lethal illness, particularly among the old and young and those with immune deficiencies. It was responsible for the plague of 1914–18 that killed thousands and left many with the incurable Parkinsonism that Oliver Sacks describes in his vivid, firsthand account in *Awakenings* of the use of L-dopa.) Of the insect encephalitides, equine is the most dangerous since it affects more people, and of these about two thirds die or are left with severe disabling abnormalities, such as mental retardation and various emotional disorders. And it was equine encephalitis that Jeffrey suspected.

Then there are the twenty-odd herpes viruses—i.e., nongenital herpes—such as chicken pox, Epstein-Barr syndrome, cytomegalovirus, herpes simplex II, and—the most dangerous of all in terms of disabling residual effects—herpes simplex I. It was for herpes simplex I that Ara-A had been devised, with which Andrew was being treated—in case he had this disease and because it was the only one for which there was a treatment. Just what the aftereffects might be, I had no desire to know, as long as that was only a possibility. The mind simply clamps shut at the hypothetical; the real is taking up all the available space.

By Sunday evening, the end of the second day of hospitalization, Andrew was still speaking, though none too clearly, and his statements had begun to take on Delphic overtones.

"Everything is more a shared experience than one is led to expect," he said, which I took to be an expression of irritation at the spurious familiarity of the staff, their way of collectivizing everything into a shared experience—"We must take our blood pressure" and "Let's sit ourselves up"—as if "we" were all in the same sickbed.

As I was leaving for the night, Jeffrey cautioned that they would probably move Andrew during the night into the Neuro Special Care Unit—a modified intensive-care unit for acute neurology patients. I got home and had an exhausted drink with Mother; we had just finished dinner when the phone rang and it was Sam Gessner. The two days of his absence, the two days of terror, had been a century. He'd called the hospital as soon as he'd come in, and talked to Dr. Kempinski or Dr. Ramir, and he was reassuring: he thought Andrew would be moved, but wouldn't necessarily go into a coma.

It was Jeffrey who called early the next morning to say that Andrew had been transferred to the Neuro Special Care Unit and that he was in worse condition. He hadn't gone into a coma, but had blacked out for a while, and when Jeffrey stopped by, he was generally confused and his speech unintelligible.

I rushed down to the hospital, only to find myself barred from the special-care unit by brusque nurses who were in the midst of performing a procedure on someone—Andrew, as it turned out. The Neuro Special Care Unit is a compromise between an intensive-care unit and a regular room—a single co-ed room, large enough (barely) to accommodate four patients and the numerous machines that their emergency situations demand. Visiting hours were limited, and suspended automatically if the nurses were treating any one of the four patients in the room.

We families huddled together in the alcove outside the room, I the newcomer, they the initiates. One, a young woman whose mother had ALS, was being taught how to care for the patient at home; the other was a woman in her fifties whose twenty-year-old son had Guillain-Barré syndrome, the mysterious creeping paralysis Joseph Heller had (and would eventually write about) and from which he was, unbeknownst to me, recovering at that very moment. From them I learned everything I needed to know in a very short time.

When I finally got in to see him, Andrew had a wild look in his eyes, and although he recognized me, he had difficulty talking. His agitation was reflected in a desperate desire for control.

"I can't figure out a single set of priorities and stick to it," he said, using that strangely impersonal language, the lingo of middle-management marketing executives on elevators and airplanes when they're discussing flow charts and cost-effective plans.

He was trembling and agitated, and endlessly preoccupied with the objects in his immediate vicinity—the whirring of machines, the tubes; like a child, he was engaged by everything in his direct line of vision, objects more than people, and no one thing for very long.

"It's okay to get mad at all of this," I said.

"It's just that it's so hard to figure out what's reasonable to get mad at and what isn't," he replied, not illogically but again in that flat, un–Andrew-like way, as if somebody else were writing his dialogue and directing him.

"This room is an avant-garde play," he said, almost echoing my thoughts, "but it's not clear whether people are acting according to the script."

Since I couldn't imagine Andrew speaking complete nonsense, I began to listen for hidden meanings, and scribbled his words in the journal I was keeping. Not that he was above banality. We were both babblers, leaping back and forth from major to minor matters, and when it came to the ambient conversational noise that takes up a good part of marriage, nobody could beat Andrew for platitudes. Far from seeking a novel way to express weather forecasts, insights about the traffic on the Long Island Expressway, the paucity of pedestrians on a Saturday in November, or his love for me, he took a kind of ritualistic pleasure in the very ordinariness of these subjects and the repertoire of stock phrases he kept burnished for them. Something about their diurnal predictability—both the occasions and the reactions they called forth—was a source of comfort, a sign of continuity. I, on the other hand, scorned routine and craved novelty, not having learned to appreciate the virtues of repetition. In a sense, we were both fleeing our pasts, but in different ways: I wanted to find different routes, an emotional adventurism to escape my ultra-civilized world, where emotion had been suppressed by the ceremonial and the liturgical; in Andrew's operatically ethnic family, self-expression had overruled manners, etiquette, nuance. Platitudes and rituals were his way of bringing this unruliness under control. If Andrew had a horror of delving into the psychic depths, he nevertheless brought a rich sense of the past to bear on the world, as his endlessly fertilizing mind interpreted the matter of daily life. He was, in Graham Greene's words, a "mass observer," confident enough in the complexity of his own synthesizing mind to enjoy the mental vacation of banalities. They were the verbal equivalent of Pablum, Jell-O, milk, and white bread, a retreat to an earlier and enveloping mode of love.

He and his mother used to have long conversations on the phone in which they simply played back catchphrases, in Greek, from the "good old days" at Howard Beach. I would be three rooms away and hear Andrew talking to his mother, then peals of laughter, that raucous and heaving laughter he had copied from her as a child and was now stuck with, and know it was one of their Howard Beach routines. On a rainy day, Andrew loved to remind his mother of those desperate weekends when they hadn't rented a single rowboat, sold a Coke or a hamburger, and wondered how they were going to get through the coming week. The comic juxtaposition of images of destitution, and their comparative present comfort, was an endless source of hilarity; the horror of the past was transformed into a family joke by the joy of survival.

But these comments in the hospital were not from his familiar litany of platitudes: they were sly and ornate, they had a kind of goofy elegance. To the doctors his aphorisms had no interest. They were medically irrelevant, but to me they were precious pearls, virtuoso tropes, smoke signals from a marooned man in a language I couldn't understand.

That evening, the doctors reported that he was failing all the neurological tests. His Babinski sign was still present: his toes still shot straight up. When Themis came in on Tuesday she was shocked at how much worse he'd gotten since Sunday. It was the trembling and jerkiness that bothered her most, whereas for me it was his deranged mental state.

Suspicion bordering on paranoia is a Greek national trait to which Andrew, under the healthiest of circumstances, was inclined, and his was flowering like a wisteria in May there in the hospital, an institution, after all, where persecution is a way of life. I felt sure that some part of him was highly satisfied, like the xenophobe who finally visits a foreign country, is treated abominably, and is secretly thrilled to have his prejudices confirmed.

"They're always telling you something, throwing you off stride," he said at one point, mentioning a conspiracy. "You're never secure."

He then looked at me accusingly. "Our apartment is the only place I can function," he said. He was convinced that whatever was wrong with him had been induced simply by my bringing him to the hospital. And I began to wonder if perhaps he was right; or at least mightn't he be just as well off, and happier, at home?

They talk of women and animals with nesting instincts, but it was for Andrew that the word *homebody* was invented. He hated to travel, he hated change. He was what the French affectionately call a *pantouflard*, a man who goes through life in his bedroom slippers.

Then he said some words that sounded like Greek. I took them down phonetically as *eypari panieta mileppi*, and later had them interpreted as *I-panayitsa vlepee*, "The Madonna looks down and sees." Was this a benediction or a threat?

If a struggle was going on inside him, I wasn't in on it. Though his words may sound pitiable and heart-wringing as I write them ("I don't know what to do to get better," he said at one point), I didn't *experience* them as such, because the circuit between us had been broken. One suddenly realizes how much communication is a business of shared rules, a give-and-take that is conveyed less in actual words than in emotional tonalities, the expression of the eyes (keen or glazed over), gestures, one mind's leaning toward another in empathy and good faith. When communication between two people breaks down, the rupture can rarely be conveyed by a simple reporting of what was said; everything has to do with tone of voice, the presence or absence of humor, the quality of listening, of hearing and *being heard* in a very particular way. Craziness is simply anxiety brought to a fever pitch, in which one plugs up all the frequencies, imposes one's own version of reality on the world.

Now, with the transmission jammed between us, it was as if I were compelled to see and feel Andrew differently. The deep-level love was there but the immediate affect was gone, suspended. Without expecting or waiting for an answer, or remembering anything I, or anyone else, said, he spoke in the querulous, self-absorbed way of a child, but with an unchildlike, witheringly sardonic delivery.

For three days, Andrew was in this agitated, befuddled state. Dr. Carrington, Ramir's temporary replacement, a highly regarded neurologist, was standing by, seeing Andrew but saying little. By now, word was out and the phone at home was ringing constantly. It was a great comfort to know friends were calling, but I simply couldn't talk: I was too distraught and the news was too bad. Mother, who had become my right hand and surrogate, was invaluable as phone answerer, and, I think, rather enjoyed it. There's something intoxicating about being at the news center during an emergency—it's one of the little dividends tragedy throws our way, and Mother, tracking the course of the hurricane, was in her element. She was "meeting" many of my friends for the first time. She had no way of knowing, however, which voices on the telephone were those of intimates, which mere acquaintances, and which business contacts (categories that tended to blur in my life in any case), therefore who wanted the full account, who the high points, and who a brief thumbs up/thumbs down notice. On the principle that it is better to avoid offending good friends than to worry about wasting the time of a lesser acquaintance, she gave the most complete and current account to whoever called. Mother wasn't a garrulous woman *except* when she was in an information-giving mode and her compulsion to tell the truth and get it right came out in lengthy precision. As a result, a good many people got more than they bargained for when they called, but they were all charmed by Mother. Once Robert Benton, the director (an old friend, also a Southerner), called from California, and with the supreme delicacy for which he is known, never mentioned the fact that he was calling long distance until forty-five minutes of spirited conversation and commiseration had elapsed.

Even without a diagnosis, talking about Andrew's illness, giving it words, helped allay anxiety all around. There were juicy new terms to play with, like "encephalitis" and "paranoia." Paranoia wasn't exactly new to Mother, but it wasn't a word bandied about in Richmond, and she seemed rather pleased to be able to tell a friend Andrew was "paranoid." She was startled, though, I think, when he answered back, "But he was always paranoid!"

To my artistically liberated but sexually straitlaced mother, the whole psychoanalytic vocabulary was something odious and alien. The sexual etiology of neurosis was bad enough, but then there was the whole concept of the unconscious, the implication of an adversary within, hidden emotions that were at odds with the facade not only of good manners and good taste but of love itself. I once tried to instruct her in the idea that the mother-daughter relationship was fraught with ambivalence, but she would have none of it. It was bad enough that her daughter's book was entitled *From Reverence to Rape: The Treatment of Women in the Movies,* and she couldn't discuss it with her friends, though she bravely put it on the coffee table. But when the book came out in 1973 I could tell there was something else bothering her. I pressed her.

She finally broke down. "You used the word . . . *penis.*"

"Mother," I said, exasperated, "that's a Freudian term. Penis envy."

"But, Molly," she said, more in sorrow than in anger, with the quiet authority of someone who knows there's a lack but it isn't in her, "we don't read Freud in Richmond."

I loved to tell this story to my friends, yet I knew the joke wasn't entirely on Mother. A large portion of the cultured and semi-cultured world reacts to Freudian terminology as if it were a loaded gun, and are more offended by "bad" words than by the most horrific imagery.

Though she never much supported my writing activities, Mother felt that if I was going to be a writer, why not a writer of nice, polite, well-bred books—preferably novels—that people would be proud to put on their shelves along with the biographies of their Confederate ancestors, the classics, books about antique silver, and the fiction of such approved local authors as Edgar Allan Poe, Ellen Glasgow, and Tom Wolfe, a particular hero to Richmonders for his Yankee-bashing, though not to Mother.

Mother didn't approve of his attire. "Why would anyone go around looking like an ass on purpose?" she asked, never bothering to read him.

"Because he wants to be noticed, Mother?"

"But Richmonders don't want to be noticed. They're happy where they are."

"Maybe he was from the wrong side of Grove Avenue"—one of those geographical/social divides that in Richmond are subtle but profound. "Or maybe he didn't come from the Right Family. Or go to the Right School. Or, more probably, maybe he went to the Right School in the wrong clothes." In fact, I had read that he went to St. Christopher's, Episcopalian brother school to my own St. Catherine's, but perhaps he was poor and wore hand-me-down knickers, like Trollope humiliated and in rags at his upper-crust British public school. Whatever, Tom Wolfe in resplendent and conspicuous white, the gadfly as Gabriel, was now a beloved and cherished hometown boy who—reportedly—would go down and sit on various front porches in the west end, chewing the fat with the old ladies, having a good laugh about the sleaziness and hypocrisy of Sodom and Gomorrah on the Hudson.

When I went in to see Andrew on Wednesday, the Fourth of July, I felt an immediate difference. He looked almost cheerful and for the first time showed something beyond mere recognition when he said, "Hi, you look wonderful." But when I asked him if he wanted to hear all the messages from friends who'd called, the sourness returned: "No," he replied tartly. Since he was the mail opener and phone answerer in the family (I could happily go for days without doing either), this lapse of his normal curiosity was a sign of the lurking suspiciousness.

This was also the day of his first visitor. After one of her three-year disappearing acts, my cousin Annie had suddenly materialized, all bright good humor, concern and support. Annie was a ball of fire, a live wire, a comic performance artist who could light up the room with her presence. Six years younger than I, she had grown up wavering furiously between emulating me and detesting me for my utter indifference to her. Of the ten cousins in our generation, Annie and I were the ones who had most in common, and should have been closer than we were. Maybe we had too much in common. We were both writers, both expatriates, and we shared a gallows humor about our cousins and the various skeletons in our family closet. We would get together—always when she decided and on her terms—we would laugh wildly and adoringly, she would make herself indispensable, and then disappear. Raven-haired and green-eyed after her mother's side of the family (her father and mine were brothers), extroverted, undisciplined, Annie was a superb raconteur with a fiendish memory for all of our dirty secrets, who poured all the energy and imagination that should have gone into fiction into tall tales of the Haskell family—Southern Gothic by way of magical realism—with which she entertained her friends. She was an admitted "fabulist" (it was what the unvarnished truth deserved), though, she insisted, a harmless one. I imagined, from the stories she told me about *them*, what she must be telling them about me. This may be why I was just as comfortable with the distance we kept between us as I remained in the city and she shuttled back and forth between Richmond and upstate New York, where she had a farm near—but on the wrong side of the track from—the landed gentry who were her mother's clan.

What I worried about was how she would publicize Andrew's

condition to the world at large. After all, for an inveterate gossip who wouldn't have minded scoring a few points at my expense, the image of a loony cousin-in-law was pure gold. I could see her working up Andrew's relatively mild symptoms into a drooling, bug-eyed routine. On the other hand, she truly loved him—if anything, she felt a good deal more uncomplicated affection for him than she did for me. When everyone else in the family had opposed our marriage, she had been a staunch fan and ally. She had a huge portrait of him hanging on the wall of her house that a painter friend had done for her from a photograph before she even met him. And she had produced the invaluable Jeffrey.

And so in she came.

"Molly!" she exploded, once she'd gotten inside the Neuro Special Care Unit and cast a critical eye around, "how *can* you let Andrew stay in this *awful* room?" (As if a room at the Plaza had been an alternative.) In the struggle between silence and self-expression, between decorum and the promptings of the raging unconscious, with Annie there was no contest.

On the other hand, she had a point, I thought, as I looked at it through her eyes. For the Neuro Special Care Unit was startlingly ugly, like a makeshift ward in a war zone. It had neither the reassuring high-tech sheen of an ICU nor the personal "effects"—flowers, cards, books—that made the regular patient rooms more human. The four patients were in various stages of decline and degeneration: the anonymous unvisited old man in the corner was dying even as we spoke. But I had grown blind to the dark lights and the barrenness of the walls, the absence of even an enlivening print, the aesthetics of internment.

It was a self-blinding process that had occurred not with Andrew's illness but during my own hospitalizations, for I had developed a kind of hospital version of the Stockholm syndrome, the phenomenon, observed by Swedish psychiatrists, in which captives of terrorists gradually lose their connection to the outside world and enlist in their captives' cause. Identifying with the aggressor rather than the victim, I was on *their* side, the doctors' side, not one of those complaining patients at all. My "bonding" with the hospital had become a kind of bondage in which I saw torture as love, craved indifference as what I deserved.

And now, as I suppose Annie saw it, I was busy dissociating from Andrew by being a Good Wife. "Annie," I said, stating what I thought must be obvious, "special-care units are strictly functional. This is not the Plaza. Nobody is here for the comfort and beauty of the place."

But Annie was not one to permit peace of mind when there were veins of negligence and guilt to be mined.

"Your doctor must be a criminal. How could he have gone away for the weekend and not put Andrew in the hospital!"

Now we were second-guessing the past. A cunning double play this, meant to drive a wedge between Sam and me with one jab, and challenge my love for Andrew with the other. I still felt that Sam had done what most doctors and I what most wives would have done. But did I want a doctor like most doctors? Did I want Andrew to have a wife like most wives?

Then she moved in for the kill. Watching as I hovered over Andrew, smiling and talking encouragingly, she suddenly exploded. "Molly, I don't believe you, smiling like that? How can you not show him how you really feel?"

"But this *is* how I feel," I argued. "I walk in and I see him and I smile because I'm so grateful he's still alive!"

To Annie, anger was mother's milk. She lived it, breathed it, cultivated it. It was the source of her near-demonic energy. Years of therapy and current vogues in pop psychology provided her with a rationale, but she operated always at the boiling point, with a generous supply of anger on behalf of her friends. All they had to do was mention some irritant in their lives, someone who had conned them or done them dirty, and Annie would be off frothing at the mouth. Actually there was something rather magnificent about her anger: she was a goddess of wrath sent down from Mount Olympus to wreak vengeance, to get action for us spineless mortals. The deep well of her rage found surrogates everywhere, whereas I was well behaved to a fault, as temperamentally incapable of exploding as Annie was incapable of holding it in. Perhaps, in some uncanny way—for Annie was nothing if not intuitive—she was acting out my own anger. Like our mothers, we were extremes in relation to each other, perhaps opposite sides of the same coin.

Those two women had argued in their time, violently, on the issue of child raising: Annie's mother, with Spock as her authority, believed in letting her children, as my mother put it, "run wild," whereas my brother and I were the products of strict discipline. In my mother's value system, anger was not only unseemly, it was "unworthy." Thus a failure of character.

Annie and I had both grown up in Richmond but had been influenced by it in different ways. Richmond was one of the great cities of the South, but I always felt its glory as something long gone, a shadow over the present. We were the child of a famous father: the capital of the Confederacy. It had once been, like the Dublin Joyce's protagonist looks back to in "The Dead," a city of "spacious days." One felt the spaciousness in the Civil War memorials and museums, in the Capitol building, and especially on Monument Avenue, paved with cobblestones, bordered by stately columned mansions and guarded, in the island that ran down the middle, by statues of the great Southern generals. Richmond had gotten bigger, moved west, away from "downtown," and shrunk in the process. It was no longer elegant or startling; it was healthy, benign, civilized, and complacent. It was a perfect place to grow up in, and perhaps that was what was wrong with it: its ideal wonderland atmosphere was artificial, like a climate-controlled Astroturf playing field, gained at the expense of keeping the rest of the world out.

Growing up in the shade of those great old elm and maple trees, in yards guarded by fat boxwood hedges, polished green and robust with virtue, there came over some of us the sense of being overprotected, and finally overwhelmed by the weight of what was beng shut out, excluded by privet hedges, the country club, the debutante balls.

There were some things Virginia did so beautifully—gardens, funerals, and Smithfield hams . . . and friendships. In Richmond, friendships were for life, and people formed packs, like elephants, at an early age and traveled everywhere, did the same things, from then on, went to the same vacation spots year after year, to the same club on Saturday night, talked on the phone daily. The tone of voice was cheerful, calm; no one ever broke into a sweat over a passage in a book, or was struck speechless over a painting or a concert, got excited by a movie, or talked in a loud voice about politics. Everyone agreed implicitly; therefore there was nothing to examine or analyze. A surfeit of belonging made introspection unnecessary.

My mother was about as eccentric as anyone got, painting modern nonrepresentational paintings that baffled most of her friends, and in which they took little interest, thus giving her a kind of "secret" life. They were astonished when she exhibited, earned favorable reviews, sold elsewhere—but unswayed in their resistance to her washerwomen without faces, which wouldn't have "gone with" their rooms, would have looked odd alongside their ancestral portraits and horse prints.

Richmond inoculated one against unruly emotions and indiscreet divulgences.

Yet there were those few secret deviants and misfits, for whom the inoculation hadn't taken. Some of us left, if only to get a better look at what was going on inside. Those who stayed got drunk more often than was allowed, or more conspicuously, or turned dull with depression or went crazy or died. There was a disproportionately high number of unusual and early deaths for so secure and traditional a community: weird happenings, suicides, car crashes, houses burning down, bizarre and untimely and unseemly.

Annie and I had left, but in different ways we were still tethered, still occasionally slipped and called Richmond "home." She lived in upstate New York, Manhattan, everywhere, but kept going back to the dentist, the country club, to see family and friends. Her anger was a refusal to play the game by polite rules, a battle against shallowness, but it was also a way of holding on to a love-hate relationship—with her parents, her hometown—and keeping it at a fever pitch. And I in an opposite manner had been imprinted for life. Reticence, keeping the lid on my emotions, had been branded into me with a hot searing iron, along with the prohibition: Don't spill the beans. The charm of that well-ordered life is so powerful, and with it the taboo against probing, that to talk of it even now makes me feel stalked, as if an invisible hand were reaching out to muzzle me.

So there were Annie and I, across a fence, becoming more extreme in reaction to each other. At the moment, we were holding fast to nonnegotiable positions with no middle ground. The qualities in ourselves we are most proud of are often neuroses in disguise, and therefore least tractable to argument.

According to Annie, my good cheer was a form of deceit that would worm its way into Andrew's unconscious and corrode our mutual trust. I saw it differently: if I seemed to be playing a role—gallant Greer Garson in *Mrs. Miniver*—it was because I *was* in a war zone where battle readiness, stoicism, rather than "being in touch with your emotions," was the required mode.

By Friday morning, Andrew had so improved that the decision was made to transfer him the following morning into an ordinary room. The fever was down; he'd asked for the *New York Post* (under the circumstances, this was taken as an encouraging sign), had taken an interest in Wimbledon, and could carry on something resembling a normal conversation. The crisis was over. I planted a kiss on Andrew's forehead. I could breathe again.

Then, as I was riding the First Avenue bus, I suddenly felt a huge letdown, as if I'd fallen down a chute. Whatever had kept me going psychologically—stiff-upper-lip cheer, adrenaline, followed by relief—evaporated. The wind went out of my sails, and now that I could relax, I was engulfed in a depression all the more disturbing for its inappropriateness. Everyday life, with all its accumulated chores, its unpaid bills and unfulfilled assignments, would now resume. Though we rarely admit it, crisis lifts us into a sort of "high"—I'd had one of those "peak experiences" that the druggies and the cultists crave—and now it was over. My husband had reentered the world of the living, and I was . . . miserable.

I understood the letdown soldiers feel after returning from war, that nostalgia—the evocation of which is the real lure of the war movie, however pacifist the message—for the exhilaration of battle, the warmth of camaraderie, the fusing of the selves into a single, selfless, and noble self, risking death for a higher cause. To be at war is to be momentarily undivided, guilt-free.

If war provides the ultimate testing and measuring for a man in his most "masculine" identity, then surely nurturing, "rising to the occasion," has been the equivalent heroic activity for a woman.

For one brief moment, I had played the traditional heroine, been relieved of all the contradictions between my egotistical (i.e., "masculine") drives for fulfillment and my "feminine" disposition to live through and for another.

For a week, questions of self and ego had been suspended: every nook and cranny of my being had been filled with Andrew, giving me a sense of strength and solidity. My face had no doubt radiated that glow that one sees in the faces of wives whose sense of purposefulness comes from living through and for their husbands; it's a borrowed strength, however, which comes from ministering to a higher being whose superiority valorizes our sacrifice.

After living on a higher plane, I was falling like a meteor; my selves, generally held together by Andrew, my center of gravity, splintered in every direction. Like a reflection in a mountain lake, in which the reflected trees are clearer and more defined than the trees themselves, I needed Andrew to give me my clarity of outline, to show me who I was.

Normal life would resume: friends would make ordinary calls instead of sympathy calls, and ordinary insomnia would keep me awake at night.

And then gradually my depression began to turn into annoyance—at Andrew. At Andrew for forcing this thing on me, first the illness, then the depression, and then this horrible sense of my own unworthiness that had been the final blow. He had called on my "strength," then exposed me to myself as a sorry ignominious creature.

When I went back to see him that evening, I was in a state of fury, hardly understanding what it was all about, perhaps enraged most of all that I didn't have him to complain to, to help me understand. He seemed so much more himself, and yet—it was this that infuriated me—he had no sense of what I'd been through. I told him I would only stay a short time, as I was tired.

"Yes, it's been a tiring week," he said, casually, the way he might have complained of too many screenings back to back. I was brooding about this—and feeling ashamed of myself—when Sam came in, and I told him how I felt.

"Get used to the idea that he may never understand what you've been through," Sam said. "Even when he's well."

I was horrified. It was unimaginable that my soul mate, this genius of empathy who understood me better than I understood myself, wouldn't grasp—if only vicariously—the most intense experience of "our" lives. That I somehow couldn't convey to him what I'd done and felt!

This idea, shattering at first, unbearably lonely, began to work its way through my consciousness, growing on me as it did so. The notion that I could have some secret woe, apart from and unintelligible to Andrew, filled me with a subversive excitement.

We weren't soldered together anymore. We were like the parts of a knife that had recently come apart in my hands. It was beautiful, one of the solemn heavy knives with the Doric-column base that was my favorite wedding gift. I'd never known I shouldn't put knives in the dishwasher, that, unlike other pieces of flatware, they were constructed of two pieces rather than one. This object I'd always looked upon as seamless and indivisible simply fell in two, the blade separating neatly from the handle, now revealed as two discrete units. They could be rejoined by a silversmith, to all outward appearances a unit again. The difference was, I now knew. Like some Jamesian protagonist, I had seen and in the seeing lost my innocence, gone over to the other side.

My oneness with Andrew was not a thing of the past, but there was a crack of light between us. It was terrifying and exhilarating, "the pathos of separateness," compensated for by that sweet taste of freedom as the mind takes possession of ground it has never occupied before.

3

Early Saturday morning, a week almost to the hour after having been admitted, Andrew was moved from the Neuro Special Care Unit to a private room on the same floor. From there he would be moved to a semi-private when one became available, all logical steps in the orderly progression from acute illness to recovery, and I should have been relieved. Yet why was it that as I watched him over the weekend, I couldn't suppress stirrings of doubt? Yes, he was sitting up, but when he attempted to feed himself, his hand trembled so violently he couldn't get the Jell-O to his mouth. I asked him to write something on a piece of paper to see if he could sign checks, and his handwriting was indecipherable; it jumped up and down on the paper like chicken scratches. True, it wasn't very legible to begin with. One of the problems with Andrew was that a lot of his "normal" physiological and behavioral traits looked like symptoms. They had noted a "swelling of the left jaw" when he was admitted. What they didn't know was that his face bulged asymmetrically because he chewed his food on one side of his mouth, to compensate for a structural defect—a "roller-coaster bite" (the dentist's words). The handwriting was especially disturbing; I couldn't read the jagged lines of an EEG (electroencephalogram), but I could "read" this poignantly clear map of a disconnected mind. And though his words, when he talked, made sense ("I feel like I've been down deep somewhere and am coming back"), they were hollow. He was posing, once again, and the words grew more slurred

69

and he grew less alert. He then became violently ill, vomiting all over the floor, a possible reaction, the doctors on duty thought, to the powerful Ara-A drug.

Admittedly, I was hypersensitive to his symptoms, especially now that it was Saturday, and with the deadly weekend pall descending, I felt I had to maintain extra vigilance. Hospital life is composed of alternating bouts of frenzy and stillness, of the busy-ness of procedures and attentiveness on the one hand, and great gaping silences on the other. At four o'clock every day, for instance, when the two shifts of nurses overlap and are in conference, the earlier bringing the new group up to date, the halls are deserted, no one is available, and an entire floor could go into cardiac arrest without a summons being heard or answered. When you are being done to, all you want is to be left alone—until night descends or the weekend arrives, and the doctors go home (smiling behind your back, all dressed up and eager to go, like parents to a party, leaving you with the baby-sitter). Then anxiety prickles the back of your neck, you sense you're on automatic pilot, and, like a passenger on a lurching plane, you begin searching the nurses' faces for signs of imminent disaster.

I felt that Andrew was definitely deteriorating: his head lolled when a nurse tried to shave him for the first time in a week, and he seemed weaker on Sunday, when he was moved into a "semi-private" room, New York Hospital's quaint designation for a four-person bed-room. This room was typical of the hospital's accommodations, and although I'd been in rooms like this myself, I never quite got used to it, always understood the look of dismay on visitors' faces the first time they walked into one. Our images of hospital rooms, like our images for so many of the locations of life's great dramas, have been formed in the idealizing laboratory of movies and television. In our imagi-nation, the archetypal hospital room is a spacious and sunny private (i.e., a *single*, not a double, and certainly not a quadruple!) in which tragic or uplifting encounters, last rites, miracles and births, go on without such unseemly interferences as the taking of blood, the chang-ing of urine bottles, noisy roommates. The altogether grimmer reality was a crowded, impersonal bunker, originally designed for two patients and now crammed with four, featuring such antiquated equipment as hand-cranked beds. (In the newer wings, the rooms are slightly larger.)

The furniture—four beds, four bedside tables, and a few visitors' chairs—took up most of the available space. Flowers ended up on the window sill, as did visitors. The cramped space and the sheer ugliness of the rooms seemed part of New York Hospital's reverse snobbery, like the inedible food: "We're so good we don't have to worry about things like that," the decor seemed to say, or "We spend our money on doctors and technology, not on cuisine." There was, no doubt, some economic justification for the shabbiness, and Sam, in endless and legitimate complaints about the hospital's struggle to make ends meet under the increasing shortage of funds and the baleful dependence on government and state health-care funding, expressed this view. Still, it was the very validity of these arguments as he saw it that made Sam and the other doctors—blinkered anyway, by definition, to problems of discomfort—immune to the cheerlessness of the environment that so affected the patients and their visitors.

There are, of course, practical reasons for having roommates: along with relief from loneliness, there's the advantage of a buddy system, of one person being able to summon help if the other is in trouble. And there's the theoretical comfort and stimulation of other people, but in the wildly heterogeneous ethnic and temperamental mix that is a New York Hospital room, sinking into solitary apathy might be preferable to messy togetherness.

As Andrew had said in the semi-lucidity of delirium, "It is all a more shared experience than we are led to expect."

His roommates in Payson 616 were, so far, extremely quiet, a young bearded man, a Japanese, and a man about Andrew's age who'd had a stroke. I wasn't really taking them in, too preoccupied with making mental notes of Andrew's status to report to Sam and Jeffrey.

When I called them on Monday and told them of my concern, they responded in identical fashion: this was the sort of up and down pattern that one should expect in an illness like Andrew's. The symptoms of one day or two days weren't important; only the overall pattern of progress. Jeffrey said it could take months. If it was equine encephalitis, which was his conjecture, it might be shorter; if sleeping sickness, longer.

On Tuesday morning, July 10, the telephone rang and it was Andrew. He could talk a little, but I knew when I looked at the clock—6:00 A.M.—that he was disoriented. Andrew was famous for being able to sleep—he was the only person I knew who could drop off after breakfast. In his career in the armed services at Camp Gordon, Georgia, in 1953 (an image that was in itself heart-stopping: the idea that Andrew was the only thing standing between my country and the enemy gave me insomnia in retrospect), he claimed that he was the only person who ever snoozed while marching in formation. I was the sleepless wife to his dozing Jack Sprat, and I might have been resentful of his easy relationship with Morpheus (sleep competition being a chief source of friction in many marriages) except that he was the one who worried over my sleep, told me stories, cradled me. Of the various magical rituals he performed, the back rub was the specialty, an elaborate nightly massage in which his hands always found the tight spots, the places where tension had collected during the day. For me, each morning was a dramatically different event according to whether or not I'd slept till six or seven, and Andrew, with his astonishing empathy, understood. For him to call me at six was the surest indicator that something was wrong.

When I got to the hospital, they had him sitting in a chair, looking pale, his head lolling again.

I then went to the solarium in hopes of finding Helena, a woman I'd met on the floor just the day before, an extraordinarily wise and comforting veteran of hospital life. She was an ex-pediatrician whose mother was there because of a derangement produced by a mixture of drugs. The sensors that we use in everyday life to seek out the people we need to love, protect, even torment us, turn radarlike in a hospital setting. Milling, waiting, keeping their lonely vigil, are wives, sisters, and daughters, anxious to bond, exchange information. Helena, to whom New York Hospital was practically a second home, had been sent to me by Providence. She usually hung out at the solarium, talking to patients and visitors, cheering them up and providing counsel. The guru of Payson 6, she knew the names and reputations, comings and goings of the entire staff. I was intrigued by her story—she was one of those straightforward, no-nonsense people who are ultimately mysterious—but I was never to know anything more than that she'd been a practicing pediatrician, and retired because of "burnout" (the sight of suffering children, she said). Within twenty-four hours, we'd developed an intense rapport—the intimacy of the shipwrecked, of war buddies, of people underground during a blackout—that carries with it the special poignancy of knowing it can't survive the unusual conditions that created it. Friendships should begin slowly, on neutral ground, and, if they are so destined, work their way into deeper waters. If the opening chords are the life and death notes of Beethoven's Fifth Symphony, there's no place to go from there. The aftermath lives in the shadow of a profundity that normal life can't sustain. Even more important, perhaps, the memories that bind you are ones you want to forget.

Helena, when I found her in the usual place, agreed with me that Andrew was worse. She said Dr. Carrington had been on the floor, but hadn't seen Andrew, which both of us thought strange. I was afraid to go home. Helena hung around with me well past the end of visiting hours, and offered to have Clarissa, her mother's private-duty nurse, look in on Andrew. She was a beautiful, playful Irish girl, and when she said she would bring him ice cream during the night, I felt he was in good enough hands that I could leave.

Wednesday morning, Helena called early to report that when Clarissa had gone in during the night, Andrew had yelled at her and refused the ice cream. Then Andrew called about eight, and I barely recognized his voice as he mumbled something, then went silent. I waited till nine, and in desperation called Dr. Carrington.

"But I'm not responsible for him anymore," he said. "Dr. Ramir is back."

Another changing of the guard, without my knowing it.

"But haven't you noticed a deterioration since Sunday?" I asked.

"I was officially off the case Sunday," he said. This meant that Andrew had had no neurologist for three or four days. Horrified, I called Ramir's office, left a message, and when he didn't return my call decided to go down to the hospital and see him myself. On the way, I stopped by Andrew's room. He was in the armchair, but unable to hold his head up at all; he was reaching for the bed, whimpering like a baby, and there was no orderly in sight to put him back.

I rushed directly to Ramir's office on the floor below, and after some argument with the receptionist I simply sat down in a chair in the waiting room until, an hour later, she let me see him.

When I entered Ramir's office and told him that Andrew was much worse, he looked back at me, startled.

"Mr. Sarris?" he mused, apparently racking his brain to remember the patient. "Oh, I thought he was up and around."

"Well, no," I said. "He's in a stupor, he's incontinent, he has no interest in anything at all, and he can't even sit in a chair."

He looked up with something resembling surprise. It was now I finally realized what gave his face its furtive aspect. It wasn't in the expression of the eyes so much as in the way he held his face, forward and at an angle and very still, with only the eyes moving, so that he always seemed to be looking up at you—even if he was standing, towering over you—a position that automatically made his face take on a guarded, suspicious look. He promised he would check on Andrew later and call me.

He did, as did Sam, and both agreed that Andrew had indeed gotten worse. Ramir seemed to think it might be the liver, some "second insult" as a result of the virus, or even a reaction to some medication, rather than the virus itself.

Unable to understand what could have happened, I talked to Jim Gwathmey, the young neurology resident who, with the intern Ed Falberg, was in charge of the floor for July. These two doctors were probably no more than a year or two apart, but Gwathmey, a stocky, bespectacled young man with a heavy sense of earnestness, seemed much older than the collegiate-looking Falberg. The story I got from Gwathmey was that once a patient is placed in the recovery category, he ceases to be followed with the same intensity, is relegated to the back burner, so to speak, in favor of more urgent cases. Andrew had simply fallen through the very large cracks between the dying and the mending.

Over the next few days, he underwent tests, tests, and more tests: EEGs, spinal taps, blood tests for liver function, chest X rays, as the great juggernaut of medical technology turned its attention back to Andrew.

The results were confusing: there was a disparity between the clinical status (temperature and mental state) and the lab evaluation. When the cell counts were up (meaning increased inflammation around the brain and meninges), the temperature was down and his actual mental state was improving, and vice versa.

Meanwhile, Andrew was still on an intravenous line, through which he was being given Ara-A and fluids for support and was receiving supplementary oxygen from a little blue face mask. He was getting worse, not just daily but hourly. By Thursday, July 12, he was agitated and in constant motion—scratching his scrotum, pulling out his IV and bladder catheter (Foley tube). I had been coming down in the morning, going home for lunch and the afternoon (when Themis would spell me), then returning at about four or five to remain until eight or nine. Now I spent most of the day by his side, leaving only for lunch, talking to him, trying to soothe him and keep his hands still, and catch them when they went for one of the tubes. Mother was covering for me at home, but she came down and we went to a movie—*Ghostbusters*—whose only advantage was that it was so mindlessly unsatisfying that I didn't have the yearning to share it with Andrew. On the way back to the hospital, Mother and I talked about the fact that we would now need round-the-clock nurses to restrain him. I was going to get nurse's aides, at half the price of registered nurses, until I discovered that the red tape required by Major Medical to reimburse for aides was so complicated, requiring elaborate paperwork and testimonials, that it would be preferable to get registered nurses (then $125 an eight-hour shift), for which a simple doctor's authorization would suffice.

The doctors were trying various things: they took him off the IV, in case the insult to the liver was being caused by the Ara-A drug. His motor control seemed worse than when he first came in, yet he was hungry and asked for a banana and chocolate milk. The most recent electroencephalogram showed diffuse abnormality as opposed to the previous one that was practically (and according to the doctors, astonishingly) normal. The next EEG and spinal tap were better . . . and he was worse. Ramir said it might be the Dilantin being given him for seizures; they took him off that and said if he didn't get better in a couple of days they would start him on steroids. I knew enough about steroids to know—and Falberg confirmed—that while they reduce inflammation, they destroy the body's ability to fight off infection.

There would be moments of relief, when he seemed to be calm and lucid, perhaps improving. On Saturday after a Friday (the thirteenth!) of such hopeful signs as a falling fever and relative tranquility, I had taken to bed, in a merciful state of collapse, and Mother was preparing to leave. She had her feet out the door, on her way back to Richmond and a much-needed break, when the phone rang. It was Jeffrey. Andrew's fever had shot up to 104. At first I couldn't react. Mother asked if she should stay; reflexively I told her to go now (while she still had the chance), it would be all right. But all I could think of was "How will I get up? How will I get from here to there?" My body was halfway into that state of exhaustion that was almost trancelike. I was like those old people—usually stroke survivors—who can't move in the morning until someone pushes them. I needed a jump start to get my bones and muscles moving.

Yet somehow I dragged myself down to the hospital, and then, when I saw Themis sitting there by the bed, the adrenaline started pumping. Something about her presence, Buddha-like and unflappable, drove me into a silent fury. I knew it was ridiculous, but I couldn't help it. Why wasn't she exhausted, or half hysterical like me? Instead of having a calming effect, her placidity pumped me up with a kind of enraged energy. Where was her worry? Part of it was a matter of simple and unshakable religious faith. She and my mother, so different in most respects, were alike in that they had that instinctual belief in God of so many of their generation and a lightness of spirit that came out of it. It was not a matter of scriptures or doctrine, of religious observance. They didn't need church or fellow worshipers to believe that God was in the firmament, overseeing His creation, and that if He/She didn't get it quite right, it was the Deity's responsibility, not theirs.

Andrew and I belonged to a generation shaped by the disillusionments of the Holocaust, psychoanalysis, modernism, and the myriad dislocations, spiritual and geographical, of the last half of the twentieth century. If Andrew and I worshiped anywhere it was at the "secular humanist" shrine of art and culture, but art that couldn't take religion's place and no longer even tried. We had no communal ideology—Christianity, Marxism—to organize the world into good and evil, to give us a fixed place.

Unlike Mother and Themis, who lived within a morally conservative theology in which there were "sins" to confess and atone for, our guilts were vague and inexpiable. If, in a liberal and permissive society, nothing we "do" is wrong, then the sense of moral transgression we can never escape settles into what we "are." Our defense against chaos was one another, and if there was anything religious in our lives, it was our mutual love.

Our mothers' belief in God's authority was a way of acknowledging—and forgiving—their own limitations: a moment with them and one knew intuitively that they felt their own sins and lapses and shortcomings less severely. Moreover, a sense of divine sanction had enabled them to cope with deaths that had left us psychologically bereft. They had been able to find, even in terrible tragedies, a purpose, and indeed, they never lost their loved ones in a religious sense.

In most deaths there is some degree of liberation for the survivor, if only because every relationship imposes burdens and limits on the individual. Themis was one of the few people I knew who admitted it openly: she was firmly convinced that the deaths of her husband and younger son had enabled Andrew and herself, but primarily Andrew, to survive and succeed, that those deaths had been the economic and psychological salvation of them both. It was a cruel judgment and probably a just one, and for it she made no apologies.

As a young girl in North Carolina, Mother had gone one day to the Presbyterian church of her parents, listened to their hymns of wrath, sermons of judgment, warnings of an angry God, and never gone back. My father had grown up in the more relaxed Episcopalian faith, but neither had been more than casual churchgoers until my father's illness. The irony was that it was I, a God-besotted adolescent, who had been the churchgoer in the family. Every Sunday I would hitch a ride with a relative to St. Mary's, a tiny white-frame Episcopalian church, nestled in a clearing in the woods just large enough to allow the sun to blaze through its brilliant stained-glass windows. There I discovered God; there I also decided that when I grew up, I wanted to be a minister. I didn't see it as a sex-specific vocation, since I didn't see myself as sex-specific yet. I was one of those children who was always on fire to be *something*, but what the something was seemed to change with the hormonal dynamics of each passing season.

But of all my ambitions, preaching was the one that seemed to miraculously combine everything I enjoyed doing: writing, telling people what to do, showing off in front of a crowd, reading the beautiful words of the Bible and psalter, singing the gorgeous hymns in the Episcopal hymnal loudly, and worshiping God, for God was very much at the apex of my yearning. I didn't respond to the mediating figure of Christ, nor to his mystic "bride," St. Catherine, the patron saint for whom my school was named. Feminists justly complain that, unlike certain Eastern religions, Christianity contains few sacred female models, but even when they are there—and St. Catherine of Siena was a force to be reckoned with, an organizing spirit and dynamo in the early Church—we turn away from them, having already thrown in our lot with the male principle as the active, powerful force in a society in which to be active and powerful is to be superior. For I was too much in thrall to the patriarchal tenets of Christianity to *want* a sacred female model; my eyes looked upward to the one and only God, the masculine power, who, like my own father, would take care of me, allow me to fuse with him, in a union in which sex was sublimated into spiritual yearning. Sitting in the pew, gazing on the lilies, the gleaming brass cross, the interior warmed by the panes of cerulean blue, and singing my favorite hymns with their gorgeous crescendos and slides, their varied expressions of love, I was exalted.

To my adolescent and rapturously religious heart, there was nothing more exciting than the itinerant preachers who used to visit Richmond and do guest stints at various churches or in the Mosque. These were our rock stars, our Rudolph Valentino, Frank Sinatra, Mick Jagger. They were not men of the Bible-thumping evangelical mold, but an ethereal breed of "celebrity" orators from Anglican churches in Scotland, Wales, England—Leslie Howard types whose rhetorical flights allowed for the transformation of troubled teenage feelings into religious passion. I can remember one, in particular. A Welshman, very slight in size, with a pale ascetic face, and a diagonal of light brown hair that fell backward and forward across his forehead as he spoke. Way up in the balcony of St. James Church, my fellow groupies

and I would sit transfixed, spellbound, and then all our pent-up adulation would overflow into the hymn, his signature hymn—we
clutched the mimeographed pages in our hands, tucked it in our diaries
afterward—"In my heart there rings a melody, there rings a melody
of love."

At the other no less thrilling extreme were the exuberances of the
Holy Rollers, whose meetings we occasionally sneaked into, and the
unbearable but profoundly cathartic pain of Negro hymns and spiri-
tuals:

> *Were you there when they crucified my Lord?*
> *Were you there when they crucified my Lord?*
> *Sometimes, it causes me to tremble . . . tremble . . . tremble . . .*
> *Were you there when they crucified my Lord?*

Those three morbidly vibrating words, implacably marching
through three verses, forced us to feel, at gut level, the resonance
between two great infamies, one against Christ and the other against
the race that surrounded us, served us, rode in the back of our buses.
There were no sit-ins yet, no boycotts of lunch counters, but if there
had been I'm not sure I would have participated. I didn't have the
singleminded moral fervor, the activist's ability to put on blinders, to
blot out the feelings of one race or cause for another. Like many white
Southerners before and after me, I felt the shame of my heritage as a
terrible irreconcilable contradiction, i.e., not just the sin of slavery
and racism (the latter simply a casual part of everyday life), but slavery
and racism on the part of a people who put such store by moral
rectitude, and who were in other ways such fine specimens of humanity, distinguished by an intense sense of personal honor, loyalty,
generosity, charm, humor. Ultimately, the only response to this di-
lemma is not to a solution but an escape: to leave town or write your
way out of it.

Thus the gravitation of Southerners to certain literary and conversational forms. Feeling alienated from ourselves and from the rest
of the country, whose forgiveness we seek, we turn to the Gothic, the
grotesque, to self-parody. Now, of course, the situation has altered
dramatically: the South, with its record of accommodation and progress

over the last twenty years, has exposed the hypocrisy and ingrained racism of the North. But in those years just prior to the great civil-rights movement of the sixties, we were wrong, we were the bastions and beneficiaries of a criminally unjust society, and no amount of rationalization—our parents talking about "conspiracies of the Yankee press" to put us in the wrong—could erase the crime.

And so for me, religion and its rituals gave expression to a great many needs and feelings I couldn't even acknowledge, much less articulate. But then my father got sick. And I began to lose my faith just as my parents were finding theirs. As the light began to dawn, as his strength deteriorated daily and we knew the disease was fatal, my mother and father began reading books on faith healing and looking into all the paths of spiritualism. They discussed it together and with others who believed, and these two proud and social people began taking me to small Baptist churches and meeting houses in odd sections of Richmond.

No magical cure was forthcoming, but religion had "taken" in a deeper sense. My father, until he became sick, had been an unin-trospective man, a man of this world who loved his wife, his children, his farm, his tractor, the land. But illness changed and purified him. When he was walking with a limp, then sitting in a wheelchair, then confined to his bed and no longer able to go into the yard, or laugh, or eat, or talk, he found religion. As his muscles degenerated and his flesh turned pale and translucent, his soul expanded.

I would go in every afternoon after school and talk and laugh with him, though I was cringing inside. I couldn't grasp what was happening, perhaps didn't want to, and felt twice abandoned, first by his illness, then by the peace he had found, that allowed him to leave us instead of fighting to stay behind. His imminent death—the very thing that was bringing him close to God—was so terrible that I resisted believing in the conversion Mother insisted he had undergone.

She, too, had been transformed in some way. Sometime after my father's death, Mother startled me by announcing she'd been given a message from God. Toward the end of the illness she heard a voice, "as clear as a bell," which told her that "they" wanted my father in heaven for some purpose of their own. That God would prize my father above all human beings I could easily believe, yet how could I forgive Him?

But it had reconciled her to the loss, and formed the basis of a relationship that, as she described it, was a kind of running, intermittent dialogue with God, or an internal monologue, in which, like Saint Augustine, she would address Him directly, argue, confess, turn away, come back, plead for forgiveness and beg absolution.

She would make her confession or complaint (What could it be? I didn't ask. Some breach of decorum on her or someone else's part). Then she would, in effect, throw up her hands. "Okay, God, you're responsible," she would tell Him. She had a kind of jaunty informality with God that she had with no one else. "You made me, so I'm in your hands. You take care of me now." And then she would feel relieved, and she would relax and sleep.

Themis's faith was more of a constant; it filled her and defined her the way air fills a balloon. It came out not as piety but as humor. She was a large, handsome woman, short auburn hair framing a joyous face, her whole being irradiated by a zestful acceptance. Life had been a vale of trouble but she was having the last laugh—a laugh at the expense of all the people who were scurrying around like ants, working and slaving, while she sat and looked out of her window at the passing scene. The scene that passed, on the skein of thruways and parkways that surrounded her Queens apartment, was nothing but cars, but to her the breezy eyrie of her fourth-floor living room was the Taj Mahal.

Themis seemed to have no need of the worldly pleasures that to most of us become addictive, and depression was unknown to her: she never complained of ailments, of the infrequency of our visits; her voice always sounded as if she'd just won the lottery.

But there seemed to me, in Themis's nonreaction to Andrew's illness, something that was not just faith but that was perhaps physiological, a slowing down of the reactions, possibly attributable to old age.

I acted like a child, became peevish. For instance, in a comic scenario played out daily, the thing on which my irritation focused— also one of the signs of her waning acuity—was her increasingly, but selectively, poor hearing. Though she rarely missed a word of Andrew's, with others she was less attentive, and she had gotten into the infuriating habit of never hearing the first words out of my mouth.

"Themis, Andrew seems to be doing better today," I might say.

"What, dahling?" she would reply in her accented English, treating my opening sentence as a wake-up call. Either I would have to repeat the sentence, or—something I found myself doing more and more, to my own chagrin—I would maintain a stubborn, childish silence. A frantic mother-in-law, hovering and barraging everyone with questions, would have been impossible, perhaps, but more *normal*.

This was our first twenty-four hours of round-the-clock nurses. The nurse who came at four was a pleasant Irishwoman with whom I felt comfortable leaving Andrew and I went home relieved. Then at 5:00 A.M. on Sunday morning, Andrew called.

"The night nurse never came," he said. I was alarmed, wondering how such a thing could happen and who I could call at this hour, when a female voice got on the telephone. It was the nurse. She'd been there since 12:00 midnight. Andrew had been awake and confused most of the night; his fever had soared to 104.8 but they'd gotten it down to 103 with Tylenol. His breathing was labored and gasping, however, and his speech and mentation were erratic. When I arrived a few hours later, they had him in the chair. Moving him around and sitting him up was necessary to get the circulation going and activate the muscles, which shorten and stiffen from disuse. It takes twice as long to regain the use of a muscle as to lose it, so in lying down you're losing ground by the minute. But Andrew was too weak. He began sweating profusely and turned ashen, looking so faint they immediately put him back in bed.

He was in one of his dire moods. "I think I'm going to sue them," he said of the hospital, the staff, everyone.

Meanwhile, the diagnostic mystery persisted. One of the people who'd become increasingly important to me was Alan Seltzman, the infectious-disease man, an eager, research-oriented young doctor whose best quality, as far as I was concerned, was that he was *available*. He spent a lot of time on the floor, he had the air of urgency and good humor of someone who enjoys being in several places at once, and he could always be relied on for the latest facts and figures. He reported that the chest X ray was clear, the urine clear, ditto the blood and the spinal fluid—all terrific, except that such "good" news left us more in the dark than ever. They simply didn't know what was causing the fever. The only possibilities were drug reaction or something in his brain not working.

Sam explained this as a metabolic encephalopathy, meaning something could be happening elsewhere in the body that was causing the brain problem; just as the consumption of alcohol changes one's mental state, so one sees brain disorder brought on by drugs (a tranquilizer like Valium), or an accumulation of toxins in the bloodstream, or kidney or liver failure, or excessive calcium; even the effects of fever itself can derange the brain. If Andrew's disorder was being caused by one of these "secondary" problems (rather than a brain tumor or encephalitis—primary brain problems), once the source of the bio-chemical abnormality was detected, it could be corrected. But this source continued to elude us. I began to feel the first murmurings of despair. Even Helena seemed less sanguine.

"The residents on duty say they all expect him to pull through but are mystified," she said. *Pull through?*

Gwathmey had said that when Andrew "came to" his mind would be as good as it was in his lucid moments, but these were few and far between. Dreading each new day's developments, and unable to call Andrew myself in the morning, afraid of what I would hear—or not hear—on the other end of the line, I had developed my own modus operandi. At 8:30, I would call and ask for either Gwathmey or Falberg, and whichever of them was available would let me know how the night had gone and what to expect.

On Monday, they told me that Andrew had aspiration pneumonia, and I was actually encouraged. This was something concrete, something that could be treated, and when I got down there, he was the clearest and keenest he'd been in several weeks. But by Monday afternoon, only a few hours later, he had changed completely. For the first time, he began to have hallucinations. He saw cats in the fan in the upper corner of the room, and he whispered that the Japanese man in the bed underneath the fan had "women in his tent."

I was horrified, but fascinated by his hallucinations. Here was this brilliant mind pouring out stock "loony-bin" fantasies in feverish technicolor, the sort of psychotic narratives that are the stuff of cartoons and teenage jokes. I remember how a group of us used to go visit our friend Mary Ellen because she lived near a mental institution, and we'd watch the inmates through cracks in the fence.

"One woman thinks she's a fried egg," Mary Ellen reported, "and she's looking for a piece of toast." And we would laugh too loudly. Madness is always fascinating, for it reveals the ungluing we all secretly fear: the mind taking off from the body, the possibility that the magnet that attaches us to a context in the world can lose its grip. Feeling our own adolescent identities as such fragile, not-yet things, we found the insane our dark doppelgängers. Institutionalized, they seemed to be a race apart and therefore definitely Not Us . . . but we felt some sneaking identification. There was the vicarious exhilaration in the madman's silliness, his irreverence for the rules of adult logic.

With Andrew, sexual themes dominated. "The food is oversexed," he muttered, and then, "Everything I see I turn into something else." Not a bad description of the transforming property of madness, and of his own active role in the process. He was the victim of all sorts of persecutions, but an active victim. If he couldn't beat his tormentors, he would simply turn them into something else.

He was becoming more uncontrollable, more insistent in his demand to be taken away, and I began to worry about physical violence and what countermeasures might be taken.

When I called the next morning, Gwathmey said Andrew was in very poor condition, and having "behavior derangements," and began talking about "getting authorization" to "restrain" him—their euphemism for tying him down or putting him in a straitjacket. I rushed down to find him sitting in a chair over a breakfast tray, waving a knife in his hand. He looked at me with that horrible, scathing look of a "mean drunk" and announced that he would kill himself if they didn't let him go, and that he wanted to get dressed in his own clothes. He hadn't been this hostile before, and the sight of him with knife in hand was frightening. I tried to talk to him softly and quietly. He went on about his clothes, and I finally realized that the hospital smock had become a symbol of his imprisonment. I helped him get into his own pajamas and that calmed him. He went uncomplainingly back to bed, the knife and the threats forgotten.

He changed personality so rapidly, it was hard to recognize Andrew in all of this. His hostility, his withdrawal, weren't symptoms for which I had any frame of reference, with which I could establish connection. I was frightened, yet it wasn't the normal fear or the empathy of the wife of a husband in pain. I was really watching a horror movie in which we were both at one remove from our true selves. Andrew was an absentee husband sending hostile messages through an intermediary. And I was The Wife, improvising with the only means available, a set of responses, clichés, instinctual moves that came to me from who knows where. There were no reference points in this scenario, only existential moments that had to be filled. Someone had kidnapped Andrew's soul and all I could do was minister to the anti-Andrew that remained.

Unable to relax, I was feeling as tightly wound as a rubber band. Because of Andrew's turn for the worse, Mother had come back. Her presence always had a calming effect on me, but I couldn't relax— even less now than earlier in the illness. Well-meaning friends are always cautioning you to rest, not to "overdo it," without realizing that overdoing it—spending long weary hours in a cramped space, tense and hovering, ignoring the rest of your life, is what keeps you going. That, and the fear that if you once lie down and breathe deeply, you'll never get up again. For when I did, that one Saturday, it was as if a lifetime of tiredness were weighing me down, covering me inch by inch like sand. I was up to my neck in it, soon it would reach my face, I hadn't the will to rise. Now I never sank down to that layer of tiredness, but remained in a state of exhausted alertness, in continual preparation for the worst.

So far, Andrew's hostility wasn't directed at me but at the doctors and his condition. Gwathmey, however, had warned me:

"He may turn on you. If he does, just leave the room. Even though you know he's not himself, he could say things that will hurt you."

In fact, madness itself sets up barriers, affronts us with charmlessness so that we keep our distance, and don't go mad ourselves.

I would be numb, emotionally protected when with him, but

when I got away from the sight of his rage-filled face or his mad incomprehension, I felt lost, desperate, and I cried my eyes out. How long could this go on without driving us both insane?

I went to another movie with Mother—Joe Dante's kinkily lurid *Gremlins,* but this time as I sat there, mildly distracted by the carnage wreaked by the movie's malignant toys, I thought of Andrew, I thought Andrew and I were never going to go to a movie together again. He was bound to die: how could anyone so sick *not* die? Happier images of the past, threaded through film, came up to haunt me. Our first date: a screening of Claude Chabrol's movie *Les Bonnes Femmes,* followed by "tea" at Howard Johnson's.

I was working at the French Film Office, and had gotten my first glimpse of Andrew when he appeared on a panel on Jean-Luc Godard at Lincoln Center. He wasn't the elegantly seedy professorial type (Oxbridge with a dose of Village Bohemian) I'd imagined behind those marvelous, wryly confessional auteurist critiques that appeared under his rubric "Films in Focus" in *The Village Voice.* He was rumpled and professorial but more Queens than Oxbridge, with a funeral-director pallor and great circles under his eyes, but when he opened his mouth and began to speak, his physical being faded. He was an artist of improvisation: the music of his mind took over as he spun arias of insight, leaving his co-panelists in the dust. Arthur Knight, beaming and sweetly officious as the moderator; Pauline Kael, nattering and breathy and combative; the filmmaker Ernie Pintoff, best described by someone as a huge man who made tiny movies. These were the days when critics took bites out of each other for hors d'oeuvres. At one point, poor Ernie had the gall to refer to himself and his fellow filmmakers as artists, at which Pauline snapped, "Don't call yourself an artist until we critics call you one!"

It was a while before we met. The late Helen Scott, my formidable predecessor at the French Film Office, had gone off to work with François Truffaut and left me to fend for myself. I loved the writing part of my job—putting out a bulletin and newsletter on French films for the American press—but was never much good at its public-relations aspect and waited for journalists and critics to get in touch with me, while they, imagining me as a second Helen Scott (monumental of size, bossy, chain-smoking, bilingual, old-line Leftist, Resistance heroine) had been in less than a rush to establish contact. I was a fan of Andrew's column and longed to meet him, but it was some months before we found ourselves at the same screening—of *Scorpio Rising*, Kenneth Anger's legendary echt-sixties underground movie. Andrew had talked to me on the telephone (he'd made my day when he called for information on Jean-Paul Belmondo), but he had never seen me before. He took one look at my legs—these were the days of the mini-skirt—and asked Rudi Franchi, the publicist, who I was. When Rudi reported that I was Helen's replacement at the French Film Office, Andrew looked startled (I was observing all of this unobserved) and rushed over. With elaborate courtliness, he introduced himself and called me Mona—a name he apparently preferred to Molly—and continued to do so when he began phoning, until I finally got up enough nerve to correct him.

Our first date was at Howard Johnson's, at 4:30 on a March afternoon, not a classic rendezvous spot, nor was it a tryst that the great lovers of history—Troilus and Cressida, Antony and Cleopatra —would have survived. Andrew really was just beginning to make a living wage: he had a teaching job at the School for Visual Arts, a spot on the selection committee of the New York Film Festival, was writing his movie-review column for the *Voice* and doing a broadcast on WBAI—a weekly half hour of extemporaneous movie insights, during which, as fans still remember, he rarely stopped for a breath. But WBAI paid nothing, and the rest, all together, paid only a few thousand a year. Nevertheless, this was a good deal more than he had made in the previous year, while lying on the sofa in his mother's apartment in Queens and ruminating on a piece for *Film Culture*, the tiny quarterly published by Jonas Mekas. He was determined to impress me with his "berths" and his prospects, which he outlined at great length while wolfing down a banana split and a chocolate soda, during which recital I sat there, drinking my black coffee, waiting for glittering insights while this sensibility I'd fallen in love with turned into a crass careerist before my eyes. We were definitely at cross-purposes. As he told me later, he was the victim of bad timing: heretofore, he'd been going out with women who soon made it clear they were interested in his bank balance and his future. Now he'd stumbled on a woman interested in ideas, and he was talking bottom line.

The next day, after *Gremlins* had failed to relieve my despair, I was having lunch with Helena at a favorite hamburger joint near the hospital when she offered to call in, as a consultant, a doctor whose very name was magic in these parts. When she uttered the name of Crenshaw, tremors went through the room. You could almost hear the stethoscopes jangling in the breast pockets of white-coated interns as they wolfed down their burgers and slurped their Diet Cokes. Aaron Crenshaw, world-famous neurologist and luminary of the New York Hospital roster, was a name to conjure with, celebrity salvager of celebrity brains (among them Patricia Neal's and Mary McCarthy's), scourge of elusive tumors, aneurysms, embolisms in some of the prime-cut cerebral hemispheres of the Western hemisphere. Helena not only knew him, but he owed her one—something to do with a rather large charity contribution she'd landed for one of the hospital's departments.

I accepted without a moment's hesitation. The arrangements were made quickly and he arrived, leading a retinue, that very afternoon. When he descended on Payson 6, it was like Moses coming down from Mount Sinai, a Handel triumphal march. A hush fell over the corridor as the neurological delegation strode up to Andrew's room. People stood in doorways—the ambulatory patients, who must have caught the excitement in the air, as well as residents and interns—gaping, sighing, everything but chanting "Hosanna." He made his way—after a nod to me, hunched over in the appropriately grateful supplicant's position—into Andrew's room. Some twenty or twenty-five minutes later, he emerged, paused before me, and announced, "We're going to take action. That's a very sick man in there." There was a brief pause. He turned and led the procession a few steps back up the corridor, then turned and rounded off his apostrophe in a stentorian tone: "And I don't like to see somebody that sick for that long."

Oh, the thrill of those words, both alarming and reassuring: only someone capable of extinguishing the fire would have called such dramatic attention to its enormity. These were not the wait-and-see words of a wimp, but the battle cry of a man of action. This was what American medicine was all about. This was what America was all about!

Oh, I know, there are things to be said for the low-key style—country hospitals in Kentucky, gentle hospices in Southern Italy, where the treatment is both professional and humane. Francis Steegmuller, in a *New Yorker* article of a few years ago, described in lyrical terms his amiable encounter with the Italian medical profession in a small Sicilian hospital. After a knee injury sustained in a vicious encounter with motorcycle thieves, he was received with a courtliness all the more remarkable for its contrast with both the ugliness of the robbery and a subsequent dehumanizing stay in a New York hospital. The trauma of the incident may have led the author to idealize a bit: we can stand brutality from almost anyone but the Italians, and Steegmuller would have needed welcoming arms indeed to erase the horror of that vicious encounter in the streets, and restore Italy to its status as most beloved country. I'd want to be in an Italian hospital, too, if the situation was routine—to deliver a baby, for a hernia operation or knee surgery, but who would want to be in Sicily with a heart condition, or a mysterious, life-threatening disease?

Did I want charm and compassion instead of wizardry and machinery? Did I want doctors who would smile, throw up their arms in a delightful gesture of *dolce far niente* instead of bearing down ruthlessly on the enemy? This was big-time stuff, drastic measures were called for. Bring on the heavy artillery, the high-tech problem solvers. I wanted to kneel on the ground, kiss Crenshaw's coat, believe that a god favoring our cause had come down from the mountain breathing fire and brimstone.

What course could intervention take? The two possibilities being raised were brain biopsy and steroids, both presenting sizable risks. With the first, there might be infection or actual brain damage; and steroids, while reducing the inflammation of the brain, would not only suppress the body's immune system, inhibiting its ability to fight infection, but would also mask signs of infection like fever and white-cell count, and the body's ability to feel pain (if the abdomen was pressed, the patient wouldn't feel tenderness or soreness). They wouldn't be done except as last resort or until a little more was known.

There were at the time various hypotheses circulating, out of my earshot but filtered to me through Jeffrey. People were beginning to doubt encephalitis—it shouldn't wax and wane that way—and the four leading contenders were: 1) edema in the brain; 2) parasites; 3) small blood clots squirting off into the brain, producing little strokes, and 4) vasculitis. This last, an inflammation of the blood vessels, and edema were two diseases that would benefit from steroids, but the appropriate blood tests did not indicate such a problem. It was like the parable of the elephant and the blind men. Each doctor had hold of a different part of Andrew and was coming up with a diagnosis of the whole in accordance with his specialty.

While they were arguing it out, I was trying to keep my head above water on the home front by answering the most immediate demands of deadlines, bills, calls from friends demanding a response. The writing I managed to squeeze out while going to and from the hospital, waiting in the solarium, between visits. Money matters were, for me, less easily dealt with, and I was beginning to feel a rising panic over how much all of this must be costing, when my younger brother, the financial planner in the family, made a timely visit to spell Mother. John, known to the family as Chevey—a nickname for Cheves, his middle name—had become closer to me in recent years and I wasn't even sure how or why. Something to do with our both getting older, or with my various setbacks and his perception that I was more vulnerable than he'd thought. Or maybe it was just a lucky accident: we had gotten past needing to see each other through a haze of childhood resentments and liked what we saw. Tall, shy, and reserved, as young and unmarked by age as a teenager, Chevey was a sort of Anne Tyler character, a putterer, a man who would have happily done without everything but a wife and a computer. He was an odd sort of businessman; he had started his own financial counseling business to which he brought the patience and missionary zeal of a saint and the secretiveness of a CIA agent. It was a low-key enterprise and he seemed to want to keep it that way. His practicality and frugality were legendary: it was a family joke that to economize, Chevey would buy his Christmas tree the day after Christmas. His presents, which tended toward the functional and practical, were also a source of amusement. When I was a single girl in a New York walk-up he sent me, on three successive years, a fire extinguisher, a smoke detector, and a battery recharger. Early on, we nicknamed him Mr. Perversity, and indeed, his determination to persuade people—me, his clients—to *save*, to increase their income by actually holding on to money and keeping records, revealed a passion for logic in an area most given to illogic and self-deception.

Still, when it came to reading and interpreting financial statements and fighting through the jungle of health insurance, no one would know better than he where to begin, what questions to ask, and therefore it was a great relief when he promised to look into Andrew's medical plans to see what, and just how much, they would cover.

When I left for the hospital in the morning, Chevey would be in the pose most characteristic of him: sitting in the living room, a mug of black coffee in hand, looking out the window. I knew he would sit there for hours, replenishing the coffee cup with coffee made fresh every hour to his precise specifications, sitting and pondering life, and then move on to the paperwork he had so generously undertaken to do for me. We barely talked of Andrew, of the terror we both felt, of the horror of this day-to-day not knowing, but Chevey's methodical and painstaking examination of our records, his calls to those responsible for our medical plans at Columbia and the *Voice*, was his gift, a form of emotional security that only he could offer. I would sit with him briefly, in a comfortable *solitude à deux*, drinking coffee. There were so many things we had never discussed that they came to seem undiscussable, taboo. We were afraid of the woundedness in each other.

In different ways Chevey and I were both children of the sixties, representative of a whole generation of rebels who split off from the world of their parents with an anger that was seemingly out of all proportion to the ostensible cause.

In the late sixties, Chevey had distanced himself by moving to the country with his first wife and they lived on a farm, completely and, at first, happily isolated. After having made a great show of renouncing the rules and obligations of society, they had formed ironclad ones of their own, discouraging family relations by limiting contact to visiting days and telephoning hours as restricted as a hospital's. Having met and fallen in love very young, and virtually never gone out with anyone else, they had grown up together, had evolved a collective identity, were each other's defense against the uncertainties of the world. She had enabled Chevey to survive his father's death, but gradually their relationship had become claustrophobic: they had stopped breathing the air of the world outside, and when a child was born, the marriage, too much a twosome to become a threesome, broke up.

We had both fled into intense coupledom with its attendant risks. The couple that withdraws into itself, in which each partner is "everything" to the other, is a social danger—the *amour fou* of the French that subverts society by ignoring its laws—but a danger to itself as well. Having no one to account to, no neighbors, either literally or metaphorically, in whose eyes we must find approval, we live now in an excess of privacy. The rise in wife-battering and other intrafamilial crimes surely springs from this intense isolation, this lack of any sense of the community as a recognized authority. We love or kill, find salvation or perdition, with one other person.

A lot had happened since then: Chevey had remarried, established strong ties with me and Mother, opened himself up in other ways, yet some part of him, some abyss, was sealed over forever. He had learned to live without great expectations. I dared not approach his secret self, fearing, as supposedly strong older sisters often do, that their younger siblings are made of glass. Thus, our rapport was in our reticence, in the lonely echo that passed between us, and we were never more companionable than when we were simply being silent with each other.

Along with Mother and Chevey, alternating with each other, it was friends who were my family and friends who kept me going.

It was extraordinary, the outpouring of sympathy and concern, how people would call, then call again, especially considering the difficulty of a situation that changed from hour to hour, and to which I could give no name. Cancer and a stroke we can at least pretend are known quantities: there are hundreds of success stories, miracles of therapy, remission, cure. But confronted with this ever-changing mis-

ery, there were no words. Yet they found them, my friends, mysteriously, abundantly.

The flow was constant, a replenishing process that, as all my
emotional energy went into Andrew, infused me like an IV. And this
wasn't a small town, where friends all know each other and gather
round, organizing themselves into a network. This was New York,
haphazard and individualistic.

Our friendships didn't align, like couples at a square dance, the
way they do in the suburbs and other cities. We didn't have a "group,"
but a wide assortment of friends who reflected our own eccentricities,
oddball mixtures of writers, academics, hybrid couples, mostly people
we had gotten to know professionally, best friends we'd met only six
months ago and others who had dropped by the wayside and reemerged.

There are people you hardly know who suddenly surface, a sort
of underground of "resistance workers" who are geniuses at this sort
of thing, and others whom you do know but who unexpectedly blossom
as caregivers. Mostly, the adepts are women. With their inborn sense
of suffering, women move as instinctually toward the sick as ducks
toward water. We are never so unambivalently close as when we are
putting our arms around each other over a misfortune. Envy and all
the harsh judgments that, as heirs to mother-daughter rivalry, we visit
on each other daily, are suspended as we return to some primal bond,
where nurturing preceded rivalry. But even among the women, there
were vast differences in the patterns of response, in the rhythms and
colors of sympathy.

Some friends reacted by descending into the depths with me;
others by trying to pull me out; still others by standing quietly and
firmly on solid ground with open arms. I found myself gravitating from
one to the other as my own needs dictated.

Among those unafraid to call, and keep calling, remarkable for
their constancy in facing, and continuing to face, the horror, were
Toby Talbot and Betty Rollin, each familiar enough with tragedy to
be at ease with it.

After having shared a walk-up on East Forty-ninth Street in the
mid-sixties, Betty and I had parted company but kept up. She had
become, in her own wryly self-mocking words, "Miss Breast

Cancer"—she had written the best seller *First You Cry* about her ordeal, and written it in the same ruefully gallant tone with which she approached everything else in life. She was now a featured correspondent on NBC, but in our days together as bachelor girls, Betty—then a feature writer for *Look*—was funny, warm and briskly no-nonsense when it came to her floundering friends. I was working in a public relations job, struggling to become a writer, and it was through a contact of hers that I found my dream job at the French Film Office. We played Scrabble, gave parties, with mostly males in attendance, mourned each other's foolish choices and failed love affairs. As much on the lookout for me as for herself, she was judiciously open-minded when I started going out with Andrew: the analysand in her was skeptical of a man who had lived with his mother for thirty-seven years, but the matchmaker was prepared to give him the benefit of the doubt.

After a marital misstep, Betty had found—and been found by—Mr. Right, a charming and witty mathematician named Ed. Like my mother, Betty was always there in important and practical ways, and that summer she seemed to have a sixth sense of when to reach out to me, perhaps because she was writing a memoir about her own mother, whose death by suicide (she had ovarian cancer) Betty had helped plan and carry out. Ida Rollin, bursting with zest and motherliness, had been a major figure in my life, too.

And so with Toby, translator, writer, and intellectual conscience of the Upper West Side, a woman with uncanny feelers for friends in distress.

I had known Bella Tolpen, too, the subject of Toby's memoir, *A Book About My Mother*. So had everyone who hung out at Dan Talbot's New Yorker Theater in the sixties. Bella worked behind the candy concession that stood in as confessional to the worshipers in the house of cinema that the New Yorker had become. Between Mizoguchi and Howard Hawks, after Buñuel or the melancholy Swede, Ingmar Bergman, was Toby's mother, confidante to blocked writers and socially maladjusted movie buffs. Was it from Ida and Bella, overwhelmingly present mothers, that Betty, who had no children, and Toby, who had three, had learned to mother their contemporaries, the daughters of distant mothers?

Bella had died in New York Hospital and I'd felt, in reading

Toby's book—though I'd never asked her—that she had never quite forgiven herself for not being there, early in the morning, at the moment of death, and perhaps one of the reasons she followed Andrew's progress so closely (telephoning the hospital regularly, unbeknownst to me, for a status report), called me often, and made her presence constantly felt was that she didn't want that to happen to me.

Then there were flowers and gifts that always seemed to evoke their senders. Periodically, from Deborah Mason and Amy Gross, my editors at *Vogue*, an extraordinary arrangement would arrive, not for Andrew but for me. We got gifts of flowers at the hospital for Andrew, nonstop and glorious, but the ones from *Vogue*'s florist were like no others—fanciful, composed of impossibly unseasonal flowers choreographed into whimsical positions that somehow held their poses through days during which the mere sight of them would lift my spirits and make me smile.

Deborah, my immediate editor at *Vogue* and a splendid writer, was a little like those flowers—beautiful, alert, her sharp features and acute mind softened by the overall arrangement: a feminine roundness, the lucidity and patience of someone who saw the humor in the absurd situations in which she found herself.

If Toby and Betty, veterans of suffering, descended into the pit with me, Deborah was the one who stood, firm and caring, at the shore, a little less involved because her boundaries against suffering were firmer.

As a corrective to those friends who, like me, saw a pretty grim picture, I had my silver-lining optimists, chief among them being Lucinda. Lucinda Franks lived a block away. She and Judy Rossner and I had become friends at the Writers' Room and had found office space on the West Side, which we rented with five other writers. Until Andrew's illness, Lucinda and I used to walk across the park together whenever our schedules coincided—agonizing over our literary and dietary struggles, analyzing our pasts and presents, gossiping, moaning, laughing, and generally helping each other to confront our various bêtes noires.

Now Lucinda would stop by or call with words of cheer she drew out of a thin sky of hopelessness.

"It's awful," I would say, reporting some fresh disaster.

"He's going to be fine, Molly. I'm sure of it. A friend of mine's husband was in a coma for a month, and he's in perfect health now." Or "So-and-so was in *much* worse shape, and pulled through." Or some other example of triumph wrested from the jaws of seeming hopelessness.

And I felt this prickle of irritation. Now, don't get me wrong; I needed such reassurances. Things weren't so rosy that I could do without them. All the same, Lucinda's determination to find a silver lining would occasionally annoy me. I didn't want patented threads of hope. I didn't want to know that people in *even worse* shape than Andrew had pulled through.

I wanted to wallow a while in the valley of despond, to dwell on every lurid detail. I wanted to think that Andrew's illness was beyond all imagining, was the most baffling, cataclysmic, mysterious, earth-shaking illness that had ever befallen anyone. The idea that there were people in the world who'd suffered far greater horrors and recovered diminished Andrew's suffering . . . and mine.

The thought that we are enduring the unendurable is one of the things that keep us going. We become proprietary, even "proud" of the magnitude of our disasters. As time went on and we got to know each other better, I came to understand that Lucinda's optimism was a conditioned reflex, as inevitable a part of her as her blue eyes and apple-cheeked complexion, an echo of her own past: her mother, when Lucinda was a child, had reacted to *her* complaints in the same man-ner. When Lucinda skinned her knee, was hurt by a friend, her mother had invariably bypassed sympathy and gone right to the consoling mode:

"Oh, you'll be fine, darling, you'll be fine." Such a strategy, though meant to reassure, makes the complaint seem paltry, not worth mentioning. It's a subtle but all-important question of timing: you want to wail with self-pity for a moment, *then* put up a front, whereas the bearer of instant cheer forces you to be brave before you're ready.

In situations like the one I was in, all we have is our heroism. We are sustained by the imputation of bravery with which those outside the situation credit us even if we secretly feel we don't deserve it, that there is something "in" us, or "outside of" us—some force that isn't quite *us*—that keeps us going.

I still wasn't up to much in the way of social evenings, and could only be with close friends because I had a way of suddenly losing control, breaking down in the middle of a conversation or a meal. Yet in my memory, those dark days have pockets of brightness when the blessing of love flashed out like a fire, pierced my misery and warmed the bones. On one occasion, some of my women-writer pals—Lois Gould, Nancy Milford, and Judy Rossner—came over and we gorged on barbecued chicken, Schrafft's Heavenly Hash ice cream, and mangoes, never talking of Andrew at all, but nothing could have been more sacramental, more indicative of truly unselfish commiseration than this orgy of gluttony and cholesterol and saturated fats among three diet-conscious friends.

Andrew, even if he felt my love, was hardly in a position to acknowledge it. He didn't take in the messages I was conveying or the flowers that arrived daily. The first real reaction I got from him—and it was a high point—was when I told him about Joseph Heller. The news of Heller's illness came from director Robert Benton, who came by the apartment one night with his wife, Sallie. Benton (as everyone calls him) and Sallie were another intensely married couple—as many of our friends were—and we used to have lively dinners together once every six months, gossiping about the latest movie-business fiascoes at some Italian restaurant or other on the East Side. Sallie, sharp-tongued and pretty, a painter, was the skeptic, the "bad cop" of the duo, while Benton so radiated goodness that when he gave dollar bills to panhandlers they didn't just thank him, they hugged and kissed him afterward. Benton, director of *Kramer versus Kramer* and *Places in the Heart*, was an odd combination of the saintly and the hip, but discretion always prevailed. Asked about another director's new picture he would say something kind and noncommital, while Sallie would rear back in her chair.

"Oh, Benton!" she would explode. "How can you *say* that? Do *you* know . . ." and she'd give us the dirt. Benton and I had a special rapport: we shared the same birthday, September 29, and we felt our likeness rather too keenly for the comfort of our spouses. Each knew what the other was thinking before he said it, and I felt behind Benton's Southern geniality and humility (both real) the same secret drivenness, conceit, selfishness I felt in myself. This made me sometimes wonder, as Benton played furry saint to Sallie's bad girl, if the two of them didn't occasionally feel they'd gotten locked into their roles. Did Benton sometimes want to doff his wings and halo and take a bite out of somebody? Did Sallie get tired of having to provide the cutting edge to Benton's virtue?

It was typical of Benton to make the one gift—a gift of information—that got through to Andrew and buoyed him up. Heller, according to Benton, had been walking down the street when he suddenly became paralyzed (in fact, it wasn't quite as abrupt as that, but almost). Like Andrew, he'd contracted a sudden and scary virus (Benton wasn't familiar with the diagnosis, Guillain-Barré, at the time). When I told Andrew about this, and the fact that he was now recovering physically and writing again, Andrew was instantly cheered. It was remarkable how this one anecdote penetrated the thick fog of his brain: here at last was something with which he could identify. This was a miracle story that hit home, that said a writer could lose it all and then recover, and it was a message of hope in the war zone of the hospital, where he was surrounded by enemies who, by not recognizing who he was, made a mockery of his claim of being a writer, and reinforced his own doubts that he would write again. Heller's story lodged there, and every so often, in a lucid moment, he would refer to it. His anxiety about writing had become all-consuming.

"Do you think I'll ever write a review again?" he asked in one of his plaintive moments. He was now obsessed with his writing, particularly the weekly column in the *Voice*, about which he had always been compulsive. It had to do with continuity, with the ego satisfaction of seeing his name in print, and with the missionary zeal of keeping faith with his readers. It was one reason we rarely went away for more than a week at a time, and now he was tormented with the notion that a gap would appear and he would gradually be forgotten, disappear.

He had been writing the column ever since we met. In fact, it was with his column I fell in love back in 1965. Andrew, I came to realize, was something of an anomaly—a late-starting and not particularly radical writer appearing in a journal committed to the youthful and far-out fringes of politics and the arts. The *Voice* itself was a wildly heterogeneous assortment of individual voices, and Andrew's was one of the most individual.

Under the influence of the New Wave French critics—François Truffaut, Jean-Luc Godard, Eric Rohmer, Jacques Rivette, writing for the small French periodical *Cahiers du Cinéma* before they began making films—Andrew came to champion visual style and directorial signature, and to "rediscover" American movies in ways that would help form the tastes of a new generation of film buffs. Because of this he was assumed to belong to the form-over-content school, yet by temperament and instinct he was a classicist, a man of the word rather than the image, and the movies to which he applied the new criticism were traditional narratives that had emerged out of the Hollywood studio system, not the personal, grainy, diaristic, or surrealistic works of the independent cinema.

He was a contradictory mixture, a polemicist with a moral, humanistic slant, a visually oriented critic who nevertheless appreciated not only narrative and character but all the fleshly and sensual delights that had drawn him to movies in the first place. Going out on a limb was what he did best and most lyrically, extolling the virtues of Raoul Walsh over Stanley Kramer, of *Psycho* over *Through a Glass Darkly*, acknowledging personal preferences. Of the chic masculine splendor of *Lawrence of Arabia*, he complained, parochially but charmingly, "Where are the girls, girls, girls!"

It was an exciting and infuriating time in film criticism: harangues in *Esquire* and *The New York Times* "Arts & Leisure" section, attacks from such self-appointed cultural czars as Dwight Macdonald and John Simon, which raised the temperature and lowered the tenor of the debate as readers complained and licked their lips over the squabbles. Pauline Kael had entered the fray with a no-holds-barred broadside against Andrew in a tiny film quarterly, in effect putting them both on the map, defining the terms and weapons (*ad hominem* attack) of the debate that was to last for a decade, a duel that, for all its windy excesses and embarrassments, spoke to the feverish excitement in film at a time when films and film criticism were at their most exciting, something to argue about, alive.

Disdaining the "spurious facade of objectivity" behind which most critics hid, Andrew saw films in the context of a directorial aesthetic through the acknowledged bias of his own tastes. He loved certain actors and actresses more than others—the cracky-voiced gallantry of Margaret Sullavan, the slanting green eyes of Vivien Leigh, were inflections of the soul. He embraced films that contained multiple points of view, character complexities, agreeing, with Renoir, that *"tout le monde a ses raisons."*

He understood subtext before the term was ever used: saw the underlying sexual pathology that gave Hitchcock's films their eternal and unsettling power—icons Jimmy Stewart and Cary Grant, who were impotent or duplicitous beneath their godlike facades; the frigid blondes who attracted and frightened them; the whirlpool of ancient, childish fears at whose mercy we move day and night.

Reading his column, I assumed that this man who understood life's paradoxes would understand me. Also, I had a passion for good critical writers and essayists, the best of whom had taken on the virtues of the nineteenth-century novel—moral girth, historical resonance— abandoned by twentieth-century fiction. Andrew's voice was a large- souled "I" expanding into the world with insight and epiphany. He articulated my own half-formed thoughts, redeemed my taste from shapelessness and mere intuition. For a woman—at least for the woman I was then—there is nothing more erotic than being under- stood.

At that point, I was in the process of becoming, a transplanted Southerner full of vague yearnings, pumped up on New York adren- aline. Like dozens of other literary hopefuls of my generation, I'd come to New York with a B.A. in English, a need to get away from where I came from, and a burning desire to write—if only to prove to the place I'd left why I'd left it. Only at work and in a professional setting did I feel any sense of ease and belonging—first in a PR job, then at the French Film Office—but at parties, on dates, my stomach clenched, my mouth chattered nervously. Where men and women, often Southerners, were smoothly on the lookout, I felt exposed, awk- ward, as if I were wearing a headband that said "Unmarried." "Why aren't you married?," often stated but always implicit, hovered over every encounter. The specter of spinsterhood hounds us into marriage—it had my mother, and I was determined to avoid those scenes, parties and hometown weddings, where I would feel, or imagine I felt, sneering, pitying, probing glances. I was more at ease with the men I met through work, where a sense of purpose absorbed our erotic energies, absolved awkwardness. And so it was that movies came to the rescue for me and Andrew, as two "courting" adults, as they had for us earlier in our lives, in movie houses in Brooklyn and Richmond, where men and women from opposite ends of the earth came together on the screen, and love miraculously dissolved the boundaries of class and geography.

Our courtship was conducted on the streets and in the theaters and coffee shops of New York. We would see two, three movies on a Saturday, on Forty-second Street (safe, if raunchy, in those days) or on the East Side, at Andrew's lectures at the School for Visual Arts or at some person or another's apartment where sixteen-millimeter films were always being screened. In those days, before there were film courses and revival houses everywhere, before the advent of cassettes and VCRs, one caught old movies wherever one could. It was in the byways and back alleys of cinema that I first met members of that strange underground species, the film buff. They were weirdos, specialists, solitaries in the company of other solitaries who knew at any given moment where to see an obscure thirties movie with Constance Bennett or Helen Twelvetrees, or when a rarely seen silent with Richard Barthelmess or Evelyn Brent would be playing: at film historian Bill Everson's apartment, or more probably at the Theodore Huff Society, a floating film-viewing group that usually met at a small office in a building on Union Square.

These were the antisocial and the just-plain unsocialized, the misfits who hadn't dated in high school. These were the sort of people you never see or read about, people the media has passed over because in our high-profile success-obsessed world they are invisible, "losers." As a group, they were almost entirely male—probably because voyeurism is essentially a male activity, as is complete surrender to fantasy. For women, marriage, and the socializing impulse that accompanies it, is ingrained from a very early age and leads us away from solitary pursuits. Hence the parting of company that comes in adolescence, when a sudden disparity in math and science scores appears, when brainy girls suddenly reorient themselves to boys, reality, and society,

and their opposite numbers—boys who fall through the social net—
retreat into an asexual world of computers, or movies, or baseball
scores. These were men who lived without women, without wives or
girlfriends to hold a mirror up to them, make them spruce up, eat
decent food, get fresh air, spend a few hours away from a movie theater.
They were sweet, civilized, educated men, but their ties might have
food spots on them, their white shirts show signs of having been worn
the day before. They were of an age in which the obsession with old
movies was also a search for their lost childhood and adolescence.
Their dreams and the people with whom they spent their vicarious
lives were stars, and their conversation was full of movies, dates, lists,
memories, comparisons.

Yet Andrew, though resembling them in some outward respects,
wasn't quite one of them. For one thing, he was more interested in
good movies than obscure ones. Once there was a choice between
seeing Hitchcock's *Shadow of a Doubt* and a rural B picture called
The Girl of the Limberlost, and Andrew's was the only hand raised in
favor of the former, the latter—"better" for being unseen—was the
near-unanimous choice. Andrew was archival in his attempt to see
everything, constantly promoting the cause of film preservation, but
he was continually refining his tastes, whereas a good many of the
buffs collected information quantitatively—indiscriminately and ex-
haustively. Yet we had wonderful evenings in the lap of this collective
obsession and because of it. I remember seeing and being stunned by
Buster Keaton's great *Sherlock Jr.* at the Huff Society, and Bill Everson's
courses at the New School were a gold mine of obscure but revelatory
thirties films. The buffs were a sacral community, joined by religious
fervor, and if it hadn't been for their weirdness and dedication and
sunless pallor, there wouldn't have been that glorious abundance of
cinematic gems and jetsam.

When I met him, Andrew was already emerging from the
underground—"Godzilla clambering from the depths," Dwight Macdonald had once said of him in a funny and peculiarly apt evocation of the primeval ooze of buffdom and, presumably, the kinds of
"sludge"—American genre films—Andrew brought with him and held
aloft for us to admire.

When Andrew asked me to marry him in 1969—we'd been going

together for over two years—I said yes, but halfheartedly and with a shrug and a shiver of apprehension. He was going to Paris and the Berlin Film Festival and he wanted me to go with him, and I was still conventional enough not to want to cope with the awkwardnesses at home and abroad of traveling as lovers, and brave the disapproval of *hôteliers* and *concierges* and my mother. Yet I had no real desire to marry. I'd grown up, like any little girl, with the appropriate romantic yearnings for the man who would share and define my destiny and the ritualistic appurtenances that went with it: the engagement ring, the wedding, the white dress, the bridesmaids, the going-away suit. But then I'd gotten over wanting those things, and the habit of mind of joyful surrender, that went with the traditional wedding. I wanted this man precisely because he hadn't swept me off my feet, made me walk on air, lose my appetite, my concentration, my self. Yet without these chemical inducements, without the irrational charms of romantic love, what was there to override my objections to marriage, persuade me to give up my freedom?

But my freedom weighed heavily; independence and fulfillment seemed to lie within the bounds of matrimony rather than without. If marriage represents a certain acceptance of convention, a solidifying of one's ties with the community, a narrowing of roles, mine would be the opposite. Lady Jane Wilde, as quoted in Richard Ellman's biography of her son, said of marriage, "I would not allow my great soul to be imprisoned in a woman's destiny." Yet I had felt more imprisoned by my singleness, by an anxiety and a sense of not knowing where I belonged.

Instead of closing off my paths of freedom, Andrew *was* my rebellion; instead of initiating me into a conventional home and marriage, an acceptance of the rules, he liberated me from conventional wifehood. By choosing a man of whom my family disapproved—painful though that disapproval was—I was released from their claims and the expectations and orthodoxies that went with them. Living in an "unsanctioned" marriage would be a little like not being married at all.

How little I understood! Like everyone else, I made the most important decision most of us ever make abruptly and intuitively, with a shrug of the shoulders, conning myself that I was making a rational choice but propelled forward by obscure and perhaps irreconcilable needs.

Half of me wanted to marry, the other half wanted not to marry, and this seemed like a perfect compromise—a marriage that wasn't quite a marriage.

And so we pledged our troth before God, blind to how peculiar we were, or perhaps thinking that other people were just as peculiar. And then I had nightmares. And then I fell truly in love.

4

On Wednesday, July 18, Andrew, perennially anxious over his column, was in a state of apoplexy, convinced he had actually written one, which had gotten waylaid: either a messenger had picked it up but lost it on the way back to the *Voice* or I had misplaced it. In fact, there was always a grain of plausibility to feed the suspicions; once a *Voice* messenger had gotten arrested on his return route and had wound up at the police station, busted on a drug charge, with Andrew's column in his pouch. And yes, once, just once, I, in my desperate and Sisyphean struggle to keep books and papers from overwhelming us, had thrown an important document away, and thus had given Andrew lifetime license, whenever he couldn't find something, to point the finger at me.

Totally convinced himself, he was very convincing. At one point, he called Karen Durbin, his editor at the *Voice*, who described the incident to me the next day.

"He sounded just like himself," she said. "He said, 'Karen? This is Andy Sarris,' as he always does, formally, using his last name, as if I wouldn't recognize his voice or a simple 'Andy.' "

Then he asked her to send a messenger for his column. It wasn't until she hung up the phone that she realized he wasn't at home at all, couldn't possibly be, but was still in the hospital, and his talk of a column was pure fantasy.

His attempts to fight feelings of powerlessness focused on two things: his typewriter, and the Foley tube. The typewriter, representing literary potency, was the object he most wanted. The Foley tube, on the other hand, was the thing he most wanted to get rid of. The symbolism of the tube was obvious, and it was his bête noire, especially as it was always being inserted by virile young interns. If, as Freud suggests, paranoia is a cover for and defense against homosexuality, there undoubtedly was a touch of homosexual panic in Andrew's feeling that his manhood was being toyed with by what must have seemed to him an endless supply of young men. How could Andrew, or any man so reduced and threatened, not fear for his maleness? He would demand, plead, almost cry to have it removed, and someone, usually Ramir down for his five-minutes visit, would agree. After all, he wouldn't be around when Andrew failed to urinate and it had to be reinserted.

Ramir was equally cavalier on the subject of the typewriter. "Oh, Mr. Sarris wants to write?" he would say. "Then by all means, bring him his typewriter." And I would go home, schlepp the forty-pound so-called portable down, watch while Andrew, having utterly forgotten he'd asked for it, ignored it, and then, because anything that wasn't nailed down was likely to be stolen during the night, would schlepp the thing home again.

I understood what Ramir was doing, and I was all for reassuring Andrew, but I was annoyed all the same. Over the years, each doctor develops a sort of professional-persona, his own variant of the "bedside manner," a face he turns to the patient that is a compromise between the patient's insatiable need of him, and his to keep back something of himself . . . *for* himself and for the other patients. These personalities—Ramir's humor-the-patient nonchalance; Sam's joviality and talk of tennis and family; Crenshaw's Olympian chill; Seltzman's schoolboy eagerness—had a broad-based majoritarian utility: they worked well enough most of the time. But there were other times and other patients where a more fine-tuned approach might have served better.

There was also the matter, in Ramir's case, of having orders countermanded at every succession of shifts and changing of the guard, and the turnover of personnel was almost unremitting in the summer months, when doctors would suddenly disappear for a week's vacation or conference. An inside "joke" making the rounds of the solariums was the axiom that there are more deaths in July than in any other month because of the influx of new graduates.

I was told by the neurology resident in charge, Jim Gwathmey, to mark the periods of lucidity (growing less frequent) because it was to that state that Andrew's mind would return when (and the unspoken "and if") he recovered. I couldn't quite understand this—it left so many questions unanswered. For instance, he was startlingly lucid on anything to do with films. I was going to look at a tape of Kurosawa's *The Seven Samurai* one night, to write a review for a video magazine, and I asked him, as I often did, what to look for. He was on a gurney, being taken away for an X ray, but his mind had turned like a flash to the movie, summoning up insights, dates, context.

"The interesting thing about Kurosawa," he replied, as I trotted down the corridor after him, "is that he's robust and intellectual at the same time." He was discussing Mifune's bravura performance as the elevator doors closed behind him.

Yet his conversations with Gwathmey were gnomic and circular, taking place in a phantasmagoric world in which Andrew had ensnared the young neurologist.

"Mr. Sarris," Gwathmey said at one point, "you told me the balloons were after you."

Andrew: "I didn't exactly say that. I said they seemed to have a life of their own."

Gwathmey: "You said you wanted to murder us. We don't hold it against you."

And Andrew: "No, I didn't." And, then, contradictorily: "And I'm sorry." (He wasn't foreclosing the possibility he had.)

As in everything else, Andrew was crazy in his own original way. He was precise to a ludicrous degree, and for some categories of information, he had total recall. When asked to name the presidents backward, he rattled them off, stunning the doctors and stumbling only when he got to Franklin Pierce, but he could never correctly answer the question "Where are you?"

"Atlantic City?" he volunteered once, and again, "Los Angeles?"

looking hopefully at the doctor. Sometimes he identified himself as being in Manhattan, but never in a hospital, and never in New York Hospital.

When I tested him it was on his home ground of movies; when they did it, it was with inane-sounding riddles that had no doubt proved valuable as a lowest-common-denominator test of what they call baseline mental function but that Andrew greeted—rightly, I thought—as a trick to be gotten around.

"Mr. Sarris," Jim Gwathmey began, in a typical Q and A session, "what do a dog and a cat have in common?"

To which Andrew replied, "A dog and a cat have in common that they define each other by their differences."

With the stubborn dignity of a superior though baffled mind bearing down on a moronic interrogator, Andrew's answers had a wonderful Alice-in-Wonderland logic. When asked, "What's the similarity between a table and a chair?" he replied, "That they are used to put things on so a person can work at it."

I saw instantly what was behind this elaborate dodge: he had in mind a person and a typewriter—himself, in other words—but he wasn't going to give the show away. Since they were out to get him, to finish him once and for all as a writer, it wouldn't do to let them know his plans.

Ah, the cunning of the mad. Andrew was imagining various people as agents of the KGB, but it was he who was spying, hatching escape plots, imposing a confrontational grid (destroy or be destroyed) on the world around him. Someone wrote that there is a parallel between modernism and madness, and I was struck by the truth of this analogy. The world that Andrew's madness manufactured was self-referential, anti-humanist, a closed system, pretending to communicate but, like the writings of some of the more obscure academic theoreticians, intended actually to close off discourse. He was sneaky, cryptic, superior in his opacity. After all, to be understood, to speak in universal terms, would be to furnish the enemy—the hospital staff, the bourgeoisie—with ammunition for one's capture. To be enclosed within a system was power and protection. Theory—and insanity—were systems of language built on islands, labyrinths within which the initiates enclosed themselves in ever-narrowing paths of thought. Once one had taken up the cause, the vocabulary, one was inside the labyrinth, there was no bridge back to the mainland.

Andrew's great quality as an intellectual was his openness, his status in what was either no-man's-land or the best of both worlds.

"I'm too much of a journalist for the academics," he once said, "and too much of an academician for the journalists."

He wasn't modish, had no ax to grind, but because he was an insatiable rediscoverer and explorer of the past, even if it meant confronting his own mistakes of judgment and revising them, he was unafraid of the future. *Auteurism*, the director-oriented approach to films, was the least ideological of "isms," a way of comparing and classifying, of expanding film dialogue, rather than a closed system. Teaching three film courses in Columbia's School of the Arts, he'd held his own for over a decade, filling his classes and ignoring the academic vogues that came and went. But in the trauma of the moment, he was taking refuge in a rigid black-and-white world, where everyone was either an enemy or a victim of the enemy. To communicate would be to compromise his own integrity.

Milan Kundera wrote somewhere that, like actors without a script, we're constantly going on "cold," maneuvering through life feeling helpless and exposed. On the contrary, we spend our lives arming ourselves against precisely that feeling—that nightmare—of being caught off-guard, in the spotlight, our scripts lost or forgotten. Madness is but an extreme version of the character armor we employ to give ourselves a sense of control, to keep chaos at bay. Our roles and the selves we exhibit are collages, as we collect bits of personae like artifacts—from books, movies, real-life characters—and keep them groomed for the unexpected. We arrive on the scene as actors, authors, and directors all in one, equipped with phrases, prejudices, attitudes, mannerisms, props, all burnished and shiny and ready to be placed around, like cherished personal possessions in a hotel room, to render the unfamiliar familiar, to stave off being overwhelmed by too many possibilities. We even cultivate small doses of anxiety in order to ward off existential panic, like a vaccine that contains cells of the disease it is an inoculation against.

Andrew's madness seemed like the ultimate defense, as hard and as unyielding as granite as it converted everything, everyone, into an enemy. He was like Leontes in Shakespeare's *A Winter's Tale*, who, having suspected, them convinced himself of, his wife's treachery, seeks out proof of her perfidy everywhere, a confirmation of his malignant vision in which he takes a positive relish. Her beauty itself becomes evil, an instrument of betrayal.

Madness as a liberating experience has had its apostles through the years, generally artists and philosophers who are standing sanely and safely on dry land, who see it as a way of breaking through false selves to freedom, shedding the personality armor and "vital lies" of daily life.

When written about, it sounds majestic, desirable, a badge of authenticity and thus something no self-respecting intellectual should do without: as the deepest and darkest of introspections (Kierkegaard), or the acceptance, as in Ernest Becker, of the reality of death. In Jung, the refusal to idealize in order to become truly and wholly oneself. Even Virginia Woolf managed to treasure the specialness of her descents into a mental netherworld, until the repetitive horror of actual madness finally overwhelmed her.

I'd experienced my own break with reality at college in the sixties, a near-psychotic depression that came about when, in a delayed reaction to my father's death, I began traveling in a different direction, took a scholarly path that led directly away from the friends and interests that had marked my life until then.

It came on suddenly, a vertiginous terror in which I seemed to be falling through mental space, like a plane suddenly dropping in a wind shear. The person that others called by my name lay in bed, staring at the ceiling, her only urge to be swallowed up by the earth. There was no "I" to contemplate suicide, to act. My days were like notations in a diary from which the first person pronoun and all affect have been removed: Went to class. Ate lunch. Actions were done, gone through by a human being that looked like me, but was an impersonator. There was a psychiatrist in residence at the college, but I didn't go to him, giving myself all sorts of reasons, but really afraid of "being found"—as the British psychiatrist D. W. Winnicott so beautifully puts it in describing adolescent neurosis—"before being there to be found."

The breakdown had left me with no redeeming insight, no hallucinatory images or poetic souvenirs, only terror of a recurrence. Madness, loss of self, was the monster I was fleeing in coming to New York, the monster that I would evade if I kept moving forward, the monster that Andrew slew, or kept at bay, in marrying me.

We seemed to have all the benefits of marriage with none of the drawbacks. We had the security of that white piece of paper, yet never felt stuck, engulfed by routine or imprisoned by that sense of knowing exactly what the other will say or do. We hadn't yet begun repeating ourselves; living together was endlessly rich and surprising. Our lives didn't begin when we met, but they began to take shape.

The part of me that loved Andrew felt like the best and most serious part of me, so that my marrying him, whatever it implied in terms of rejection of a former life, was less a reaction *against*, than an action *toward*. We choose people for reasons that aren't always clear at the time, and then discover that they have pushed us in the direction we already wanted to go.

But once again, I found myself at odds with the times. It was the late sixties and early seventies, unhappy wives were denouncing the evils of the patriarchy and the sexist brutalities of marriage, and I was aglow with newlywed joy, I had a man who delighted in my career— was in fact my mentor—and stood behind me in every way. At gatherings of my sisters in which the inequities of domestic life were itemized, I sat in the corner, silenced, a capitalist among the Trotskyites. Their husbands made outrageous demands, turned a blind eye to their efforts at self-realization, betrayed them with their best friends. My heart went out to them, but what could I say? I was the victim of a happy marriage.

Andrew genuinely cared about women as people. Although he was known for lushly romantic paeans to actresses as objects of a frankly lustful desire, he was no less interested in their psyches and their social position. He often spotted an instance of the double standard, or an injustice to women, before I did, and no man was more fascinated by the twists and turns of a woman's intelligence. He had little of the misogyny that afflicts so much American writing and was immensely comfortable with the female half of himself—more comfortable, in fact, than I was with the female half of myself.

And yet, how truly liberated was I? There's a wonderful, little known British film, *Passionate Friends* (called *A Woman's Story* when it was released in 1949 in America), that tells the story of a woman (Ann Todd) torn between her first great love, Trevor Howard at his most captivating, now a biologist who keeps reappearing in her life and reawakening her passion; and the safe, secure businessman husband played by Claude Rains, who gives her her freedom. Of course the two men, as so often in the woman's film, represent the two irreconcilable sides of herself. As Todd, married to director David Lean at the time and framed in an aureole of light, looks shimmeringly beautiful and torn, Rains explains to Howard that she has chosen him, Rains, precisely so she won't lose her self in marriage. "I give her independence, affection, freedom," he boasts, whereas with Howard, she would have had "romance, fulfillment, togetherness. She doesn't want that." Since marriage based on passionate love was the holy grail of the woman's picture—and the reigning social myth—it's remarkable to see a film that so clearly shows the penalty of such a love where a woman is concerned and the advantages of the practical match. The power of being loved; the powerlessness of loving.

With Andrew, I thought I was marrying Claude Rains and I ended up with Trevor Howard.

And now Andrew was fighting for his identity. I suddenly remembered the article he had written from Cannes. The one about the tear gas . . . why hadn't I thought of it before?

We had come down one morning from our hotel room to find a strange odor in the lobby. We didn't think much of it, went on over to the Palais where the screenings are held, but gradually, during the day, our eyes began to tear and we felt a strange buzzing in our heads. Later, we found out that in the early morning, some roughnecks from a sleazy bar across the street had grown threatening in the hotel lobby and the night watchman had sprayed them with tear gas.

Andrew had included the incident in his column, not only describing the end-of-the-world feeling that Mace induced, but hinting that no one would know what had happened until they analyzed his remains at the Centers for Disease Control in Atlanta. Now here he was, and there in Atlanta were at least some of his insides, being tested and reviewed.

When I told Gwathmey and offered to bring in the column, he was interested, but not in the ways I'd hoped.

"Sure, bring me the article," he said. "We don't think he could have gotten this from Mace. But we'd like to read it just to see the way he thinks, what his mind is like."

There was certainly no evidence of the breadth and luminosity of his mind in his current behavior, but there was a cryptic quality that was not out of character. Threatened on all sides and utterly helpless, madness was an act of aggression. Suspicion was his weapon.

"Are you still seeing the Mayor of Quogue?" he asked, imagining a "titled" enemy, an antagonist powerful enough to be worthy of him.

We all make peace with horror. As terrorists' victims become their allies, we cozy up to torment in the hope of exorcising its dangers. I was playing out a strategy of appeasement, while Andrew was beset by fantasies of escape, persecution, and emasculation. A man in a red shirt had been "very unfriendly," he told me, and had said to him, "What makes you think you'll ever teach again?" This sounded pretty horrible, but I tended to discount it—as much for my own peace of mind, no doubt, as for his. He lived in an endlessly metamorphosing world in which his fears took on weird shapes and narrative fragments. The Japanese was having orgies, and the young intern had taken Andrew's penis and put it in a tube.

"It's sitting in the next room," said Andrew.

"That's okay," I said.

"That's okay?" he asked, and when I nodded, he repeated, "Okay," apparently mollified.

Like a dog, Andrew had no sense of time, whether I'd been away for an hour or a week. But unlike a dog, he didn't automatically pant with joy when I walked in the room. He would be seething with some grudge he'd cooked up during the night. That morning he had called me over and, in that horrible, conspiratorial voice, said, "I've got to get out of here. I offered a man ten thousand dollars to help me. Are you coming with me or not?" He paused menacingly. "Otherwise, I'll divorce you."

"Who'll take care of you?" I said, exasperated, but trying to humor him.

"My mother," he answered confidently. I tried to laugh, but

paranoia's icy fingers gripped my soul. Might there not be something between them to this effect, some determination to carry out this wild plan? Her love of Andrew took precedence over all other loves, and in any conflict, the legal and moral claims of society would always rank a poor second. I began to visualize Themis, rickety on her legs, charging down the hall, pushing Andrew in a wheelchair, in a midnight getaway.

I came in one day and was told that Andrew had struck his mother. I was horrified, but at the same time, I felt a shameful spasm of relief—ah-hah! the escape plan had misfired. Then appalled at being relieved. Which of us around here was crazy anyway?

I was acting strangely myself, or so Annie said. She and her friend Patrick came over one evening, with another couple.

I was trying to hold myself together but afterward Annie said, "You were acting just like a Virginia hostess, Molly, passing hors d'oeuvres, with a smile plastered on your face, refusing to let anybody help you, but looking like death warmed over."

What did she mean? I hadn't even realized how grotesque I must have seemed. Yet . . . was it that bad, or was Annie still in part reacting to the me she had seen—and invented—when she was ten and I was sixteen, she trying frantically to make me notice her, I thinking only of boys, utterly indifferent to the pesky little cousin who followed me around. She would lurk outside when I came home from school and went in to see my father. She told me later that I would go in and laugh and talk with him, and I would be forever grateful to her for this recollection. In my own guilty memory, I had fled his sickroom constantly, invented excuses to avoid the painful sight of him dying. And then, according to Annie, I would run upstairs to my bedroom, she running after me, slam the door in her face, and play rock 'n' roll at a deafening volume. Now, Andrew was sick, Annie was still ten years old, wanting to be let into my inner sanctum, not understanding that I was still only sixteen, and that I wasn't shutting her out, but shutting my pain in.

Another night when friends were over, the phone rang. It was Andrew.

"Molly," he said conspiratorially, "I have an idea." I dreaded what was coming. "I want you to put out a warrant for my arrest. That way the police will come and take me out of here."

There was a kind of gallows humor in the situation, and in his ingenuity, and I suppose I reported it with a certain pride, like a mother whose child is a truant and a mischief-maker, but with style.

Sam was good about calling when he didn't see me at the hospital, but almost all he or anyone could say was that Andrew was "confused." He kept warning me not to pay any attention to the mood or substance of his fantasies, only to the surrounding symptoms, but that wasn't easy to do.

Andrew was more malevolent by the minute, and Gwathmey warned me again that he might turn on me. Neurologists carry more than their share of professional gloom—for one thing, because the prognosis on neurology patients is generally poor and they rarely improve or get well. Certainly that's the reason given for the undesirability of the neurology floor, often the first assignment for new nurses. With seniority they flee to other floors when they can—though I found nothing to complain about in the nurses while we were there. Then there's the terrible sense of helplessness because there's so little that neurologists can actually *do* to relieve suffering. They are primarily in the business of making diagnoses. And Gwathmey, cheerless even for a neurologist, was the sort of doctor who seemed to take pride in facing the worst, in exposing "unpleasant facts" long before they became facts. He may have been guilty of nothing more than trying to seem older, or wiser, than he was—a young physician attempting to deal with that most difficult thing for a doctor, complete helpless ignorance—but it came across as low-level sadism.

One afternoon, Themis came up to me in tears. She had still not quite "gotten" what was wrong with Andrew—as indeed, who had?—yet Gwathmey had told her that they "couldn't promise he wouldn't have brain damage." I was stunned, outraged, first, that he should say such a thing to her, and second, because it was a possibility I hadn't allowed myself to even think about. How dare he answer this question that nobody had asked! I told him from now on not to volunteer grim information unless we asked for it.

Even as their profession concentrated on the biological over the psychological, neurologists seemed to have gotten more literal-minded, more rigidly "factual," as if waging an eternal battle against the great bugaboo, the arch-necromancer and magician, psychiatry. They all thought Freud had taken the wrong turn when he left the neurology lab for the consulting room, and psychiatry, for its part, instead of sticking by its symbols and asserting its privileged insights, had gone on the defensive, straining to prove its medical (i.e., scientific) credentials. Like Andrew's dog and cat, they defined themselves by their differences.

It never came to the straitjacket, but Gwathmey's prediction that Andrew would turn on me did come true. I'd been out to have my hair cut and attend a screening. It was Friday, July 20. I'd been coming in twice a day and this was practically the first time I'd left his side to do anything connected with work or maintenance. But the minute I walked in, I knew he had "turned." He was propped up in the pillow, his face half cocked, with a murderous look in his eye, an expression that could corrode steel.

"Where have you been?" he demanded. I reminded him I'd gone to see *Country*, the Jessica Lange picture, with the Festival committee.

He continued to glare. "All you care about is your career," he said, with a viciousness that took my breath away. "You'd do anything to get ahead, even if it killed me."

I tried to dismiss this as absurd, as the ravings of a maniac, or a husband who'd had one drink too many, but as with a drunk, one can discount the vehemence of the hostility but not the underlying emotion. It was a startling moment. Had Andrew been secretly resenting me for my ambition? Did he think I had "used" him? Even that I was trying to take over? Aren't the strivings of the pupil to supplant the mentor a component in any such relationship? For certainly one reason our marriage had worked so well was that Andrew was the established one when we met, and remained the "giant" in the relationship and the authority in our mutual field, film criticism. I walked a figurative three paces behind, or sat at his feet, but perhaps I had been inching up without even realizing it.

In the late twentieth century, we no longer arrange marriages according to status and property parity—an upper-class wife for a wealthy tradesman; a woman with a dowry for an impoverished aristocrat. Nevertheless, there's a tacit system of equivalences and trade-offs, and one's failure to live up to one's half of the bargain can mean the end of the relationship. If the man slips, loses status, if the woman rises, can the slide rule adjust? Changes in the wind, shifts in the balance of power, affect modern marriages more, because they are more isolated from the community, with its built-in pressures and supports. If two-career marriages are in general vulnerable to such shifts, ours was even more vulnerable, being a marriage of two people working in the same field, and a marriage in which work was central to our lives. A writer married to a writer is unusual and for good reason: temperamentally and financially, writers are better matched with stable and stabilizing partners. I knew one couple in which the wifely wife, a fiercely purposeful Englishwoman, took it upon herself to stop her garrulous husband from scattering and squandering his insights, like so much intellectual semen. At parties, she would see him in conversation, rush up, and virtually clamp her hand over his lips.

"Henry!" she would cry, "Save it. Don't waste it," as the group looked on in wonderment. His words had cash value; he had to be muzzled.

Almost all of my writer friends, men and women, had spouses who were in other fields: psychiatry, law, mathematics, art, publishing. And of the writer couples, there were probably even fewer who worked in the same field.

Woman of the Year, the Katharine Hepburn–Spencer Tracy film about the tensions between a husband and wife who are both reporters, was based on the marriage of Dorothy Thompson and Sinclair Lewis. In the film, Hepburn and Tracy manage to overcome the strains introduced when Hepburn's smart and fiercely undomestic foreign correspondent wins the Woman of the Year award and simultaneously shows herself unfit for child rearing and egg scrambling; in real life, Lewis and Thompson announced their separation just after *Time* magazine had voted her Woman of the Year. His ego was apparently no more able than Tracy's to tolerate such competition, and the movie wreaks vengeance on all uppity career women by humiliating and ridiculing Hepburn's superachiever. The film ends with a victory for Hepburn, yet it's a Pyrrhic victory of sorts. The breakfast fiasco scene, a domestic Armageddon of ineptitude and missed timing, concludes with Tracy accepting the fact that Hepburn will never be like other women. But what Hepburn's triumph (and what Thompson's failure) confirms is that Hepburn *herself* is extraordinary; that only a woman as exceptional, gifted, and defiant, as sure of herself as both woman and suffragette, can defy the domestic gods so openly.

After a brief flurry of housewifeliness just after our marriage—poring over cookbooks and giving dinner parties—I had lost even minimal competence. I had a husband who never *expected* me to act like a housewife, but I had nevertheless internalized those gods and felt guilty over my dereliction. Andrew had nothing of the lord of the mansion or the old-fashioned male in him (my mother had once said he was the first modern man she had ever known). He gave me my freedom, urged me not to waste my time on domestic or decorative trivia, was completely "on my side" about housework. He had seen a mother, frustrated by poverty, unable to fulfill her dream of going to college. My mother was certainly no model of domesticity, so I couldn't blame her for forcing a homemaker conscience on me. Yet out of some anxiety, I always felt a giant finger pointing at me and my slovenly ways. Domesticity was both a trap and a temptation; I could never "do it right." The archetypal Housewife may no longer oppress us as she once did, but she is still there, like a phantom limb, perhaps more insidious for being intangible and indefinable, a ghost.

More insidious because she represents a deeper guilt, a past we are trying to suppress. As Freud pointed to the fantasy of parricide—the son wanting to rebel against his father and victoriously overcome him, with all its attendant guilt—so women, in going beyond and against their mothers, are committing their own form of matricide. We are the first generation of women to rebel against our mothers and the very definitions they lived by. The housewife is thus a symbolic archetype, an image we must both appease and transcend, all the more powerful for being officially outdated.

Like me, the women writers I knew were married to domestically tolerant and relatively secure men, who didn't stand on ceremony or expect lavish entertaining, who could fend for themselves. I had little excuse not to produce, not to concentrate fully on my work, yet I think we all felt a certain domestic anxiety, a pull, perhaps even an atavistic desire to pad barefoot in the kitchen. Perhaps I even needed domesticity as an alibi. Because if the house, being my domain of responsibility, was a major source of distraction for me that it wasn't for Andrew, it was also a protection. As long as I could create a pleasing environment, cook a decent meal, look and behave winningly, I wouldn't have to prove myself as a writer, or *just* as a writer. My brains would be a dividend, not the definition of myself on which I stood or fell.

As long as Andrew and I were traveling in the same direction, we seemed to be governed by an inner equilibrium, but on two occasions, we lost our footing. First, when my book came out, I was suddenly thrust into the spotlight for my fifteen minutes of fame while Andrew was inevitably reduced to "Mr. Haskell," the husband. He made jokes about Norman Maine walking into the ocean at the end of A *Star Is Born*, but there was an edge to the jokes. And for a two-year period in the mid-seventies, I was the critic for *New York Magazine* while he was first-string critic for the *Voice*, and we were going head on, week after week, reviewing the same movies and under extra pressure because our editors, terrified that one publication would scoop the other, were pushing us to ignore the opening date and plunge into print first. We had the impression, no doubt exaggerated, that we were two fighting fish in the goldfish bowl that Manhattan is; not only were we being set upon each other, but everyone we knew and didn't know was looking over our shoulders, scouring our columns for identical insights, making snide remarks or invidious comparisons. (Was Andrew the Pygmalion to my auteurist Galatea? Was I henpecking Andrew into a feminist viewpoint?) There were suddenly constraints on our marriage where there had been none before. Where before we had always gone to screenings together and talked afterward, now we were obliged to go to screenings separately and keep our thoughts to ourselves. There we were, week after week, straining to be different, to be better, to mark the boundaries between us, all the while longing to go back, to curl up in our old glued-together roles. I suddenly found I didn't have much taste for the spotlight after all, or for weekly deadlines, and though I blamed my abrupt leavetaking on an unsympathetic editor and my own inadequacies, some part of me was no doubt more than relieved when the two of us came to a parting of the ways and I could retreat into Andrew's shadow.

That experience, traumatic as it had been for me, had been perhaps even more agonizing for Andrew, who suffered for me. One of the disadvantages of two people being so much an extension of each other is that misfortune has a kind of exponential impact. We feel the other's wounds as our own, and more painfully. How much had it cost *him*—that defeat of mine, my sleepless nights, my sense of re-jection? The person who suffers defeat has the advantage: calls on inner resources, the adrenaline of battle, fantasies of vengeance, in order to rebound, while those who love the sufferer suffer in silence, feeling the pain twice over.

How much had worrying over me in general cost Andrew? For in his role as mentor and support, had I perhaps depleted him? If there is the threat that every pupil will supplant the mentor, isn't there also a secret hope that this role reversal *will* take place, allowing the mentor to breathe free of the burden of responsibility and escape the ideal image the disciple has formed of him?

All writers need stroking, of course, and for New York writers, sex pales beside the ecstasy of having someone wax enthusiastic over one's literary effort. The real love scene in *Hannah and Her Sisters* is the one in which Dianne Wiest waits breathlessly for the response of Woody Allen to her screenplay and he gives a rhapsodic "I love it!" But I seemed to require a good deal more than Andrew. I saw him as one of what Freud termed the "conquerors," those sons of doting mothers with an unshakable inner confidence. There was an ideal reader, himself, for whom he wrote, and what he wrote gave him pleasure. It took him a pathologically long time to get there: he would lie on the sofa all week ruminating, then rise at midnight before the column was due and type it out, one draft only. He would then chuckle and laugh as he read it over and over, first in typescript, then on Wednesday when the *Voice* came out. I, on the other hand, would cringe at columns, at my words falling so far short of my hopes. Andrew played doting mother to me, and my "confidence," such as it was, came late and from the outside, from Andrew—a kind of vitamin-replacement therapy that he supplied with his constantly reiterated words of encouragement, but which was never permanent, and never enough, and which was a reminder, like the medications we take, of chronic inadequacy. What would happen to me if something happened to my "source," if the supply ran out?

Perhaps it had. Perhaps this was precisely what was happening now. I had grown fat and sleek and smart on Andrew's love, like the character in Henry James's *The Sacred Fount* who has acquired a personality and distinction he never had before because of the sacrificing love of a woman. In this most brilliant and ruthless study of the dynamics of coupledom, James posits a depletional model in which one person grows symbolically fat—or young or beautful—on the sacrifice of the other. The one who pays for the other's miracle is in effect "cleaned out," an "intellectual ruin." Had I sucked the intellectual blood out of Andrew, leaving him an empty husk? Was Andrew the sacred fount from which I had drunk and grown powerful, a fount that in James's image has enough for one but not for two? It had never occurred to me that this insatiable need of mine, and his constantly having to buttress me, must have taken something out of Andrew. When would my ego take wings and fly on its own? Was he going to have to spend the rest of his life nursing a crippled bird? Was some part of Andrew, even now, hoping to see me break free, was the mother in him delighting in my apparent competence, even as the eyes burned with the rage of the threatened and beleaguered male?

Despite the doctors' warnings and those of my own reason to disregard Andrew's hostility, I reacted with hurt and fury. There had been so little anger in our marriage—not a healthy thing, perhaps— that I didn't know how to cope with what I felt to be true venom.

That night, Mother called from Richmond and Annie answered the phone.

"Molly can't talk to you now, Mary," said Annie. "Andrew turned on her and she's upset and angry."

"Put her on the phone," Mother commanded, and when I got on, "Molly, that's unworthy of you. You know he's not himself. How can you react that way?"

Unworthy. An interesting reaction on Mother's part. Anger was not something that just was, but something that required moral justification, thus an immoral feeling. And unseemly. Then there was her instinctual sympathy with Andrew: welcome in one respect, yet hard to comprehend in another. During my father's illness, had she never experienced anger, frustration, fury, rage, however irrational? Had she so repressed all these emotions that she found them inexplicable in me?

Still feeling bruised by Andrew's hostility, I tried to understand it in a larger context, the rage of all men who are deeply and secretly afraid of the power of women. His situation, four men lying prone while their womenfolk came and went, was a daily, hourly evocation of the fear that lurks in the hearts of all men, that they were born of women, will be overtaken by them, and that death, which awaits us all, awaits them first.

In a situation like this, where the social inhibitors no longer hold sway, those sexual fears and prejudices that lie under a thin layer of civilization rise like earthworms after a spring rain and we revert to sexual stereotypes. In this dramatically segregated arena, the division was simple and the role reversal was painfully obvious: men were prostrate and powerless; women freestanding and powerful.

To the extent that men's identities are bound up in their sexuality, being reduced in this manner is to be exposed, unmanned. Inevitably, hospitalization desexualizes a man, whereas women are not "unwomanned." Theoretically we are used to playing a passive role and being cared for, to being on our backs, whether figuratively or literally, and however we may hate the position, we are not socially humiliated or sexually compromised. I say this in theory, yet in fact I had been completely shattered by my first hospitalization, in a hospital outside of New York, where I had been listed as Mrs. Andrew Sarris, denied my own name and working identity.

The truth is, some surgeries and illnesses cut closer to the bone than others. Unlike the later abdominal surgeries, when I was at New York Hospital and had my own name (I was actually writing a "Hers" column from my bed), this first had been gynecological—the removal of a fallopian tube by the same doctors who were delivering babies and checking on beaming mothers with newborns in another wing of the hospital. The experience raised the whole issue of my childlessness, and, in a deep depression I saw myself as barren of offspring and purpose. It called into question my womanhood, just as Andrew's deranged sense of powerlessness was now calling into question his manhood.

I could imagine Andrew, in a more rational and self-censoring mood, or with a different kind of illness, resigning himself to the various abuses of body and soul, but in the horror film in which he now existed, the taking of blood, the insertion of the Foley tube, became the assaults of bloodsuckers and castraters on his maleness. In this scenario robust and uncaring wives were implicated, if only as witnesses, and Andrew, not usually given to male bonding, was in alliance with his fellow patients.

A mortifying scene had taken place that very day, when Andrew let loose with a loud, rude remark about another man's wife and I wanted to dive under the bed. It was the man with the brain tumor, across the room. His wife, Eileen, an attractive woman in her forties or early fifties, whom I'd gotten to know and like, had been taking care of a huge burden of immediate responsibilities: talking to doctors, making appointments, determining whether her husband should be transferred, getting power of attorney, supervising, and in general doing all the things one does in such situations. Andrew had been watching her moves intently. She was on the phone now, no doubt talking to a doctor or lawyer, and I could feel Andrew growing more and more agitated.

"Look at that woman!" he finally cried. "Her husband is dying and she's socializing on the telephone."

I could only hope that Eileen didn't hear, or understood if she did. One of the standard fantasies among male neurology patients is that their wives are having affairs, something that is particularly ironic given the fact that the wives, haggard and exhausted after up to eight hours a day at the hospital, are too tired even to eat, much less fornicate. Even a one-night stand is the last thing on a woman's mind, since there is nothing like illness, life in a hospital, or perpetual crisis to dull one's sexual appetite. You cease being a woman in any sense except that of caregiver. Yet more rational patients than Andrew allow their uncensored imaginations to run wild with images of orgies, a projection no doubt of what *they* would do—or what they would like to do if they weren't too guilty—if the situation were reversed.

"G. B. Shaw was talking on the phone this morning," Andrew reported one day. (The bearded young man to his left—who incidentally was unable to talk at all at this point—reminded him of, and had accordingly *become*, the playwright.) "And he was discussing you and your love affairs with all his friends."

He also began telling me strange stories about Soopie. Soopie, the Indonesian nurse on the night shift, was to me only a soft nocturnal voice to whom I'd talked in hushed tones—at midnight, or at 7:30 A.M. She would report his mental wanderings of the night, and his fixations. Andrew insisted once that she call our good friend Vincent Canby, the *Times* film critic, and get him to do an exposé of Andrew's predicament, and another time, Alfred Hitchcock, for whom he had a screenplay idea.

On this particular day, she told me he had held her hostage for twenty minutes and wouldn't let her go. When I came in after she'd left, and reproached him, he looked at me with surprise.

"But she was going to murder me," he said, now in great good humor. "Don't you know that?" He looked at me expectantly. "She's in love with me and wants to marry me and have my children." He paused, lowered his voice. "You think she's your friend, but she says terrible things about you."

One night—it was a Saturday night, and the usual sepulchral pall had descended on the hall—I told him I was going out to get a bite of supper with Betty Rollin and Ed Edwards, her husband.

"Oh, so how is everybody?" he asked, with elaborate sarcasm. It wasn't a question at all but a stinging allusion to my hyperactive social life, as he saw it, with all its amusing options, in contrast to his imprisonment. Betty and Ed were our good friends, and he wasn't included.

"Why don't they come up and see me?" he asked, self-pity mingling with hostility, as I shrugged helplessly.

"You seem to be getting along pretty well," he followed up, the sardonic note still in his voice.

"I'm not," I said, out of the depths of my misery, with such feeling that I didn't see how he could miss it. I looked into those hard eyes, trying to find his old soft brown ones. "Oh, God, Andrew!" I pleaded, "I need *you*, don't you understand?"

He seemed to soften for a moment.

"I need you, too," he said. And then, in that tone of melancholy that to me was so much more distressing than the craziness, he added, "I just don't think I'm ever going to get out of here." Remarks like that sounded normal, therefore "real." Sam had warned me repeatedly to ignore the content and mood of Andrew's meanderings, but for me, the hostile mood became a wholly different, and preferable, condition. It not only created a distance between us—I could *dislike* him when he was nasty and paranoid, whereas my heart went out to him when he was sad—but the craziness seemed robust, a form of fighting back. When he hallucinated, he was a warlike figure doing battle with the enemy. But when he sank back in despair, he seemed much closer to surrendering. I recognized the mood from my own habit of turning anger in on myself, falling into the dead zone of depression, and it scared me when Andrew did it. So when the seething bitterness returned, moments later, I welcomed it.

"I hope they don't fix you up with Frank," he said. I knew the "they" was Betty and Ed, but who, I asked, was Frank?

He looked at me with weary cynicism, as if I knew the answer and was feigning ignorance. "Frank Sinatra," he said, in an "of course" tone of voice. He was convinced until the moment I left that "Frank" would make one of our party that evening.

The next day when I came in, Themis was in a state of agitation unusual for her.

"Molly," she clutched at me. "They say Andrew has"—she paused, trying to get it right, finally succeeding—"encephalitis." Poor Themis. Her protective shield had finally cracked. Or *been* cracked. She had managed to think of Andrew's illness as some kind of vague emanation that her presence, with God's blessing, would soon put an end to (or what *had* she thought? Truly it was a mystery) and now somebody—Gwathmey, no doubt—had worked very hard to press this terrible-sounding and possibly no longer relevant word on her, to make her worry like the rest of us. I felt a nostalgia for her innocence, for its faith and confidence.

But then, as I watched her return to her vigil, the unpronounceable word forgotten, her faith restored, I once again felt rising that sour fury against her, like an acid coating the tongue.

More even than her faith, I couldn't stand the purity of her love, the fact that she lived totally for Andrew, while I was divided by details, claims on my attention, bills, work, trying to keep our life going. And yes, by my own ambitions and self-interest. As much as I loved Andrew, I felt I would never love him the way she did. I didn't think I would love a child of my own that way: it went against my principles. As a feminist, I felt that oceanic self-sacrifice was out of place in a modern egalitarian society, and I resented the fact that such love was almost invariably lavished on male children, not females. I wanted to have been the beneficiary of such love. I knew that Themis's love was a specifically mother-son love, and that to some degree her love for me—so generous and tolerant—was an extension of her love for Andrew.

About that time, Judy and I went to Lucinda's one night for dinner and the three of us made a great fuss over her small son, Joshua. This angelic creature—a cross between Lucinda and Saint-Exupéry's little prince—had been born shortly after the three of us had found our office space on the West Side, and Judy and I took responsibility for his birth: I had had a dream; Judy had had a fertility statue; signals and half thoughts from our three unconsciousnesses had seeped into the common atmosphere. When Bob Morgenthau, Lucinda's husband, came home that evening, he chatted with us about Geraldine Ferraro, whose selection as vice-presidential candidate had just been announced (his own dim view proved more prophetic than our elation), and began playing with Joshua. When he threw his son in the air, this august white-haired man with his ecstatic two-year-old, I felt such a longing—for Andrew, for some life born of Andrew—that I rushed from the room, feeling sick.

For us, it had seemed natural not to have children. It was as if my relationship with Andrew filled my days and thoughts, absorbed all my emotional energy, so that the desire not to have was stronger than the desire to have. I firmly believe that such decisions are not decisions in the ordinary sense; we are predisposed in a certain direction and we formulate reasons, or a philosophy, after the fact, select the images that will reinforce it.

The cultural atmosphere of the early seventies, a far cry from the fertility frenzy and baby mania of today, supported "childfree" marriages, and our lives seemed to tend in that direction. We were late starters for those days, and when we married (I at twenty-nine, he at forty) we were still struggling to get our careers going; there wasn't much money and we would have plummeted from a comfortable life to a difficult one; and then there was the tiredness, the domestic ineptitude, as if we didn't have enough energy left over for children; and finally, there was little of that social pressure from the outside that often pushes us into decisions beneficial to society. My mother never hinted or pushed in that direction, nor did Themis. Only once did Mother discuss the subject with me. It was several years after my marriage, and we were at the ballet. During intermission, she asked me casually if I'd made up my mind one way or the other. I said yes, I'd pretty well decided not to have children.

She thought seriously for a few moments. "Well," she finally said, "you may be sorry someday. I hope you won't." She paused and gave me a searching look.

"What would I have done without you?" she said softly. I knew she meant this: she really believed that I had sustained her in the years since my father's death, but to me, this was more an argument *against* having children than for. I didn't understand her love, for I regarded my performance as a daughter as pitifully inadequate, and didn't like the idea of being a mother who depended on someone like me for visits, calls, emotional sustenance. It seemed to me that in my attitude toward Mother, I had never grown up. I was so often bad, angry, and uncommunicative, a pain-in-the-ass teenager erecting an invisible wall against her. When we got together, we would spend three or four delightful compatible days, and then I would feel the dread change coming on inside me, like a human turning into a werewolf. I would become tense, ostensibly resenting her for certain irritating mannerisms, but really for loving and needing me so much, and resenting myself for my churlish refusal—or inability—to satisfy her needs.

At its simplest, Andrew and I had never become parents because, in some way that was both the glory and curse of our marriage, we had never ceased being children. And one reason we had never ceased being children is that we had never *been* children. We had been miniature adults from the start: Andrew, as a loner, with the usual ambition to be the supreme ruler of the universe, would sit on the floor for hours mulling over military schemes based on the great battles of history. I was full of beans, eager to please, my head cocked like a bird's to see what the grown-ups were up to, how I could anticipate their moods and desires. My precocity took the form of determining to be the independent little tot my mother wanted me to be, proudly jumping the hurdles she set in my path.

"Look at her," my uncle Howze once said of me as a three-year-old, as I was bustling around with some ambitious project or other. "If anything ever happens to you, Mary and John, Molly can just go get herself a job."

Mother proudly described the time when a neighbor came over for a drink and watched in amazement as I trundled upstairs and put myself to bed. I was two years old. I would go into the bathroom, climb up on the stool Mother had put by the lavatory, take the toothbrush, and brush my barely existent (and hardly in need of brushing) baby teeth (Mother was thinking ahead), then go into the bedroom, climb up the ladder attached to my crib and roll over. When I was settled in, I would call out, according to Mother, and she or my father would come and kiss me good night.

I put on a grand show and it became my "line," independence, the act of my life. I talked to grown-ups on their terms and in their language, but somewhere within was the child who craved being lifted up and nestled in her crib, being coddled the livelong day, and lo and behold! there emerged the great coddler.

Andrew babied me shamelessly. Brought home surprises for me —food, cassettes. Put me to bed, rubbed my back, was available for hugs whenever the urge seized me.

Andrew was the child whose confidence and ego had formed and taken nourishment within the mirroring reflection of a mother's adoring gaze. And now, he turned the gaze on me.

Whatever the underlying reasons, time itself had by now made it difficult to imagine a third person in our midst, and the decision had come to seem so unalterable as to be biological: as if Andrew and I literally "couldn't" have children. We had become different. Whether it's because they can't have children or because they don't want children, childless couples often become this way: so close you can't see air between them. The intensity can be suffocating but it happens gradually and pleasurably, like anesthesia or like climbing at high altitudes, so that in your euphoria you don't even realize you're taking in less oxygen than the normal person.

There was also the sense that in rebelling, we had played out a scenario to which there was no sequel. As with many "odd" couples, of different backgrounds, we were in some sense the end of the line rather than its continuation. Our marriage represented a deviation from the past rather than a pledge to carry on its traditions. How does an act of defiance procreate? If we had a child, what mongrel could we beget? What tradition could we, who had broken with tradition, give a child to react against?

I missed most of all the idea of it, of mingling our genes in life's greatest experiment, producing something that was and was not us. We had forsaken our Darwinian purpose. Right now, children would have given me something to think about other than Andrew, warm bodies who needed me alive and responsible. My friends were sustaining me, but who was I sustaining? One night, Annie, a dog lover, had urged me to get a dog, clearly—though she didn't say so—because she thought Andrew was dying and I needed something alive to keep me company. Mostly, I wanted something *of* Andrew, a child to fill his place. He would die, and there would be nothing left of him. For one brief moment, I had the bizarre thought (or, given the current technological climate, not so bizarre) to get his fluid and try to conceive artificially.

And now Themis was before me, and her massive, uncomplaining presence made me feel slight, weightless. If only she'd been "small" in some way—overbearing, or critical. If only she'd objected to *me*, competed and nitpicked in the time-honored mother-in-law tradition, arrived bearing chicken soup, but no, she loved me, struggled through my column in *Vogue* every month, bragged about me to her two friends. It had always been like that, her loving me without my consent. When we went to visit her, it was all on her extravagantly loving terms.

"Ah, Molly," she would say, after embracing me in a bear hug, her voice ringing, "you and Andrew! So wonderful. How could anything be better. God brought you together. You are so wonderful."

And I would squirm uncomfortably under this benediction and the sheer overwhelming physicality of her embrace, so contrary to my own style of emotional reticence. I used to feel her love was something of a blunt instrument, making no allowance for me, for my preference for reserve. We had different ways of loving. With Themis, as with Andrew, you were with them or against them. For me, brought up with the idea that love had to be won by good behavior, there was something almost terrifying in such unconditional love.

The memory of all the times I had felt embarrassed by Themis's effusions fed into my crazed reactions now, as my rage at Themis grew, hour by hour, taking on a strange, powerful, subterranean life of its own. During the day, I would behave and feel like a reasonable person, but at night, as I lay in bed trying to sleep, bilious feelings would rise up in me and burst forth in orgasms of loathing and detestation, frightening in their force. Oh, the nights! It came in stages: first, there would be a simple, uncomplicated anger; then, loathing; then, like one wave rising on the back of another, there would be shame: how *could* I feel this way toward this extraordinary woman who loved me so much. So much. So much. Too much. That was it. Like my mother. Like Andrew, even. How ridiculous, how excessive they were; how could they be so blind as not to see me for the shabby, horrible, deeply undeserving creature I was. Now I was proving it in this orgy of anger—see, Themis, how unworthy I am, how miserable, see, Mother. See, Andrew. Then, all the guilt I had felt as the beneficiary of their undeserved love would rise almost joyously, fed and validated by this wretched spectacle of myself as hater. It was maniacal, the intense pain and pleasure of hating Themis and hating myself for hating Themis. It was *vicieux*, Baudelairean, addictive. And then, my anger spent, my anxiety over Andrew displaced onto his mother, I would sleep like a baby. I began almost to look forward to the nights when I would steal furtively into my vice, like a proper family man and pillar of the community returning to a bordello, not just any bordello but a dangerous and unsanitary one, ridden with lice, syphilis, disease.

This ritual of anger was a narcotic, a tranquilizer at night, a stimulant by day. At night, it meant there were whole minutes, hours even, when I didn't think of Andrew. And when, exhausted by my spasms of loathing, I slept. I would awake refreshed, fortified by anger, ready to do battle. I would go to Andrew, and if he looked at me with hatred, I would glare back. It was infantile and I knew it, but it was exhilarating. I was like a child making faces at an angry and unpredictable parent behind his back, a child for whom words are no recourse, whose only defense is to mimic the attitude of the aggressor.

If he was quiet and peaceful, as he was rarely, I would sit by his bed, talk gently to him, touch his poor arm, thin now, bruised from a hundred needles, but whenever he looked at me with hatred, I would glare back, trying to outdo him. Then I would return each night to my secret vice, my Valium, and sink into it voluptuously.

Between grief and nothing, give me grief, but between hatred and grief, give me hatred! Juicy, vivifying, ferocious, inspiring, unacceptable, the secret and alien emotion that rose from somewhere within and rescued me from self-pity, allowed me to plow through each day's horrors with a hide as thick and glistening as a rattlesnake's skin.

5

On the medical front, things were deteriorating rapidly. On July 23, twenty-four days into his hospitalization, Andrew's white blood cells had increased, either a sign that they were rebounding from their previous suppression by drugs or the result of a new infection. He was weak and pale and sweaty, confused most of the time, and his reflexes weren't working properly. In the search for the source of the metabolic encephalopathy, liver, urine, and lungs had been ruled out. No one knew why he continued to hallucinate; Crenshaw said he no longer believed it had been encephalitis. Andrew's heart and kidneys were still good; the worry was that the liver wouldn't hold up. Although the doctors felt Andrew was remarkably strong just to have been able to fight such a virulent disease for so long, Sam looked worried.

He took Chevey and me into the solarium. "I don't know if you realize it, but this is very unusual—for an illness to go on this long without a diagnosis. Even when there's no prescribed treatment, we usually know what we're dealing with."

Ramir and some of the others thought Andrew was getting better, but Sam disagreed. Faced with no solution and no diagnosis, with Andrew constantly deteriorating, he wanted to do three major tests— a liver scan, a bronchoscopy, and a CAT scan to rule out infection —and then start him on steroids in the next day or two.

They had given him several transfusions because of anemia related to the illness and slow blood loss related to stress, and now, as they gave him another, I thought back to my own transfusions, in 1981 and 1982, and of the mystical overtones, both threatening and miraculous, of having the blood of another person, some anonymous donor, merging with one's own. This was before we knew that AIDS could be transmitted through blood transfusions; in fact, 1984, just before the screening technique was developed, was—as we would later find out—the period of maximum danger for this. Fortunately, I knew nothing of that, nor of the time to come when people, in one of those sudden mass panics similar to the bomb-shelter craze, would begin freezing their own blood and storing it for future emergencies. Now I could think only of the generosity of both the anonymous donors and of those of Andrew's fans and students who had called and volunteered their blood.

It struck me now how earlier blood donations, those of beloved parents, had played an oddly similar part in our lives, perhaps even saving them.

As a newborn baby, I had turned blue, or one of the doctors (whose verdict Mother had later questioned) had said I turned blue, and my father, who had my blood type, had been called on for a transfusion. This rather unremarkable event was related to me when I was an impressionable four- or five-year-old, and it had taken on magical and frightening overtones. I visualized my father's blood not as a supplement to my own, but, since I couldn't imagine my infant body containing more than a pint of blood, actually replacing it. In a remarkable feat of Oedipal transubstantiation, I had removed my mother as my progenitor and sustainer, and bestowed the life-giving role on my father. And then, there was Themis's account of the time Andrew, a three- or four-year-old, had been hospitalized with life-threatening colitis. He was in the habit of screaming whenever his mother or father was out of his sight. At a certain moment, his father was gone and Themis was out of the room, and suddenly . . . silence. Themis, at the other end of the corridor, rushed into his room, found him barely alive, and demanded that the doctor hook her up to him immediately, transfusing her vein directly into his.

"He had another half hour to live," she would say, in telling the story. "I got the blood into him and it saved his life. When it was over, they locked me up in a room with bars on the door." They would both laugh at this, the image of this ferocious mother who so alarmed the doctors that they had to "put her away."

How much of this was true? How close was either of us to death? Who knows. These were real-life fairy tales, the myths of our lives, created in childhood, kept polished and vigorous by desire: the tigress mother, the life-giving father, figures projected at a thousand times their size against the screen of memory, dwarfing all the other players.

Andrew was being given tests for every abnormality they could think of, while he was more and more disoriented and his mood fluctuated by the minute. In the midst of all this, a new and mysterious symptom appeared: a distended abdomen. His belly was swollen to triple its normal size, and, to add insult to injury, he had lost control of his bowels. He was stinking up the place; he knew it and was mortified. He insisted that G. B. Shaw, who he now thought was running the hospital, was trying to have him evicted.

"Well, that's perfect!" I said. "You wanted to leave. Now's your chance."

But Andrew, desperate as he was to escape, didn't see it that way. For the insane, as for the rest of us, shame is often a more powerful motivation than desire. Andrew wanted to leave under his own terms, or in handcuffs; he didn't want to be banished in humiliation.

But the embarrassment that his body was causing him was a terrible thing, first for him, then for me on his behalf. I wanted them to move him into a private room, where the odor couldn't disturb other patients and where he himself would be spared the shame of *their* repugnance, whether real or imagined. (And how could it not have been real? No one's sense of smell was impaired, and visitors could hardly be expected not to resent having to endure *that* indignity on top of everything else!) I talked to Gwathmey and Sam, but they said the decision had been made to keep him in the room with other people. In the Aesopian language of the hospital, he was considered better off in this "normal" environment. I began to realize that for doctors, discomfort is not a major priority. They are in the business of attending to acute illness, and discomfort, like pain (i.e., recovery pain as opposed to symptomatic pain), impinges less on their consciousness. They have, perhaps for their own efficiency, or convenience, managed to block it out. And yet, for patients it looms large, larger than many of the invisible and intangible symptoms of the illness that they can barely comprehend.

Watching Andrew made wretched by embarrassment, I began to wonder if the greatest trial of a hospitalization isn't pain at all—bad enough, but taken seriously and treated with drugs, *and* something a patient can be brave about—but other forms of torture.

Doctors, with limited time, need to deal with things you can see, touch, feel rather than states of mind. The abscess, the perforation, the fever, the suppuration, the bacteria, the thing you can X-ray, chart, pursue. To stenches their senses appear numb; of vomit, sweat, blood, feces, death, halitosis, they are no more aware than they are of the flowers on the bedside tables.

Yet for the patient, stripped of the roles and outer garments that give him his dignity, his body, and whatever respect it's allowed, is all he has left. He doesn't see the tumor in his head or the infection in his liver, but he does know if he soils the bed or if his odor is offending other patients. Andrew's state of selective awareness—in which obtuseness combined with acute sensitivity—made this particular horror a mortification. Freud points to the beginning of civilization, of cultural consciousness, as the moment when the infant, hitherto happy with his own fecal smells, realizes they are offensive to others. Andrew was crossing this painful threshold over and over again.

The habit of infantilizing patients is so endemic that in Britain, the process is rendered explicit in a language that eliminates "grown-up" articles, as in "Doctor says," and "Nurse is coming" (so that Patient, once in Hospital, will behave his little self), without anyone realizing that no one has a keener sense of smell and the social prejudices surrounding it, or a more intense sense of bodily shame, than a child.

On Friday, July 27, a new catastrophe: a high fever and positive blood cultures revealed what might be causing the bowel problem—septicemia, an infection in the bloodstream. This development, which would be frightening enough as a primary illness, was a major complication in an already very seriously ill patient. Steroids were now ruled out. Jeffrey, sounding concerned, said they might have to remove the gallbladder (a common source of abdominal infection) and treat

Andrew with antibiotics for weeks, although these new bacteria still might not be the cause of the recent fever, just of the new high (103.9). Sam more or less echoed this view when he said he was sure this strain of bacteria wasn't *the* one, and the bronchoscopy would just have to wait.

Andrew would seem better, then worse; less, then more, jerky. "I don't ever want to be alone. Ever," he said ominously.

I began to think of calling in an outside doctor for a consultation, and put out an alert to friends for doctors they might recommend. If the New York Hospital staff was baffled, might there be someone, somewhere, who had come across an illness like this?

It was now, in one of those ironies of hospital life, that a physical therapist showed up. Andrew weighed 154, having lost over 30 pounds, and was weaker and more incapacitated than ever, yet there appeared on the threshold an attractive, blond, muscular man looking like a yuppie Tarzan, bearing the hospital equivalent of a barbell—a small metal triangle that hangs on the bar over the patient's head. He was all ready to put Andrew through his paces. Unlike psychotherapy, physical therapy is at least on the menu of the hospital, but it is honored more in the breach than the observance. Every three or four days, an overworked young man or woman will show up, offer a half hour of instruction, leave the patient with a sheet of exercises to be followed, and then disappear, promising to return the following day. He may come back in a day, or a week, or a month. Exercise and movement of any kind are immensely important, a preventive measure against bedsores, pneumonia, and other infections to which patients in their debilitated state are especially susceptible. You realize how crucial muscle functioning is when you see the radically altered appearance of a person who's been bedridden for a long time.

One of the most upsetting things was the look of Andrew's face now. Because of the loss of muscle mass, it had taken on that caved-in, teeth-bared look of a death mask, and his head fell onto his chest because the neck muscles no longer automatically held it up. They talked in such dire tones of muscles atrophying that I was afraid that even if he got well, his head would plop forward permanently. He could barely talk, much less flex his muscles, when this blond gym teacher, fairly glowing with health and optimism, showed up, a huge grin on his face and the breathlessly winning manner of one who is constantly having to apologize for missed rendezvous with disappointed patients. By nature, Andrew was not a happy pupil, but then he was one of those people who was constitutionally incapable of following any kind of exercise regimen. Watching him trying to follow exercises on videotape, as I had occasionally persuaded him to do, was hilarious: comically spastic, his legs and arms went in all directions like a windmill; then he'd be completely winded after five minutes. He wasn't uncoordinated: he could dance rhythmically and in tempo, and he could play tennis. But—perhaps it was dyspraxia of some kind—when it came to following commands, something in the signal transmission between mind and body got fouled up and turned him into a moron.

The simplest and most basic instruction of all, breathing, was to Andrew an insurmountable task. Tell him to inhale deeply through his nose—as our determined young therapist was now doing—and exhale through his mouth, and Andrew, with his own imperturbable earnestness, would suck in through his mouth, and keep sucking. Andrew was baffling to the staff, who couldn't figure out how much of his lack of mind-body coordination stemmed from the illness and how much (a good deal, actually) predated it. But once the triangle was installed on the longitudinal pole overhead, he took a fancy to it: he would grab hold of it, pull heroically a few times, and then stop, exhausted, his agitated mind on to something else.

The day after this rather discouraging episode I saw Crenshaw in the hall and ambushed him. It was the first time I'd laid eyes on him since the famous consultation, and he strode along the corridor with the swift, aloof steps of a man who did not welcome intrusions.

"Got any theories?" I asked, my heart in my throat, running along beside him, trying to sound both bright and deferential. Crenshaw had patented the manner, common to doctors making rounds, of being in perpetual motion, exuding a sense of having weightier matters on their minds, or of being on the way to a more urgent patient whose life you may very well be endangering if you halt their progress with some frivolous question. While they're at your bedside, giving you the requisite three minutes, their feet are already pointed toward the door, and the next patient. And when you accost them in the hallway, they don't really stop. They're like joggers at a traffic light, running in place.

Moreover, as Crenshaw wasn't our own doctor, he had no obligation to keep me posted. Yet how could I help asking?

"I'm very worried," he said, in peremptory answer. "I'm afraid" —he paused briefly—"your husband has a serious underlying illness."

I scurried along behind him. I was a burr that had attached itself to his lab coat. Nothing about taking action now. "Just recently, a man here died of a heart problem," he continued, glancing at me, just barely, as he continued on his way. "We did an autopsy, but we never did find out what the problem was."

If the intention was to brush me off his coat onto the floor, it worked. I was dumbstruck. And furious! I knew what he was trying to say, but what did a fatal heart problem have to do with Andrew? Was he suggesting cancer? Whatever the connection was, it was sufficiently obscure that all I could read in his response was monstrous tactlessness, designed more to get rid of me than provide information.

Of course, in thinking about it later, I realized that his remarks weren't completely gratuitous: a "serious underlying disease"—namely cancer—could cause both heart failure and mental derangement. And what obligation did Crenshaw have to spare my feelings? Or even to be correct? He wasn't professionally involved, his reputation wasn't on the line, he had come in as a courtesy, and there was no reason he couldn't say anything he pleased, including hinting—no doubt with a good deal of certainty on his part—at death. Yet by the same token he could have brushed me off with bromides or ambiguous evasions —the possibilities were limitless for a man of his experience and intelligence. He had seemed to want to shock me, in as brutal a manner as possible, but why? Medical confusion hiding behind arrogance? The habit of omniscience responding with a reflexive assault when challenged? Strangely, there was something so extreme, so almost gloating, in his bravura response that I managed, after picking myself up off the floor and thinking about it, to write the incident off as an understandable desire to withdraw from such a difficult case.

Far more disturbing were the increasingly pessimistic prognoses I was getting from the doctors whom I had come to think of as my allies, the ones like Kempinski and Seltzman whom I trusted to answer my questions as accurately as they could, without projecting their deepest fears. Kempinski had followed the case since he'd admitted

Andrew in June, as the covering doctor, and he told me he thought Andrew had an "autoimmune disease allergy defense." The idea that a body could, in effect, turn against itself was a concept I'd never heard of, and I found it unthinkably horrible. An inside sabotage job, like a computer virus, an ingenious runaway disease that is programmed to proliferate, destroy everything in its path, turn your own benign insides against you.

One of Andrew's favorite shorts was an Eastern European medical cartoon about the inside of the body as the site of an ongoing war between germs and antibodies, drawn as semi-realistic military figures in the World War II vein: the bad guys, the viruses and bacteria, are always on the move, running up and down the bloodstreams and corridors, lobbing hand grenades, while the good guys—a sergeant reading a magazine—must be roused from their complacency. In Andrew's case, the lazy antibodies had been galvanized . . . to attack themselves! The whole thing was like one of those Le Carré spy thrillers, echoing the moral inversions of the modern world, in which, at best, "our side" is as bad as theirs, and invariably the "good guy" is being framed by his own superior officers. I couldn't banish the image: instead of producing antibodies to the disease, the cells of Andrew's body, the body that I loved, were pouncing on their fellow cells. How was such treachery possible?

This all had a curious appropriateness for Andrew, who had always seen life in terms of a dialectic between the two sides of his own nature, the barbarian encouraged by his father to believe that life is a jungle, and the libertarian humanist who'd gone to Columbia and had come under the civilizing influence of such beacons of liberalism as Lionel Trilling and Charles Frankel.

Andrew tended to paint his father as the monster of the family, a tyrant who was always aching for a fight, or coming down hard on his mulish son. And from the reports of both mother and son, he could be terrifying in anger. When Robert Kennedy was murdered, and we were watching the replay on television, Andrew said Sirhan Sirhan reminded him of his father. That wiry little Mediterranean fanatic clung to his gun with such superhuman strength that it took two giant football players to dislodge it from his hand. Andrew's father may have been a man of the jungle, frothing at the mouth at the infamies of the Turks, but there was another side to him: the voracious newspaper reader and talker, the shrewd analyst of world events, the fantasizing soliloquist, the transplanted Demosthenes, the man who loved nothing better than to sit around the kitchen table talking . . . about politics, about movies. The bluffer. On days when he had supposedly been laboring in the vineyards of real estate he would come home and regale his family with this or that plot, movies supposedly seen, and recounted to him, by his friend Skimmer. This was the Depression and the family couldn't afford the price of admission, so Skimmer was the source of entertainment.

"Skimmer told me about this great movie today." He'd then launch into the story of, say, Charlie Chaplin's *Modern Times*—a movie he adored for its anti-factory message. His distaste for the idea of working for a boss was another Greek national trait that he and Andrew shared.

Or *Lost Horizons*. Or *The Firefly*. "Skimmer told me about this scene," he'd say, "where Napoleon's brother, the King of Spain, goes among the people in his carriage and he throws gold pieces out at them." Whereupon, forgetting this was a secondhand account, he'd rise to his feet and mimic the king, lips pursed haughtily, throwing the gold pieces contemptuously. Themis and George and Andrew would smile to themselves, as entertained by the transparency of the game as by the movies themselves.

"And then the proud Spaniards"—in identification, his voice would rise excitedly (just as Andrew's always did), "*threw* the coins back at the carriage"—another grand gesture. And when Andrew or Themis would tell this story, I would see and hear Andrew in his father, Andrew, the great talker, the transparent fibber.

Andrew dismissed his own articulateness as glibness; his ability to think quickly on his feet was something he was almost ashamed of. A professor! Talking all day to make money! His father would have sneered, but his students loved him.

"I confess that I might not have, over the years, collected all of Sarris's books," one wrote in a film quarterly some years after graduating, "if I had not first seen his head floating ecstatically at the front of the class, mellifluously expounding on the subtleties, hot and cool, of Josef von Sternberg, John Ford, and all the other auteurs enshrined in the Sarris Pantheon. (And his books led often to other books, sometimes to deeper structures, but always, quite properly, directly back to the movies.)"

Toward George, Andrew felt both the guilt of the survivor and the guilt of the one who is loved too much. George had died in a sky-diving accident at age twenty-eight, the younger brother who, Andrew felt, had been born under an unlucky star. When Andrew was born, the family, momentarily flush, drove home from the hospital in a Pierce-Arrow. When George was born, they were flat out again, and barely had the money to pay for a taxi. Thus were their destinies, as survivor and victim, inscribed early. George, though as much a reader as Andrew, was the physical one, active, charming, an extrovert. It was little George who, when Andrew got into a fight, went after the bullies who persecuted his idolized older brother . . . and George was always in trouble. If it hadn't been the sky-diving accident, it would have been something else. Andrew once told me that George's death was such bad luck that ever after Andrew felt he led a charmed life because whatever happened, he had lived longer than George.

I sought out Alan Seltzman, hoping he would dismiss Crenshaw's proposition, but to my dismay he agreed. If there weren't a "serious underlying disease," Andrew would be getting better.

"But isn't a dramatic turnaround possible?" I asked.

"Yes," he said. And then, "But the longer it takes, the less probable it will be."

More than anything that had been said, these words sounded like a death knell. And it came just when I thought we'd had a sort of reprieve, a moment of hope. Earlier in the day, Andrew was to undergo a gallium scan (notable for its ability to pick up inflammatory masses or abscesses or—one of those lovely medical terms that seemed to be what our lives were all about—occult infections), and we were waiting outside the X-ray room. He'd been given an injection of radioactive dye and now he was on the gurney, me beside him with two pitchers of fluid, which I was charged with coaxing him to drink. He had an hour in which to drink the two quarts.

Andrew was semi-lucid, which was rare enough, and we were

alone, which was even more unusual. After the constant, pressing presence of others, of nonstop activity, of having our lives conducted in public, this peace was a rare gift, something I'd yearned for without even knowing it. Such a simple thing—being alone and quiet—yet so hard to come by. We were talking casually, me doing most of the talking—about the Olympics, which were being televised. Andrew and I had always admired the otherworldly beauty of horses, and I mentioned that the equestrian event was on. He smiled and then gave what I thought was a wince, and I remembered that he had once complained that they shouldn't be included in the Olympics. It was too agonizing to watch them falter, fall over the jumps or into the ponds. For an hour, it was as if we'd slipped out of the universe and into our own pocket of time, a fourth dimension where the normal course of things was reversed and the ordinary had become extraordinary.

I put my head against his chest. It was still now, no longer trembling. My cheek felt the sweetness of his skin, ridiculously soft, as always, as soft as a baby's. There was no mention of love, but it lay all around and beneath us, coursing through my body, lighting me from within, like the radioactive liquid that was filling Andrew. It was strange, the giving out of love without any certainty or even expectation of having it returned.

After that brief reprieve, things went downhill fast. The plan to try steroids—which would have been effective if, as Sam suspected, the disease was an inflammatory "process" rather than an "organism"—had been indefinitely delayed by the septicemia, which might require removal of the gallbladder.

When I went home at noon, I decided to call the doctor whose name had been recommended by several friends. It was time for a second opinion, yet I was nervous. What would Sam say? How would he react? I had called two doctors at Mount Sinai days before, friends of a friend, and each had been reluctant to comment.

"Sounds like they're following the proper course," each had said, in so many words, when I went over the main points of the illness.

I understood their reluctance to comment on an unknown patient being handled by other doctors, but I felt desperately in need of auxiliary forces. And perhaps a little medical hand-holding. Toby and

Dan and the Appletons had suggested their internist, Dr. George Cavendish, a highly regarded New York Hospital doctor with a number of writer patients (a "carriage trade" doctor, Helena had called him) and a cool personality. I'd met him once at a party and liked him. Friends had alerted him to expect my call, and I brought him up to date.

He listened, then politely but a little stiffly said, "And what do you want me to do about it?"

"Uh, well . . ." I hesitated. I had expected—I don't know what. If not sympathy, or perhaps an expression of amazement, at least a take-charge attitude, a willingness to step into the breach.

"Do you want me to come in as a consultant?"

"Yes, I guess so."

"Then you'll have to get Gessner to call me. I don't think he'll get his nose out of joint."

Of course, that was precisely what I was terrified of—that Sam would be offended, walk off the case in a huff. It wasn't a realistic terror, I guess, but it served to distract me from the more rational ones.

Andrew, when I returned, looked terrible, ashen; the fever was spiking and he was in a constant state of agitation. He was obsessed with his defecation and wanted the curtain pulled at all times.

"Stay with me," he said, as they were about to draw some more blood. "I want yours to be the last face I see."

When Mother and I left in the late afternoon, it was with a sense of foreboding. Andrew was more distended than ever, and could barely talk. I looked at him, looked into those darting eyes and couldn't find him. Had the pilot light finally gone out?

Then things began to happen quickly, that ominous sense of an acceleration before a climax. Gwathmey called about nine o'clock Sunday evening: Andrew's hematocrit (red-blood-cell count) had dropped by half. He was now bleeding into his stool and they wanted to perform an endoscopy (a tube is inserted into the colon for observation) for which a signed release was necessary.

"Oh, and—" he added before he hung up, "Mr. Sarris is asking for his typewriter."

Mother and I rushed down and found Andrew in the basement, lying on a gurney, white-faced and sedated. (This was one of the few times when he was given any kind of mind-affecting drug, the need to monitor his mental status being paramount.) I sat beside him waiting for that gruesome-sounding procedure that was to become familiar to the entire country when graphic details of the presidential cancer made front-page headlines and prime-time televiewing across the country. I got through by thinking how I would phrase my question to Sam the next day. I had told Jeffrey that afternoon of my plan to call in Cavendish, and he had said it was perfectly normal to call in a consultant and had actually been wondering why I hadn't done so earlier. He said that Cavendish was a particularly good choice, as he was a specialist in vasculitis, an inflammation of the blood vessels that was one of the principal suspects in the diagnosis of Andrew's illness.

Yet I *still* lay awake half the night dreading the phone call to Sam—needlessly, as it turned out. He was altogether gracious—perhaps he even welcomed another colleague who would either shed light on the subject or confirm his own bafflement—and agreed to call Cavendish right away. Cavendish, in turn, agreed to come in on Tuesday.

On Monday night, Jeffrey was visibly alarmed and so was I. Andrew was having great difficulty breathing, and nobody seemed to know why. Both of us felt, without having to say it, that the situation had taken a critical turn for the worse.

At 7:15 the next morning, Tuesday, July 31, the phone rang. It was Sam. Emergency surgery would have to be performed for a probable perforation of the colon. X rays showed free air in the abdomen, i.e., air that had escaped into the abdominal cavity through a rupture in the bowel wall, distending his belly and pushing upward on his diaphragm, collapsing the lung (hence Andrew's breathing problem). The toxic effect of the newly disseminated infection secondary to the bacteria was spreading through the abdomen. In other words, along with everything else, Andrew had peritonitis. Sam had called Fred Gaines, his surgeon of preference, who would operate on Andrew as soon as an operating room became available.

This was terrible news. From my own experience, I knew how invasive abdominal surgery is, how totally debilitating even for a person in prime health. It seemed to me there was no way anyone in Andrew's compromised condition, weak and infected, with blood loss, fever, and peritonitis, could survive. Peritonitis, thanks to antibiotics, is no longer always fatal as it was to Rudolph Valentino and Jean Harlow, but Andrew's body was in no shape to mount a campaign against it.

Mother and I rushed down to the hospital, she going to the basement cafeteria to get us coffee and a Danish, while I went directly to Andrew's floor. As I walked along the corridor a nurse was coming toward me, hurrying to get to her car before 8:00 A.M., when the eight-hour parking limit expired. She was small, dark, East Asian. Simultaneously, we hesitated, looked at each other and then, without a word, fell into each other's arms.

"Soopie?"

She nodded. "Molly!"

"He can't get through this," I said. I began crying.

She was made of sterner stuff. "Yes, he can," she said, her tiny body enfolding mine. This was the nurse who, according to Andrew, was plotting my overthrow behind my back. We had only a minute to talk, but I clung to her, this woman who had previously been only a sound on the telephone, that low, sweet, lightly accented voice in the dark hours of the morning. She was the one of all the nurses who knew Andrew at his loneliest, craziest, most abject. Alone with him on the desolation shift, she had wiped down his feverish body and soothed him with words, had lived with the smells and the crankiness and the sorrow. Tending him in a situation as intimate as a marriage, she was both my rival and my surrogate. What—if anything—did she feel toward this man whom she had never known as a normal and pleasingly eccentric human being—witty, boisterous, kind—but only as a hallucinating and troublesome invalid. Had she, in fact, tired and irritated by his distemper, finally struck back with hostile words, bruising actions? Were the emotions she felt anything resembling normal human emotions of exasperation, empathy, love, pity? Was there ever attraction and was it possible to be attracted to a body so wasted, a mind so absent? Maybe even *because* it was so wasted, so helpless? Perhaps she who knew so little of his everyday self, his size, movements, idiom, was free to imagine him in whatever way she liked. I wondered if there had been anything more than clinical caring in the movements of her hands, the caress of her voice, thus giving rise to Andrew's dark-of-the-night fantasies. Locked away in this hospital netherworld, do the wandering minds and ministering angels ever become just male and female? Had Soopie turned against me? It seemed more probable that Andrew, feeling both desire and impotence, turned her into a betraying vamp to satisfy his fantasies and simultaneously exculpate himself. It was also entirely possible that she had neglected him altogether, huddled with the nurses eating pizza and joking about the loonies in their charge. When we hugged each other in the hallway, our rapport seemed perfect, but that may well have been a hunger for illusion on my part. For my own peace of mind, I needed to think of her as conscientious and caring, even if it meant contending with feelings of rivalry. Negligence or active malevolence I simply couldn't allow, couldn't cope with: I was too strung out to check and double-check on the nurses, and so dismissed Andrew's complaints as the usual paranoia. I would never know.

Andrew was being prepared for surgery, sufficiently non compos mentis (mercifully) not to be aware of or resist the nasogastric tube that was being stuffed down his throat. Mother and I were in the solarium waiting for various procedures and examinations to be finished. Dr. Cavendish had arrived for the consultation as promised and, when he found Andrew being prepared for surgery, had decided to go ahead and examine him anyway. I'd completely forgotten this was the morning of his appointment, otherwise I'd have headed him off. He walked into the solarium where Mother and I were standing, tall, authoritative, an unflappable professional, but obviously stunned by what he had seen.

"I've seen him and read the chart. I can't believe what you've been through," he said, with genuine concern. He promised to follow up on Andrew after the operation, no doubt suspecting that the occasion would never arise.

Then we were called in to see Andrew off. It was about 11:00 A.M. by now, and he was being transferred from bed to gurney. The last thing Mother and I remembered was Andrew, just before he was trundled off, reaching for the overhead triangle. Trying, with what was left of his depleted spirit and energies, to pull on it, resting, then trying again.

6

After Andrew was taken up in the late morning, I went home and paced. And paced. Mother and I ate lunch, made small talk, and in trying to distract each other, distracted ourselves for at least a few minutes at a time. Then I would pace some more, panic, pray.

The need to believe survives loss of faith, survives everything, and then, it's the position you're in: once something has brought you to your knees, there is nothing to do but pray.

I made deals. I would take Andrew back on any terms. I would no longer nag him about reading newspapers all day, or shush him when his voice rose in restaurants. I would cherish his oft-told tales, his doomsday economic theories, the fingerprints he left on walls and surfaces, the burned teakettles, his absentminded-professorisms, his driving.

I rationalized that Andrew was more precious to God than I was, and that it was his life I was praying for. But this was not quite true. I was praying for my life when I prayed for him. I could no more imagine eating, breathing, walking the face of the earth without him than I could imagine hanging upside down from a tree branch, or living underwater.

As the minutes and hours dragged by, I tried to picture what they might be doing to his poor belly, what demon they would find there (one genre melted into another: first the medical horror film, my own favorite, with gore and viscera, then the special-effects monster movie, in which they would find some crawly creature inside him, whose presence would explain everything). I knew, from what I could remember of my own drug-hazed experience, that the surgical chamber was a disappointingly small room, more like a dentist's office, with bright lights and high-tech machinery, than the great amphitheater of early movies, or the one pictured in Thomas Eakins's majestic nineteenth-century painting *The Gross Clinic*. Speaking of medical pornography, that's the one in which the master surgeon—a stand-in for the artist in Eakins's view—is cutting up the leg of an unanesthetized young man while the distraught mother leaps forward in horror. The medical students stand by, interested but detached. With whom are we to identify? Andrew would be the star patient that day, but thanks to twentieth-century progress, he would be happily unconscious, while I sat at home, alternating between both "onlooker" viewpoints: surges of emotional panic and the more fear-numbing and voyeuristic view of the medical students.

I was suspended in a time warp, a sort of sensory-deprivation chamber, in which there were only two possibilities: Andrew would live; Andrew would die. It was like a dividing line in the middle of my life: everything that had come before was now rounded off and given an ending, but I was in blind ignorance about the future.

Finally, at 4:00 P.M., Dr. Gaines called with great news: the operation had been a success. He had performed a colostomy, which he hoped would be temporary, and I should notice "a marked improvement in a couple of days." I cried out to Mother. A marked *improvement* in only a couple of days? This seemed hard to believe, but I would believe anything.

The phone rang again. "Hold on there," said Sam, puncturing my euphoria when I told him what Gaines had said. He was shocked at Gaines's words. "Surgeons see things a little differently. No, what we have is a very scary situation. Andrew's blood pressure has gone down to 50, he's in shock, and he has a major-league infection."

But how could—? How could there be such diametrically different versions? I had a sudden insight into the bizarre yet strangely logical thinking of surgeons and specialists in general (scientists, even artists: Eakins was right in implying an analogy). He had done his job and done it magnificently: he had attacked the problem, perhaps saved

Andrew's life, found the solution, and he wasn't concerned with the aftermath and the problems that might arise. They belonged to somebody else.

Sam hadn't told me the whole of it, only what he felt he needed to tell me at the time, and even that was a good deal worse than I imagined. I didn't know (or choose to consider) what the drop in blood pressure signaled (a heart attack or ongoing septicemia, with possible mental damage, was most likely). So while Andrew's life hung by a thread, while I waited by the phone, both hoping and dreading someone would call (Jeffrey told me later he was dreading I would call), I focused on the one aspect of the whole thing that was least dangerous, but—and?—most vivid and easily imagined—the colostomy. In a colostomy, a section of the colon is removed, and then the end is brought through the surface of the stomach wall and enclosed in a waste bag. Some of these are temporary, others permanent. Although thousands of people live with colostomies gracefully, uncomplainingly, and often unbeknownst to most of their friends, I couldn't imagine Andrew being one of them. I could more easily imagine him without an arm or a leg. So instead of praying he wouldn't die, I prayed he wouldn't have a sloshy little shit bag attached to his belly for life.

The next morning Sam called to report that Andrew was still alive.

"I got him into the surgical ICU on the eleventh floor, one of the two best in the hospital," he said proudly. These days a major criterion of a good doctor is one with the clout to get his patients onto the best floors, into the best units, in touch with the best specialists. I wasn't complaining, only when I finally got in to see Andrew, I wished Sam could have spent a minute or two preparing me.

The ICU was itself an otherworldly experience. I was the only visitor—they'd agreed to let me in for a few minutes before regular hours. It was an antiseptic enclosure cut off from the rest of the hospital and the flow of life by its restricted visiting hours (11:00 to 11:45 in the morning, 5:00 to 5:45 in the evening). It was like an airship, suspended in space, sterile because there were none of the ordinary signs or sounds of life, only the whirring and clicking of machines surrounding mummylike patients, each click signaling that death had been forestalled by another moment. I walked along the small passageway, between two glass panes, where the patients, four on the right, two on the left, were lined up side by side, with tubes of the most expensive lifesaving machinery in the world reaching like tentacles into every orifice, and with their faces, peering out from oxygen masks, unrecognizable as to sex and age. They weren't humans but cyborgs, half man–half machine, new arrivals on display from the planet of near-death.

Andrew was pointed out to me: he was in the room on the left, the last patient. He was swollen to twice his normal size, three times what he'd been the day before. He'd gained this astounding amount of weight from water that had been pumped into him to bring up the blood pressure and treat vascular collapse. His whole right side was a purplish blue due to a blood transfusion that had missed the vein and gone subcutaneous. There were six or seven tubes coming out of his body—a catheter into the heart, a drainage tube, the Foley tube, peripheral lines in various veins. And a respirator the size of a vacuum-cleaner tube was in his mouth, which was taped over completely. His hands were tied down. And his eyes, dazed in his man-in-the-moon face, told me nothing. Did he recognize me? What was going on in his head? He was grotesque, unknowable.

That night I dreamed of a Frankenstein monster guarding the gates of Hell. Only Hell was Heaven, a cartoon-blue heaven, with white puffy clouds.

The next day Andrew had swollen even more, gaining over sixty pounds from the thirty liters of fluid he was being given daily. The fluid was to replace what had been lost from the vascular system. One of the problems with sepsis is that fluid leaks out of the small vessels, the capillaries, leaving the brain, heart, lungs, and kidneys deprived. Mentally he was the same except a little more alert, the anesthesia having worn off. His eyes moved, he could shake and nod his head. When I asked him if he recognized me, he nodded. But when I asked if he loved me, he shook his head, a vehement negative.

When I told the doctors how shocked I was over his appearance, I realized they didn't "see" him as I did. Looking bad or good to them didn't mean puffy or purple or crazy-eyed; it meant what was going on "inside"—the fever and the status of his organs. Even his mental state didn't interest them now, because it couldn't be distinguished from the disorientation produced by the surroundings.

"Everybody goes crazy in intensive care," Sam said. It has to do with the weird atmosphere: the fact that, due to the twenty-four-hour fluorescent lighting, there is no distinction between day and night; with the click-clicking of the machines, the gurgling of liquids, the constant blaring and bleating of the radio that the nurses keep on for their own sanity—late-night talk, early-morning talk, the same pop tunes (Lionel Richie singing "Truly," over and over again) what keeps the nurses sane drives the patients crazy even in their semiconscious state.

The doctors were elated that Andrew had gotten this far without dying or, at the very least, his heart or kidneys failing.

"There are a thousand things that can go wrong," Sam said. One was that if the liquid filled the vascular system beyond its capacity, fluid would seep over into the lungs and drown the patient. Another worry was adult respiratory distress syndrome, when the lungs fill with water—the large concentration of oxygen required to ventilate the patient with adult respiratory disease syndrome damages the lungs even further—they tighten up and fill with water, and nothing can be done. To me, he had never seemed so alien and unreachable. His appearance and hostility were so distressing that I thought I might take a day off. I asked Sam if he thought I could.

"No," he said. "It's important for you to come in. On some level he knows you're here and needs you."

I was almost relieved by diversion that came in the form of the two-week marathon viewing of films, by the selection committee, for the New York Film Festival. At the end of July and the beginning of August, the five of us who were on the committee gathered in a screening room and, from ten in the morning until five or six in the evening, watched the offerings that had poured in since Cannes—the grim, the ghastly, and the tedious, the minimalist, the folkloric, the earnest, and the occasional, very occasional gem that supposedly justifies all the time and expense. My colleagues that year were the late Richard Roud (he who virtually invented the festival and was unceremoniously dumped in 1987), Richard Corliss, Jim Hoberman, and

David Thomson, and they were what made these two weeks in the dark worthwhile. This was a hip group of moviemanes and, under the directorship of Roud, a group that endured long hours and a very modest fee as much for the pleasure of each other's company as for the films themselves. Richard, slipping back and forth between London, Paris, and New York, elusive yet incandescently *there*, was the magnetic center of the group. He was one of the world's most charming and impossible people, and his running commentary on the generally mediocre films was the art form that held us all spellbound. He was the mischievous ringleader, but none of us was above taking a few pot shots.

It was a sort of game: who would be the first to sneer, to risk showing dislike for a movie someone else might be watching in impressed silence; or, conversely (and more courageously), who would have the nerve to defend a movie once it had elicited a snicker or a chuckle.

As if my nerves weren't already on edge, keeping up with this bunch of wiseacres was like being on a quiz show when you never knew what subject they were going to throw at you. The new film critics are an awesomely knowledgeable breed, smarter than most of the movies they review and the audiences who read their reviews, and they love to show off for each other, tossing off figures and gossip from the latest trade papers along with the minutiae and esoterica of film history, and there was a subtle atmosphere of male preening. Being with them, I felt like a peahen among the peacocks or a woman trapped in the press section of a sporting event, where the guys—in their egghead version of the macho men slogging it out on the field or the court—are reciting batting averages and recalling strategies and plays from great and obscure games of the past. It's a form of bonding and competing at the same time, a holdover from the time when boys separated themselves from girls through the numbers and lists, those male obsessions that seem to give them a handle on the world, to impose Reason and Order as a defense against death, birth, the unruly world of the emotions.

This summer, Andrew's demise and/or my emotional breakdown were an ever-present possibility, and their "facts" and *bons mots* and gossip and showy *aperçus* were a blanket of comfort—their way of distracting me. When I came in each morning, they would look at me awkwardly, then look away, with a barely audible sigh of relief: if I was there, Andrew wasn't dead yet. None of us mentioned Andrew, but I felt their unfailing compassion.

I could sense them slumping in their seats at certain scenes— death scenes and hospitals were very big that year—worried as to how they would affect me. Actually, these didn't bother me at all; on the contrary, they enthralled me: it was boring scenes and the tedium of bad films that threw me back on myself and my misery.

They shared the tension with me, and no doubt wondered, as they looked at my haggard, distraught face, how long I could go without collapsing under the strain. I felt their awkward, silent sympathy in all its complicated forms, the tension of all of us keeping up a front, so that it was almost a relief when, one day, I finally did break down.

Strangely—or not so strangely—it was over Mother, not Andrew. It came, seemingly, out of nowhere. The committee and I were having lunch at our hangout, Wolff's Delicatessen on Broadway, now gone, like Richard. I'd left home early that day, without seeing Mother, and having tried to get her on the telephone all morning, I went down to the pay phone to call her once again. When the phone rang and rang and she still didn't answer, I became upset, grew overwrought, then hysterical. I had visions of her lying in ashes, one of her cursed cigarettes having smoldered all night and finally set the bed on fire. That and emphysema were the two terminal fates my brother and I had always imagined for Mother, and now, as I displaced my anxiety for Andrew onto her, it seemed more than possible, it seemed absolutely *certain* that she had died in the night.

The two Richards took turns coming down to the phone booth with me, reassuring me as best they could.

"She's out doing errands," said Richard Roud sensibly, but I would hear none of it.

"She's probably still asleep," offered Richard Corliss, a late-show night owl and workaholic, who never got to bed until 3:00 A.M.

I reached Gabor, our superintendent, a gentle, sexy, and efficient Hungarian on whom every woman in our building had a secret crush, mechanical competence being the real turn-on to us cave-dwelling wives of urban klutzes. I asked him to go up and check to see if Mother was in the apartment, and gave him the number of the pay phone. Moments later, the phone rang and his reassuring, accented voice reported that the apartment was intact, but no sign of my mother. My anxiety refused to be quieted, ran in other directions: she'd been run over, she was lying in a gutter. Call the police.

Eventually she turned up: she had, indeed, been out doing errands. I talked to her, was finally calmed, and went back to the screening room for the afternoon. That evening, when I told her how upset I'd been, she was astonished.

"I didn't know you cared about me so much," she said, pleased. It was my turn to be astonished. How could she not have known how much I loved and needed her, that I couldn't have gotten along without her these last weeks? Because we didn't discuss such things. Because —such was the early imprinting I had had at her hands—I couldn't tell her so. This was the central irony in the complicated pact between us. In fostering my self-reliance, she had created a child who believed that the best way of getting her love was not to ask for it, not to behave like a child, not to *need* like a child. I had so suppressed such needs, had so little experience in finding words for them, that I had misplaced them altogether. Was it possible that on some level I really didn't know, or hadn't accepted, how much I needed Mother, and how great was my fear of being abandoned?

Something like this had happened earlier, back when Andrew was on the neurology floor, when I "lost" Mother one day at the hospital. We were to meet in the solarium, but through some misunderstanding, she was in one, I in another. I asked the nurses; everyone thought they had seen her go home. Annie and Jeffrey took me home, hysterical, plied me with Valium, and at my insistence called the police. They went through the motions, asked at the 96th Precinct if a Southern lady in her seventies had turned up, were told no. Finally Mother appeared, having of course been waiting for me at the *other* solarium. The relief in each case was so overwhelming that it was almost as if I had constructed the disappearance—the false "death"— in order to reverse it. I had "lost" a loved one—Mother as herself and as Andrew—in order to find them again in a happy ending that would portend Andrew's survival.

People tried to distract me—Mother with television, friends with detective stories—and I had all sorts of books piled up as usual beside my bed. But nothing worked. Death, in even the most stylized detective stories, seemed real: those refined British corpses gave off a stench. Any movie, whether bad or good, provoked thoughts of what it would have been like seeing it with Andrew and was thus tainted by a connection with him. Even the things I enjoyed *apart from him*—music, philosophy, more and different books, the occasional flirtatious lunch with another man—were things, I suddenly realized, that I enjoyed precisely because they *were* apart from him, a defense against his swallowing me up completely. My life was connected to his even by the interruptions in the chain and the disruptions of the harmony.

Andrew had been in the hospital five weeks, and gradually the sense of what life was like before was slipping away. I could barely remember what reading and discussing the paper in the morning was like, or listening to each other's boring dreams, laughing over each other's jokes. I thought of the byplay between us, those routines and alter egos we'd developed, as couples do, doppelgängers with squeaky voices, animal personae, sweet and sour versions of ourselves.

More and more I felt a sense of amputation. One of the worst things was, simply, the bedroom: waking up in it each morning, returning to it each night, feeling his absence everywhere, in the sheets, the smell of the pillow, the worn place in the rug between the bed and the closet, the filing cabinet with more papers on top than in. And especially the closet, that quintessence of Andrew. Before, Andrew's mess had driven me crazy, the dozens of mismatching tennis shoes, the scuffed loafers, ties fallen from the tie rack, the hangers tumbling out, the socks stuffed into the shoes (one black, one brown), all reminders of his inveterate sloppiness. But, in that curiously transfiguring way that absence has, these mementos had taken on a holy glow, had become the still-warm relics of a saint.

And finally it came to me with the force of a revelation, clear and painful and shocking. I was dependent on Andrew, wholly and utterly. Far from being independent, an "equal" partner in a marriage of equals, I was almost wholly supported by him, emotionally, financially, and intellectually. The idea of life without him, though my mind could hold it only for a flash, was pitch black, literally impossible to imagine. How was it possible, and how had I come to this? I was a clinging vine, not in the obvious ways, oh, no! On the surface, and to everyone including myself, I was self-defining, confident, but my heart was embedded in him, my lungs got their oxygen from his. I realized that I was crazier than Andrew, that my love for him was a kind of madness more insidious for being hidden, undiagnosed.

As someone who had always prided herself on looking life straight in the eye, this came as a shock. My rather pathetic solution to my own evasion was to play a sort of game in which I exorcised the fear of death by confronting it directly, or pretending to.

"Oh, death, where is thy sting?" said I, in effect. I made plans: "Okay, so die—now, while I'm still relatively young. I'll get remarried. Die, and I'll get rid of all those books, call Columbia and get them to send a truck down for all the papers, spilling out of filing cabinets and closets. And I'll have space!"

Space? Yes, but where? In some walk-up in Brooklyn or a nice two-room in Hoboken? Until this moment, nothing had come to ruffle the vision of myself as a bona fide liberated woman, a writer slash feminist with a book under her belt, a marriage-of-equals partner. But when it came to the nuts and bolts of finances, there was nothing equal about our marriage. I now had to face the unpleasant fact that without Andrew I was anything but independent, and without Andrew's income I was anything but self-supporting. In purely practical New York terms, I would be destitute. So far, it appeared that both *The Village Voice* and Columbia, in their quite surprising munificence, would continue Andrew's salary during his illness, but if he died I became a statistic in the feminization of poverty.

And what about the image I'd always cherished of myself as a loner, treasuring those evenings when Andrew went out of town, or when I went on trips. Like most women, I was delirious when sprung from domesticity, obedience to schedule; I would go anywhere for which a free ticket was supplied. Yet the solitude that I loved was hardly the solitude of the single woman, the divorcee, the widow. It was always circumscribed by Andrew; he was the music that always played in my head, the symphonies, the operas, the show melodies, against which I lived my life.

As a test to my hypothetical widow, I resurrected from mothballs my old Village-bohemian fantasy to see how it played, and it didn't.

Living in poetic disarray in a basement apartment on Perry Street was out of the question now—too expensive; I was too old, too afraid of cancer, and too much of an insomniac to drink espresso and smoke Gitanes. Village coffee houses had been replaced by fast-food outlets, intellectuals were outnumbered by scruffy outerborough types, there were no places to hang out and discuss Mallarmé (reading and finally penetrating Mallarmé in the original was part of my Village fantasy).

And what were our finances anyway? My ignorance on this subject was one of the continuing bones of contention in our marriage. Andrew was always trying to get me to sit down and go over our situation, and I was always sidestepping the issue. Partly it was that deep-seated aversion to talking about money that was an intrinsic part of my upbringing, while Andrew, like so many otherworldly types, loved the way talking about money made him sound practical and businesslike, on top of things.

But there was also the difficulty of our opposing perspectives, and the fact that Andrew's idea of how well we were doing was different from mine. In fact, we were lucky to be where we were, in an apartment we had bought in the mid-seventies, when fuel costs were up, real estate was down, the city was near bankruptcy, and people were fleeing the impending disaster. An apartment we couldn't possibly have afforded today, in a city where more and more we felt squeezed between deprivation and guilt, between stretch limos and the homeless.

In any case, I had a Scarlett O'Hara reluctance to face facts because facts were always unpleasant. Like weighing yourself (another ritual I avoided): with one it was always too much; with the other, never enough.

And so it was with us: Andrew, having clambered miraculously out of the depths of a Depression childhood, always saw the glass as half full and counted our income a noble sufficiency. While I, who had been raised in comfort if not luxury, thought the same amount an inadequate shoring against what I saw as a statistically probable solitary future. He saw us living well, flying to Paris every six months, or at least taking taxis down to the Film Forum. I saw another image: myself in isolated decrepitude, having outlived Andrew by many years, standing at a Broadway bus stop, waiting for the driver to lower the pneumatic stairs while everybody on the bus groaned; returning to my barely heated SRO hotel room, reheating my Meals-on-Wheels daily repast that had been dropped off earlier in the day and reading myself to sleep with . . . Ken Follett in large type, the only book legible to my cataract-afflicted eyes or comprehensible to my enfeebled brain.

A well-heeled relative made a tactful offer of financial assistance through a close friend. For the moment, I thought we were all right, assuming the hospital and doctors' bills were going to be covered by either Blue Cross or Major Medical, of which Andrew had two policies. But for how long? He had a $250,000 lifetime ceiling on his plan at Columbia, but it was now only August 6, and obviously nowhere near the end of the illness: Sam predicted this was going to be one of the most expensive illnesses on record. There was not only the astronomical cost of the ICU and all its technology, but because of the length of the illness and continuing bafflement, the need for more tests, more specialists. Columbia was pressing to know whether Andrew would be able to return for the fall term; unable to face the obvious—that even if Andrew didn't die, he would hardly be up to teaching anytime in the near future, I put them off.

What terrified me most was also the most shaming. It was my intellectual dependence on Andrew. He was a walking reference book, a live-in fund of insights and erudition, and a sounding board for my ideas. I rarely wrote an article without discussing it with him, calling upon his sweeping sense of the past, his instinct for spotting and defining social phenomena. Our lives and our work merged and cross-fertilized, a long-running talk show in which we stimulated and inspired each other. My reliance on him was a secret canker. How could I know if I could get along without him since I had never tried? And whom would I write for? Andrew was my reader, his the eyes I wanted to see light up with pleasure, not mine.

Strangely enough, I suspected that most of our friends would have been startled at this glimpse of our marriage, would have thought that if one of us were to die, it would be my death that would devastate Andrew. But I knew now it wasn't so. As crazy about me as Andrew was, as theatrically devoted—an anxious look if he lost sight of me at a party, a hangdog voice on the phone if I was away—it was I who was more deeply in need of him. If I had died, Andrew would have crawled back into his hole, contented himself with movies, with thinking, with his own solitary form of being: he had never quite believed his good fortune in getting me to begin with. Whereas I . . . I felt that if Andrew died, I would die, too. Not by suicide, but just automatically, as bees die when they are detached from the hive.

In this context, the act of putting one foot in front of the other each day, getting to the hospital and back, became a triumph. There were small but genuine pleasures, the pleasure of being alone in the summer, when New York's East Side was like a movie set after the actors have gone home. There was a side of me that blossomed in summer, unfolded and turned toward the sun as simply and sybaritically as a flower. I loved the sensuality of summer clothes, the cheap colorful kind. Skirts—it was the only time I ever wore them—sleeveless shift tops, sandals, the feeling of bare skin and toes. There were fewer people around and I was grateful. Toby and Betty kept in constant touch, but everyone else had disappeared. I would take a different route each time I went to the hospital, make acquaintance, as it were, with a new neighborhood, browse in bookstores, peek through townhouse windows, gaze with a kind of aesthetic hunger at the dishes arrayed in take-out places, unlikely combinations in jewellike (and jewel-priced) settings. Sometimes I'd have my lunch on free samples, moving from one food boutique to another.

Restaurants, where couples sat laughing and drinking spritzers, lingering over a late lunch, or having an early dinner, gave me a pang, as if each one was a taunt and a reminder. This one or that one was the kind of place we might have tried out, alone or with friends. Would we ever go out again?

Every day when I walked under the arches of the hospital entrance I would glance at the small Gothic chapel just off the lobby, with its brilliant blue stained-glass windows, and eye it longingly as my apostate's feet hurried past. How could I go in and pray for Andrew when I hadn't set foot in a church, except for special occasions, since we were married. I should have kept up my churchgoing as an insurance policy—say, once every three months, and on the humble Sundays, not Easter and Christmas. Then I could go in now, my conscience clear, my premiums paid up to date. But finally I could resist no longer: I'd go in with an unclear conscience. I'd pretend it was a

European cathedral, a Michelin One Star of minor architectural or historical interest or a small-town cathedral in Tuscany or Umbria. With a tourist's alibi, we wouldn't think of missing one of those religious shrines that form the heart of every Italian village, those dark, dank places smelling of incense where the kitsch and the sublime jostle each other unselfconsciously. One went in for aesthetic reasons and allowed religious feeling to come in the back door.

I went in quickly, looking over my shoulder in case someone I knew—a doctor, a fellow skeptic—should see me, and took my place in a pew, sheepishly. I wasn't seized with the rapture of that old-time religion, but neither did I feel a hypocrite. What I felt was slightly absent, the way, during the first chords of a symphony, or lines of a play, your mind fiddles, not yet having given in to the mood. I didn't even try to pray. But as I sat there, I felt a kind of acceptance that came either from without or within. That is, the spirit of the place hadn't "seen through" me and called my bluff. Perhaps it was holiness or perhaps it was the change in the atmospheric molecules that I had introduced, or just the cool smell of wax and stone, but I felt my shoulders relax and my lungs expand, and I breathed more freely.

I began to stop in regularly. Sitting alone in that pew, I was as close to the still waters as I'd been in many years, yet the peace was short-lived. When I emerged, I found myself overtaken by uncharitable feelings, fighting back rage and hostility toward people I hardly knew or didn't know at all. Toward everyone I passed who seemed well and preoccupied, the nonsufferers—doctors, nurses, patients on their way home with their families. I begrudged them their freedom from anxiety, felt their indifference to me as an affront. I thought of Breughel's Icarus, falling from the sky in Auden's "Musée des Beaux Arts," while nobody notices:

> About suffering . . . they were never wrong,
> The Old Masters: how well they understood
> Its human position; how it takes place
> While somebody else is eating or opening a
> window or just walking dully along. . . .

The sun was shining outside, the flowers in bloom, the early blossoms on the linden trees had turned into leaves, people walked through the hospital door as if life were normal, and Andrew and I were "falling out of the sky," our wings burning in the sun.

Yet my fellow victims in suffering made me even more uncomfortable. The very people with whom I'd passed companionable moments in the early days—Eileen, wife of the stroke victim, Martha, mother of the patient with Guillain-Barré syndrome—I now avoided. We'd all been around this place too long. If I saw them coming toward me, I'd turn to the wall, let them go past. (And how many times did *they* look the other way, pretend not to see me?) We were like children who start out in school together only to find themselves locked in competition not of their making. Was one of their men better? (I didn't want to hear it.) Was one failing? (Even worse.)

Then there were friends, two in particular, who had been through terrible ordeals themselves, but theirs ended in widowhood, and I couldn't bear the association. Not that Billy, whose wife had died of cancer that spring, or Martha Lear, who wrote the immensely moving *Heartsounds* about her husband Hal's death of heart disease, pushed the comparison. They were wonderful, they gave me advice, took me out, brought me chicken salad and never mentioned death, but that particular death—of a wife, a husband—was always present in their very kindnesses, their intuitive grasp of my grief, the very tact with which they refrained from saying "I know how you feel." The fate they had suffered, the one I refused to accept for Andrew, lay between us, as painful for them as it was for me.

At the end of the first week of August, one week in Intensive Care, Andrew still had a low fever and was being maintained by machines.

The doctors were uncertain as to which had come first, the perforation or the infection. It was conceivable that just lying in the hospital and not moving the bowels could cause the intestine to perforate. When I came in, Andrew's hands had been temporarily untied and he reached for me, the first show of anything like affection in weeks. I leaned over and kissed his taped-over snout.

"You're going to live, you know," I said, assuming that if he'd survived for five days he was free and clear.

But then I added, "I can't bear any more of this, any more anguish, Andrew." He seemed to understand. Then the eyes and the mind wandered, went inward no doubt to whatever dark imaginings that day had brought. I was still encouraged.

"Things aren't as hopeful as they look," Sam warned. "There are still seven hundred and twenty things that could go wrong."

This was at least an improvement, down from a thousand. Some of the tubes were out. He was being given hyperalimentation.

A night or so later I walked in and Michael, my favorite of the nurses, had Andrew sitting up in bed for the first time and Gluck's *Orfeo ed Eurydice* was playing on the radio. As I listened to the last triumphant aria by "Amor" in which Orfeo is given a reprieve, I felt both the elation and the terror that myth had always held for me, of two people who couldn't take their eyes off each other even if it meant death.

Michael had had a tray set up in front of Andrew—this was a major step forward—and Andrew kept motioning for a pencil and paper. I was as excited as he was: what would he write? What would his first words of reentry be? Would he ask for his typewriter, or had he some comment on the political campaign that was gathering steam? I gave them to him. He seized them eagerly and after a laborious effort, held up the paper.

I looked at it. His writing, never too legible, was almost indecipherable, but I finally made it out. "Write Morse code," it said. Andrew, who couldn't even pick out S.O.S.! I managed a wan smile.

Andrew alternated between extreme agitation, when he was often wild-eyed and manic, and tired peacefulness, some of the mood swings dictated by the condition of the surgical incision and what had to be done to it. It was horribly infected, and every morning and afternoon the nurses had to scrape off dead cells, a process so painful he required steady doses of morphine, which in turn left him limp and half-sedated. They were also taking him off the respirator for a few hours at a time, so that he was often so tired when I came in that he slept for most of my visit. I almost preferred those times, when I could at least imagine him as peaceful. When he was awake, I tried to soothe him, to ease his agitation, since relaxing was an important factor in the bowels returning to normal, but the moments of serenity were short-lived.

Then, finally one night he was off the respirator, with only an oxygen mask to assist his breathing. He was making those beautiful respiratory sounds on his own, a soft, just audible hissing. He didn't say anything for a long time, but at last he reached out—his hands had been temporarily untied—and took mine in his and grasped them tight. Then said, "I love you so much."

I felt such a rush of happiness, a physical sense of life coming back into me. Just as his lungs had finally begun to push air through his body, just as his organs were beginning to tremble with life, so some frozen-over pool of sane emotion had thawed. I fell over him, leaned gently across his bandaged body, listened to the miraculous sound of his breathing, and as I did so it was as if we had found each other in some place that was neither life nor death, sanity nor madness, some hole in the universe where we were joined each to each, and through each other to the dead. It may be that Andrew had come halfway back from death and I had gone the rest of the way to meet him. It may be that Andrew had a stronger hold on life than I did, and was pulling us both back from the brink.

A few days later, Andrew was still breathing well but he was in full, flaming paranoia. He begged me to get an ambulance and take him to the D.A.'s office where our friend Bob Morgenthau would issue a writ to get him out. Moments later, he asked for a gun. I asked him why.

"I want to shoot myself, because"—and here came that absurd understatement that had become his trope—"I'm fed up." So I tried to distract him—"Andrew, you've always been an advocate of gun control"—but he just kept asking for the gun.

Now, some of the 720 things that could go wrong were going wrong. Michael said he would have to be kept in Intensive Care longer because the infected incision wasn't healing. Despite the scraping away of dead skin to encourage the cells to start regenerating, Andrew's weakness and anemia were delaying their growth. The morphine he needed during the scraping process slowed down his body functions and depressed the activity of the lungs and bowels. His hematocrit had now fallen from 32 to 28 (normal is 40 to 47) so they were transfusing him and increasing the hyperalimentation he was being given intra-venously. According to the hematologist, the drop could be attributed to any one of a number of things: a loss of white blood cells, which could be a reaction to the drugs (they had stopped administering the possibly offending antibiotic vancomycin); an underlying disease, what-ever it might be; or the infection. The decrease in red and white cells could mean bone-marrow suppression. Yet, as Sam put it, the disease was so ominous and multifaceted, if some of these things weren't going wrong, something would be wrong—with their perceptions. Andrew's wasn't an isolated infection, but a multiple one, its ramifications show-ing just how interdependent all the systems in the body were.

Now the thing that I had been dreading was upon us—the August exodus. Sam would be going to Martha's Vineyard Friday, and on Thursday, when all of this was happening, he was preparing me for his departure. We were standing in the small hallway of the ICU going over the details. Medically, Andrew would be in the best hands: all the specialists who were already dealing with him would continue and a new man, a Dr. Davis, would take over for Sam and act as coor-dinator. My fear expressed itself in a sudden anxiety over financial details.

Money is a subject rarely discussed in illness memoirs or auto-biographies in general, as if the "triviality" of such anxieties would diminish the magnitude of the drama or taint the author as ignoble. Yet except in rare cases of the patient for whom it's no object, money presses on the brain constantly. The hospital consumes money like water, bills arrive daily, the meter is always ticking. Every time a doctor walks into a room and out again, it's $50 (or was then). Worrying about money was something I did constantly. I had laid out $8,000 in nurses' fees and hadn't gotten a penny back. I still didn't know what to tell Columbia, or rather, how long they should expect Andrew to be absent.

As Sam went over details I began to feel spasms of self-pity and aggravation rise in me. Sam was standing there in his white coat and a blue shirt, leaning against the paneled wall, that boyish shock of hair falling over his forehead, guiding me impeccably through what might be expected to occur in his absence, when in the midst of it I let out a sigh. A sigh! I was ready to collapse, fall to the floor, sob, throw myself in Sam's arms for comfort, rage at him for deserting me, but I did none of these. What I did was sigh. A poor, pitiful—but socially acceptable—sigh.

And how did Sam react? He shook his head reprovingly. "None of that now," he said.

I was cut to the quick. He wasn't just saying "Buck up"—that I could have taken; he was rebuking me, he was saying that my sigh was excessive, my implied complaint out of place. I felt breathless with embarrassment. Had I been troublesome? Called him night and day? Asked for emotional support? Painted myself a martyr? No, none of the above. On the contrary, I'd been a model of restraint. I'd even thought to get points for my stoicism, perhaps unconsciously hoped for a little praise ("You're doing great, Molly, keep it up!"), and instead I stood there with egg on my face, humiliated.

But hadn't that small sigh been a huge appeal, which his unconscious had heard for what it was? Didn't I want him to take me in his arms, say "I won't go." Tell me he'd give up his vacation, his family, to stay by my side.

Doctors, almost by definition, aren't comfortable with emotional intensity and the irrational. The conventional wisdom now has it that it's a professional hazard, and young doctors should be schooled in human relations before they become inured to the needs of patients as a result of the numbing horrors of hospital life. From what I can see, however, it's not so much that medicine makes them that way, as that distinct personality types are drawn into medicine to begin with. Sam, for instance, often voiced a wariness of writers and the liberties they took. He was smart, charming, and—perhaps I should add here—quite disarmingly handsome. (Themis, who adored him, once said, "Doctors have no right to be so good-looking. It's not fair to their women patients." And there were times during my own hospitalization when it was almost worth fifty dollars to have him stop in, his cheerful masculine face lighting up the room and thrilling his forlorn female patient . . . and her fellow sufferers. "Who was *that*?" they would ask after he left, and I would smile with proprietary pride.) He got along with people well and had many writer patients, but I always felt there was a basic difference of mindset. Where writers acknowledged sub-jectivity, embraced ambiguity, enjoyed double and triple meanings, Sam went for the rock-hard reliability of medicine and its terminology.

"I love medicine," he would tell me, "because it means what it says. 'Myocardial,' 'lymphocytopenia,' myelomeningocele.' " His face would light up with an almost sensual pleasure as he offered up a platter of words and then happily broke them down into their Latin or Greek roots.

How can we bear this truth: that doctors love us for our cells rather than our selves. We can't. Hence the appeal of medical soap operas, where fantasy doctors are endlessly adoring and solicitous of their female patients. How can we be prepared for the brusque and businesslike approach of most medical professionals when our heads are full of Dr. Kildare, Ben Casey, Marcus Welby. Doctors who are never overburdened by other patients, never away in August, and who combine male omniscience with the nurturing qualities of the perfect mother.

"Wa-a-a-ah!" I wanted to say, and break down shamelessly. Hav-ing prided myself on being a stoic, where had it gotten me? I wanted to descend into that never-never-land where insatiably needy women wallow in their fantasies of eroticized hospital worlds.

Why had I held myself aloof from them, from the cheap catharses the genre provides? Those of us who pride ourselves on our stoicism are the real fools, waiting for a reward that never comes, the Nobel Prize for Women Who Are Not Nuisances.

But there was more to it, and perhaps that's what Sam sensed— that my needs were so cavernous, that they went beyond him, even beyond Andrew, that to have responded would have endangered us both, washed us away, like a hurricane hitting at high tide.

At that moment I felt only fury and humiliation, a defense that had its advantages. Yet there were advantages: I now turned away, withdrew all sense of dependence on him, ready to cope with August on my own. Now that Sam was written out of the script, I missed him less than I might have otherwise.

Andrew was now alternating between periods of hallucination and a proximate lucidity, i.e., he had developed some vague sense of his predicament, but still saw it as something that had been inflicted on him by his enemies, or by friends who were now deserting him. One of the most consistent symptoms of his madness was that he never knew where he was, a peculiarity that seems to be generally true of people with delusions or brain disease, as if to admit to where they are would concede important ground to the opposition. Actually, I think the simplest explanation would be that their wandering minds literally are elsewhere, back in the town where they were born, on the high seas, anywhere but here. Andrew could answer questions of a historical nature: the name of a movie, the year of a war, who killed Jack Kennedy. But to the question of where he was (i.e., recent memory; awareness of surroundings) he never gave the same answer. Now he thought he was in Nebraska and asked the nurses why nobody came to see him. He threatened to kill himself again. He was in his bitter sardonic mood one day when Mother came in, the first time she'd seen him since surgery nine days earlier.

She came out after a brief visit and told me she felt he looked better.

When I went in later, Andrew said, "Your mother looked worried."

"But no," I said. "She told me she thinks you look better."

To which Andrew, without a trace of irony in his voice, replied, "Maybe that's why she looks worried." He mumbled something bitterly about the cream of the jest, and the next day, when I came in, he said he'd had a "bad fantasy."

"Your mother prefers a statue of me to the real thing." He paused. "Also, she wanted to cut off my head."

There was a marvelous and uncanny appositeness to this fantasy, intertwining the fear of castration at the hands of the "enemy" mother, with Mother's abstract art, her style of painting figures without faces, without features.

Next to Andrew was a woman in her sixties who'd also had a colostomy—one of those hair-raising horror stories in which a doctor had given her a barium enema, sent her home, and then, when she reported, and continued to report, bleeding and pain, he kept ignoring the symptoms and telling her to lie down and rest. By the time she came in she had a perforated colon, and now peritonitis.

Her visitors—a husband, children, nieces—provided rich material for Andrew's fantasies. Her husband had stolen her pocketbook, Andrew reported, and was pawning her eyeglasses. He also thought they had stuck an umbrella down his throat, and insisted that I look at his bottom to see if it had come out the other end. In fact, though I didn't know it at the time, he was developing bedsores on his rump, which may have provoked this striking image.

He had gotten numerous letters and get-well cards from friends and fans. Most of them he ignored, but his face lit up over one of them, a card with a stunning photograph of Garbo on the front. He was even more pleased at the message, affectionate words from a fan who missed his column. I taped it to the wall so that he could see it from his bed, but he frowned.

"That doesn't count for anything here," he said morosely, referring both to the glorious Garbo and to his own status as a Garbo-worshiping critic reduced to the status of a nobody. His attitude toward me was less one of rage or fury than the exasperation of someone who has lost all hope of persuading the other of the reality of his world. The classical Hitchcock hero/victim whose own mother and/or wife refuse to believe him.

"I love you," he said sadly at one point, "but you and I are talking at cross-purposes."

And another time, he said, "I have a selfish suggestion. Could you be the one to suffer ninety percent of this torture?"

He was being given transfusions and the white cells were down, nothing of major significance, but it always seemed to me he just wasn't getting any better. On August 12 his spinal fluid showed a rise in white cells. Dr. Davis, the covering doctor, said the fever wasn't high, that it could indicate either an infection of the wound or a slight case of pneumonia, both of which would resolve themselves as Andrew improved.

Then, out of left field, came a blow of surreal proportions. On Tuesday, August 14, they discovered that Andrew couldn't move his legs. "Flaccid paralysis," they called it, and planned to do X rays. Wouldn't that just be the normal atrophying of the muscles? I asked, but Dr. Ramir thought it was more than weakness. He speculated it might be something called porphyria, a metabolic problem in which, because of the body's abnormal ability to break down hemoglobin (which makes up a good portion of the body's blood), abnormal products build up. But Andrew didn't fit the diagnosis neatly, so it could be some aspect of this carried to an extreme . . . or something else altogether. The abnormality, according to Ramir, was not in the spinal cord itself, but in the nerves leaving the spinal cord. It was unbelievable, yet it wasn't. A paralysis of the legs? Andrew, if he survived, might never walk again? I mean, after all, why not? And walking seemed small potatoes compared to living.

At 4:00 P.M. Ramir called. Tests showed that nerves were disconnected from the muscles. There might be a small abscess within the spinal column. The next day they would do a myelogram—a spinal tap in which the patient is placed at an angle and injected with a dye that's heavier than spinal fluid. Jeffrey, who'd been away for two weeks, saw Andrew two days in a row, then called to confirm the paralysis and say that his legs were worse the second day. I had kept hoping it might be some kind of temporary immobility, but Jeffrey assured me that it was a real paralysis. It could be any of a number of things (Jeffrey doubted it was porphyria), one of which was Guillain-Barré syndrome. This, of course, was a familiar term to me now, and, as far as Andrew was concerned, a dreaded one. There was no way, it seemed to me, that anyone in his condition could survive a paralysis that traveled upward from the legs to the hips, the chest, the lungs, all those organs that had been living daily under siege.

It was at this time that I began to dread going to see him. The craziness, the weakness, those wretched moods, never a moment of lightness or hope, of normal discourse—it was more than I could bear. I told Jeffrey I didn't think I could go in one more day, and he agreed, saying he didn't know how I'd been able to keep it up until now. The strength that enabled me to trudge down there twice a day, day after day, only to see that blighted body and familiarly unfamiliar face began to seem a mixed blessing. I longed to break down, have an excuse for not coming in. I dreaded it, yet something—morbid fascination, perhaps—kept me going. I *had* to see him, see what twists and turns he had taken that day, that hour.

* * *

The results of the myelogram were to come in on Friday, August 17. On Friday evening, still not having heard, I sat through a screening of Milos Forman's *Amadeus*, trying to get with the antic playfulness of Tom Hulce's Mozart and hiss at the mordant envy of Salieri, but feeling, even in the divine Mozartian score, only tragedy. Jeffrey called me that night with the results—negative—but he pointed out that this was not so good: it could mean a Guillain-Barré-type "ascending paralysis," which would develop within a week.

The plan was to move Andrew from the ICU on Monday to a private room on F7, supposedly the best nursing floor in the hospital. In addition, he would have to have round-the-clock registered nurses to dress the wound, which was still dangerously infected—dangerous to Andrew and dangerous to those around him. On Saturday and Sunday he was extremely tired, and weak, and thin, but he seemed to be more interested in the outside world. When I told him about the DeLorean acquittal and Reagan's gaffe over bombing the Russians, he wanted to know if the election was over.

"How long do you think you've been here?" I asked him.

"Six months," he said. (It wasn't yet two.) Nor could he tell me where he was when I asked him. When I came in Sunday evening, he was still hallucinating. He looked at me with surprise. "I thought you'd had an operation," he said. I explained that that was several years ago. Then I mentioned his mother, and he looked even more shocked.

"But she's dead," he said. I argued back and forth with him for half an hour before I could convince him otherwise. That night, prior to the move, he was very confused, insisting that he was in Auschwitz, and he slept with his eyes wide open, the pupils rolling back in his head while he murmured and mumbled. When I told him he wouldn't remember any of this, he said, "I remember all too clearly through a hole in my stomach."

His mind had hatched yet another striking image to integrate and organize the horrors he experienced into a poetically apt metaphor. He was like those lunatics who believe they are receiving position papers from God or messages from outer space through their bellybuttons, only he really had a hole, a giant crater of a receiving dish —a womb, or a missile launching pad?—for his transmissions.

There is always an undercurrent of anxiety and suspense before a move, and Sunday, the day before Andrew's, was fraught with both. The woman in the bed beside him, the woman who'd also had a perforated colon, died. I couldn't tell if Andrew quite took it in, but it was a blow to the rest of us. She had never really come back, yet here was Andrew, talking gibberish, seeming far sicker in many ways, but apparently determined to elude the Grim Reaper.

The evening before Andrew's move, I said good-bye to the staff of the ICU with emotion. He would have his own nurses, and the regular nursing staff but we'd be more on our own now. A small miracle had taken place here and I didn't want to leave those responsible. Michael, my favorite, had hoped to come down with us as night nurse, but Andrew's stay in the ICU had been longer than expected, and he had to return to school. Finally, I shook hands with the intern who'd seen him over the last two weeks.

He was standing by Andrew's bed, looking first at him, then at me. "You know," he said, "he came as close to death as a person can come without actually dying."

I looked over at Andrew, still in some twilight zone of his own. Why hadn't he died and what was it in him that had brought him this far? His darting eyes and baleful mutterings weren't going to tell me. And certainly the doctors, who still didn't know what he had, couldn't tell me. Through some phenomenal combination of medical technology, first-class nursing, and his own incredible constitution, Andrew had—so far—survived. But it wasn't over yet, as the doctors and nurses assured me.

I left the room and, glancing briefly at the patients on the left, surreal, isolated, and unrecognizable (were they the same ones I'd seen nineteen days ago? no way of knowing), I walked along the corridor, and out the door of the surgical Intensive Care Unit and I never looked back.

7

I went directly to F7 the next morning, and found Andrew installed in a private room, the first one on the left as you entered the corridor. It was a large, unconsoling room, whose only concession to decoration was a wall color of pale yellow that tried unsuccessfully for a sunny feeling. It was more spacious than the rooms on the neurology floor, but unlike the rooms in the "Tower," it still had a makeshift feel about it, less a bedroom than a vacant space into which a bed had been arbitrarily placed.

I hovered over Andrew, looking for signs of change. Would his removal from the ICU show up in a sudden improvement of his mental state? Although the rational part of me knew this was unlikely, I had some vague hope that one madness—the more recent ICU-induced madness—might dispel the other one, as a storm dissipates smog. He would emerge refreshed and sane.

But as I watched him, I had only to see the fierce gleam in his eye as he watched Gloria, the nurse, move around the room, to know that the demons were still within. Gloria was a highly qualified Asian who'd been with him during the last week in the ICU and who had agreed to come with us on day duty.

Andrew had been muttering suspiciously about her for several days, and as soon as she left for a moment, he looked at me.

"Did you see that nurse?" he asked, in a voice loaded with malevolence. "She hates me. She just tried to burn me with a hot breakfast."

Then he changed tack.

"I am, however, not without guilt," he announced. "I had an affair . . . with a movie star's sister." He then hastened to add that he "couldn't handle it" and it "was the only time."

He was out to prove his tattered virility in having had an affair, and to get back at me for my promiscuity a month earlier that had allegedly been bruited about by his fellow patients on the neurology floor . . . and perhaps for who knows how many infidelities I'd never had but he suspected I'd had, or ought to have had.

Then, no less aggressively, he asked for his typewriter, implying that I, in my plot to undermine him as a writer, had done away with it. These two sequences were not unrelated. His writing was his manhood; it was also what had won me and made him a hero in my eyes.

He'd been told that he had a problem with his legs, which he didn't believe for a minute, and to prove that this wasn't true, he demanded to put on his shoes.

I suggested we try a few leg lifts first.

"Twenty," he said.

I held his leg. "Let's just try three," I said. After two noble tries, his legs flopped down. He was thoroughly exhausted, but undismayed, as he'd already forgotten what he was doing and why.

The signs of lucidity were themselves ambiguous. The more reasonable he sounded, as when he told his mother on the phone not to expect too much, the more you felt it was an elaborate put-on. It was now August 21. Themis had not been in since July, when Andrew had his surgery. Her physical movement was becoming more and more restricted by the weakness of her legs, so she was spared the spectacle of Andrew in Intensive Care. When I told her Andrew had suffered a paralysis of *his* legs, she didn't believe it.

"Oh, he'll be fine, Molly, I'm sure it's just from lying down too long," she said.

"Yeah, you're probably right," I said. I no longer felt any desire to force the truth on her. Her truth was as good as mine. The two of them could at least talk on the phone now, and Andrew managed to sound almost normal for a short conversation. Part of the reason was that he was still too dissociated from his body to know how sick he was, and had no conception of what he'd been through or where he'd come from.

Over and over again, I had to remind myself not to expect too much. We tend to forget that illness and recovery aren't a series of dramatic lurches forward but a spectrum of very gradual, barely discernible improvements and setbacks. We want to believe that a change of scenery—as in the theater—signals movement of the drama, progress of some sort toward a conclusion. But Andrew's illness was anything but a well-made play, so baffling and multifaceted that looking for a forward trajectory was like trying to see the curvature of space with the naked eye.

He had been in the ICU from July 31 (the day of the operation) until August 20, almost three weeks, and in a very real sense, he was still in intensive care. The low fever signaled the still flamingly infected wound, and now, out of the blue, early Tuesday morning, the night nurse called to say his temperature had shot up and he'd been ranting during the night.

This seemed to take even the doctors by surprise. He had a soaring 104 fever by late morning, and nobody seemed to know why. Gaines's assistant, Dr. Wetherby, thought it might be another abscess. These deposits of pus—infections that are, in effect, sealed-off, self-generating germ worlds within the body—must be drained or, failing that, removed surgically. The plan had been to remove him from antibiotics, but now that was impossible.

Ramir, still mystified, said he would take Andrew's charts home over the weekend and go over them. He was beginning to think it had never been encephalitis, and that whatever it was, Andrew still had it.

I had never seen the wound, primarily because in Intensive Care they always changed it at a time other than visiting hours. Now Gloria came in with the bandages and solution and asked me if I wanted to stay, and I said yes. They kept referring to the "wound," from which I understood that the incision was open rather than closed. You can't sew up an infected incision or you'll stitch in the bacteria. Still, what the word *wound* connoted to me was a thin gash down the middle of his stomach. Instead, a hole, a canoe-shaped crater a foot in length and nine inches wide gaped up at me from where his stomach had been, and in it, staring up at me, like a medley of fruits nestled comfortably in a compote, were his innards . . . all pink and purple and presumably where they were supposed to be, like one of those three-dimensional anatomical sculptures in science class. Although I was told later that what I had seen was fat and muscle, I was sure I could make out the organs. It was like a house whose facade has been blown off in a hurricane. There were the rooms: the stomach, the liver, the kidneys, the gallbladder, the pancreas, the small intestine, all in place, clear as the plaster models, but where were the two little flaps of skin to close over it, the front doors? Andrew's abdomen, I was told, would somehow close and become a belly again in the healing process.

And no less exposed, and strikingly analogous, was his poor mind. The lid was off, and all the normally hidden drives and desires were surging forth.

When I came in on the afternoon of August 23, five days after the transfer, I discovered that Gloria had quit. According to the nurse on duty, she and Andrew had had a row during which Andrew had used "foul language." Stunned, I questioned one of the hall nurses closely. It had happened once before, she said, and Gloria had tried to ignore it, but the last time it had become "intolerable"—Gloria's word—and she quit. At first I refused to believe it. Andrew didn't even *know* any obscenities. It was one of the jokes between us that Andrew never said so much as "damn," while I had a streak of vulgarity a mile wide. There was the army experience, though—he had once told me that while in the army, men spoke nothing but obscenities, that every other word was F-U-C-K, an expletive spoken as casually as *a, an,* and *the.* "Foul language" was the common currency of army life, but might it not also have been an adaptive ploy for keeping collective anger on call should it be needed for battle? And now Andrew was embattled, and, reverting to army language, had perhaps gone even further than four-letter words.

For I sensed, in the extremeness of Gloria's reaction, an indication that there might even have been racial slurs. Andrew was the least bigoted person I'd ever known, but the hospital is an enforced melting pot, overrun by those Others whom we officially embrace in our liberal waking lives. Andrew, in his mind, was always in a combat zone, and what better weapons than the racial resentments that percolate beneath the surface. Prejudices are a necessary part of life, the mirror image of our loyalties and the hates by which we organize our solidarity to the tribe. We presumably outgrow them, move beyond them, but they are languages learned early, part of that primitive architecture of the mind that, as Freud pointed out, is built over by successive layers of civilization but never quite disappears. It is when we are helpless and under siege, as Andrew was, that we call on the emotions of hostility to energize us for battle.

Actually, whatever social biases Andrew possessed were directed upward, not downward. Like most children of immigrants, he had started out thinking that he was a regular, sports-loving, whitebread-eating, full-blooded American like everybody else, and with the same chances of becoming president, or funding a chair at the Metropolitan Opera, but his moment of truth about the land of equal opportunity had come during his senior year in high school. Having announced his ambition to become an ambassador (after all, he was class vale-dictorian), he was given a questionnaire by the vocational-guidance counselor. Expecting to find questions on geography or politics or language, he found instead: "What kind of boot polish do you use?" With that, his eyes were opened to the realpolitik of our supposedly classless society. A million dollars he might hope to make, but knowing the right kind of boot polish was a sartorial secret he could never hope to acquire. It was programmed in the genes by the DNA molecules governing dress and tailoring for the ruling class.

In the early years of our marriage, he would get into arguments, blow up, turn perfectly pleasant dinner parties into shambles. Any display of real or imagined privilege would set him off—East Coast preppie/establishment types, mouthpieces of radical chic, writers for prestigious and high-paying periodicals, couples just back from Greece who "adored" it because it was so quaint, so cheap. Knowing exactly what would provoke him, I would tense up and wait while Andrew, deserted by the eloquence that was his crowning glory, would grow bullying and repetitious. Even when the targets were blockheads them-selves, Andrew came off the loser.

There would be acute discomfort all round, then the storm would pass, and everybody would make excuses.

"It's wonderful to see somebody feel so strongly about something" was the usual response. Sometimes, when he grew loud, I, sensing the crescendo to come, would try to hush him up; then everyone would turn on me, the heavy.

"Let him alone!" they would cry. "He just feels passionately." As opposed to me, of course, the uptight and unfeeling, WASP-holding-it-all-in "lady." At first, I tried to see their point of view. After all, Andrew had come from an ethnically exuberant family who believed in expressing themselves (yelling, not to put too fine a point on it), and he had never learned the collective art of dinner-party conversation. But the effects were too painful, making every dinner party an event to be dreaded. Why was he doing it and why was I putting up with it? It seemed we were engaged in another of those mutually flagellating rituals, like tennis, or like the alcoholic and his wife: he gets drunk, makes a scene, embarrasses her, and she feels that in some obscure way his public outrages are designed to punish her. In a way, Andrew was lashing out *for* me, playing the rude Charlie McCarthy to my Edgar Bergen.

For at home, with me alone, no one was sweeter, more courtly, a true Galahad. Indeed, in a marriage that was like a perpetual courtship, he was a twelfth-century troubador paying homage to his lady. Andrew, seeking only to serve and adore, was the Mediterranean type, a knight of lyrical bent as opposed to the lusty and self-aggrandizing northern knight of the epic tradition. As Maurice Valency describes him in his wonderful book *In Praise of Love*, the courtly "True Lover desires not so much to possess as to be accepted," a goal to which the sexual reward is incidental. In public, we scraped and jarred each other. In private, we were two mutually accepting halves who together were more than the sum of our parts, like the mythic union of opposites in Plato's *Symposium*.

Valency traces the exalted ideal of romantic love back to the famous fable in that dialogue, offered by Aristophanes, according to which heterosexual love was born when the spheroids that originally peopled the earth were sliced by Zeus, producing men and women who were then destined to roam the world in search of their matching halves. The passage that Valency quotes might have been written for us:

"Each of us when separated is always looking for his other half; such a nature is prone to love and ready to return love. And when he finds his other half, the pair are lost in an amazement of love and friendship and intimacy, and one will not be out of the other's sight, as I may say, even for a moment; these are they who pass their lives with one another; yet they could not explain what they desire of one another. For the entire yearning which each of them has toward the other does not appear to be the desire of intercourse, but of something else which the soul desires and cannot tell, and of which she has only a dark and doubtful presentiment."

Modern psychiatry would classify such love as neurotic, the "perfect fit" masking all sorts of disruptive and repressed emotions—anger, sexual desire—that will eventually have their say. In fact, the blowups—Andrew committing an outrage, me reacting in horror—may well have been a way of backing off from an engulfing closeness, finding our way, if only for a few moments, out of the "amazement of love and friendship and intimacy." They occurred during the seventies and then, for what seemed a variety of reasons, they ceased to occur. Andrew's voice would rise, but rarely in anger. He no longer had such a short fuse. This could have been the consequence of a normal marital adjustment process: we were both surer of ourselves with each other—he was less likely to explode and I was less likely to sit still for it if he did. There was also the fact that he had discovered he had dangerously high blood pressure and was now taking medication. Finally, there was the shift in the marital narrative that had occurred as a result of my bouts with emergency surgery: from Andrew being the temperamental partner and I the one who walked on eggshells, suddenly our positions were reversed. My abdomen was a field of land mines that Andrew might set off. I had become the fragile half of the partnership, someone to worry over as a semi-invalid (Andrew's extreme view) rather than an invulnerable golden child. His sense of grievance, formerly a weapon of offense and defense, had been turned outward into a continuous, even excessive, caring about me.

Now he was under siege again. Reverting to his old self-pity, covering himself with it like a comforter, he might have said, with Elizabeth Bishop, "What's wrong with self-pity?/Pity should begin at home;/As long as I feel pity/I feel at home." For Andrew, adrift in the alien world of a hospital, self-pity *was* home.

Adding to his problems, he had now developed painful bedsores. These raw lesions of the body—actual infections from having lain too long in one position—can be life-threatening if untreated. He hadn't been moved regularly enough, although perhaps there was no way he could have gone through a hospitalization as long as this and with the enforced inertia of intensive care *without* getting them. (Even for a short-term patient, the crudely textured, overstarched New York Hospital sheets are like sandpaper—my own elbows were always bright red after three days.) Andrew needed help to be turned in the bed so the bedsores didn't get worse, and they had to be treated along with the still very infected wound.

His voice was slurred—perhaps because he was always on his side—and he was constantly sleepy (though he was being given no drugs other than antibiotics). When he talked, he made little sense, and offered little cheer. "If anything happens," he said at one point, "we had a wonderful life."

He'd been on F7 for about a week, and instead of improving he seemed far worse than he had before the surgery. He was agitated, disoriented, trembling. Instead of the picture clarifying, as the doctors obviously had expected it to do, the array of symptoms was more confusing than ever.

As the puzzle continued, my spirits sank to a kind of subsistence-level dread. I no longer had any idea what to feel or expect, and I got no help from the doctors. We were equally baffled in the presence of a mystery that broke all the rules of suspense, spraying clues wildly in all directions, no solution in sight. The whole thing was too ornately obscure, like a crossword puzzle with so many trick words that you finally throw it aside.

"How do you do it?" people would ask, as if there were a recipe or some special qualification. As if it were anything but on-the-job training. It was asked so often that I realized that behind the question was another question. "How would I behave?" each person was asking herself, projecting herself into the situation and wondering if she would have "the right stuff."

So when people ask you how you do it, you answer "I don't know" because you truly don't. In a curious anesthetizing process, the mind itself shuts down, and shuts out the answer to that question along with a good deal of the daily horror, allowing in only the necessary bits and pieces.

One of the things that bothered me was my inability, beyond accomplishing what writing tasks I had to, to concentrate on anything, to take an interest in the world. I could barely get through the paper, yet I knew if the situation was reversed, Andrew would have continued to read, and he would no more have lost his interest in politics than he would have stopped breathing. The Democratic Convention came and went with Mario Cuomo making the nominating speech for Mondale, the Olympics were over, and Andrew, by osmosis, probably knew more about them than I did. The only articles I could read all the way through were obituaries and health stories. I'd never read obituaries before, but now I turned to them first, checked the name and age to see if the deceased was younger or older than Andrew, then scoured the item for any trace of an infectious disease resembling his. Similarly with the health stories: the ones that drew me like a magnet were the very ones I should have turned quickly away from. I was enthralled by an article in the *Times* Tuesday "Science" section on "piggybacking" viruses. Surely this was what was confusing the issue—Andrew had become the host to some unlikely duet of viruses that, like a few couples I knew, were innocuous enough as individuals but were near-lethal when combined.

Andrew's condition consumed me utterly, was my life's work. In fact, living within the horror is easier than imagining it from the outside, or living half in, half out, with Life offering competition and perspective. Once inside, you cease to see the broad picture and instead become a specialist, a connoisseur of details, the tiny gesture, the word, the look, the fractional change that signals a motion toward or away from health. You lose your "objectivity," your detachment. Like the scholar or biographer, you identify with your subject, become a partisan of his life. With Andrew, it was always he who had held together the fragmented parts of my life; or perhaps we were that to each other, mutual magnets who kept each other from flying apart. And now, his sickness held me together as his wellness had united me before.

The pain and discomfort from which he suffered were bad enough, but in the midst of it all, he seemed to be receding. The connection was growing dimmer.

Then, several days after Gloria left, the moment came when I thought I had lost him. The afternoon began almost comically. We were watching television—for the first time since his admission to the hospital—and there was an Alan Ladd movie on, one that Andrew recognized. He watched it intermittently, dozing, his mind wandering, until his attention was suddenly caught by a scene in a hospital. A patient was being administered to by a nurse: the standard Hollywood regulation-model Florence Nightingale, blond, crisp of cap and de-meanor, pretty but not glamorously or distractingly so. Andrew looked wistfully at the screen.

"That's the kind of nurse I want," he said, without a trace of irony.

As the afternoon wore on, his speech grew more slurry and in-comprehensible. There came the terrible moment, the one that for me seemed to augur the end. He'd been talking morbidly, his eyes glazed, not quite seeing.

"I feel death," he said, his voice suddenly normal, "I see death." He looked toward me. "Has it gotten darker in here?" and at that instant, for me, night descended.

I knew that if I called anyone, asked for help, I would simply be told to ignore the content of his ramblings, but how could I? How could I look into those all-seeing brown eyes that never lied to me, and not *believe*!

I broke down completely and wept all the way out of the hospital and to the bus stop.

Then, going up Third Avenue on the bus, I and my fellow passengers were captive to one of those grisly little operettas that mark life in New York. A handicapped woman, followed by a male helper with her wheelchair, boarded the bus through the back door, insisting that space be made for all three. Not any space, but the special area that is designated by law for wheelchairs in a space by the rear door. For some reason—perhaps the seats couldn't be folded up properly to make room—the woman couldn't have her space, and she reacted with three minutes of nonstop tirade, threatening the driver and screaming at the other passengers. Finally, the driver stopped the bus and marched up the aisle with a menacing look on his face and . . . a very large knife in his hand! Where had it come from? I began to suspect the whole thing was staged, especially when, with her aide-de-camp at her side and occasionally chiming in, the woman claimed center stage like a veteran diva. Suspiciously steady on her feet, she swung into the climactic aria, a medley of obscenities and figures (the chapter and verse of New York City statutes regarding accommodations for the handicapped), while the passengers shouted back, in exasperation and protest. And then, without knowing what took hold of me, I exploded. I yelled.

"I have a husband dying in the hospital, you idiots," I shouted, to the passengers, to the bus driver, to the handicapped woman and her leading man, and to the people on either side of me. They looked baffled; I sat stunned at my own outburst. By now the police had arrived and the chorus was dwindling into a murmur and I just got off in a hurry and began, as I walked home, to be shocked at my own performance, what I'd *said*. I had given words, and thus a kind of reality, to the possibility of Andrew's death. I had surely tempted Fate to reply in kind.

Yet nothing could have stopped me. For one moment, however wretched the woman's condition, that Bernhardt of the buses represented the tyranny of the grotesque, the army of exhibitionistic sufferers to whom the rest of us regularly deferred. She had turned her handicap into a weapon of intimidation, her "suffering" had long since been transmuted into a schtick, and I was calling her bluff.

The whole thing, nasty and exhilarating, jogged my memory. Once I had been insulted at a dinner party by a drunken writer I'd just met, a self-important Samaritan of the Left. A very unpleasant man who was nevertheless associated with various good-works projects in poor neighborhoods.

"You!" he said, turning on me out of the blue. "You have never suffered!"

And now, in some pathetic and delayed act of revenge, I was showing him, through this wretched woman on the bus, that though I might not look like somebody who had suffered, I had.

"See, see," I was saying, "I *have* suffered. I *am* a serious person." I realized I'd been carrying this man around with me for years as a touchstone against which to gauge my inevitably failed attempts to be a serious person. Because this ogre I'd been fighting, this ogre who didn't take me seriously, was myself.

The distraction was only momentary. When I got home, I called Alan Seltzman, the infectious-disease specialist, and he agreed with me that Andrew was "sinking."

I was lying in bed with the telephone when Mother came to the door, and I told her how bad things looked. Her face sagged with hopelessness, and for the first time, I saw the strain of what she had been going through for my sake, the strain of trying not to show the strain. She looked gray and haggard, and the effort to find some consolation must have been immense.

We spoke of something we hadn't spoken of before—the possibility that Andrew would pull through, but with some permanent damage to body or brain.

"Would he want to live like that?" Mother suddenly asked. "And, Molly, would you want him back like that?"

It was a strange question.

It wasn't as if I had a choice.

"Of course," I said quickly, "I'd take him any way, on any terms. Andrew with half a brain is superior to anyone else with a whole one." But was that true?

I begged Mother to take a taxi to the hospital and go to see him, and when she returned, saying she thought he looked better, hope, beautiful hope, came flooding back into my life. If fear, once embedded, is hard to eradicate, so, too, is hope: as hard as unrequited passion, as hard as a weed, to vanquish. It was the positive drug, the steroid, that inflated me until fear brought me down.

Mother's words had provided me with immediate nourishment, which was all I needed to relegate the epitaph of the previous hour to ancient history.

Then, on Thursday, out of the blue, a thrilling leap forward:

Andrew, who until that moment had been unable to recall what he had just said or eaten, remembered a remark I'd made earlier in the day. I had been worrying about getting my monthly assignment done, and that morning I'd made some offhand comment about the movie column I was doing—that I was having trouble summoning up the perky, hyperbolic prose that was expected of me, that the review was a mess and I'd probably get fired.

"Well," he said, when I came in that afternoon, "did you get fired?" It was wonderful—the first sign of retention, and there was even a trace of humor in his voice, key signs, I thought, of mental recovery.

Then he said something that in its wisdom and breadth was so like the old Andrew: "Even when I've hallucinated," he said, "one thing I've never said is how unfair this is. I've never said 'Why me?' You play the hand you're dealt." There was perhaps a touch of self-aggrandizing rhetoric in this, but it was glorious nonetheless.

We began to have real conversations: I told him about his surgery and, taking it in for the first time, he was amazed. He wanted to know if we were all right for money. He was depressed by his staggering weakness, and obsessed with his feet, which were excruciatingly painful from what could have been a circulatory problem, or a neurological problem—no one quite knew. He hallucinated that they had turned into horses, thus detaching them from his body, and that certain doctors and nurses would come up and take them away. They were forcing him to sit in a chair for a few moments a day, and it was a torture he dreaded for hours before the fact, endured gracelessly, and complained bitterly about afterward. With the improvement of his mental state had come paradoxically a greater fear for his sanity. Now that he could remember, he began to remember his hallucinations and be frightened by them. Whereas before, he had been too crazy to be frightened of going crazy, now his awareness was driving him crazy: he would hallucinate, and in the midst of a hallucination, like the one about his horse-feet, he would be stricken with terror; then he would phone for me to come right away. One day, he saw that his room was filled with upholstered furniture, and Katharine Hepburn was sitting in a chair, then moments later wondered why he had seen such a thing. He later told me he'd had a letter from Garbo and accused me of hiding it or throwing it away. I argued that much as she might admire him, it was unlikely that the reclusive star would "come out" for him. This went on for several days, and it was after he came out of that particular hallucination that he took, for him, the unusual step of asking to see a psychiatrist. Andrew, a shrewd analyst himself and as deeply and explicitly indebted to Freud as any intellectual of the twentieth century, was nevertheless a man who preferred to let sleeping dogs lie. He wasn't interested in looking any more closely into his relationship with his mother—intense but basically peaceful, nor did he want to share with a stranger the details of a randy adolescence that still mortified him. He was basically a pessimist and a loner: he hadn't asked for the moon, and he had gotten close enough to it with me not to question the whys and wherefores. His defenses had served him reasonably well up to now, and he was, like a great many men, anti-analysis. But now the shocking idea that his mind, his unique glory, was becoming unhinged was enough to prompt him to ask for a psychiatrist.

Leaving aside the hallucinations, there was always the possiblity, even the probability, of depression, as there is with any major illness, especially one as severe and prolonged as Andrew's. Through a cousin of his, I met a New York Hospital doctor who had suffered a bout of encephalitis two years before and had gone through a depression so severe it had temporarily altered his personality. Jeffrey knew him well and said that, indeed, he had been a changed man for months, over a year, after the illness. He graciously agreed to talk to me about it and admitted that the depression—something for which he'd been totally unprepared—had been horrible, by far the worst aspect of the illness.

Another horror story came to me from a film critic friend whose associate, a man we'd both met, was currently receiving shock treatment in a New York hospital. After an operation for cancer of the larynx several years before, and a complete recovery, he had gone into a depression from which he hadn't recovered and which no one could explain. It was diagnosed as endogenous depression, the kind for which there is no discernible cause, as opposed to exogenous depression, related to external cause: illness, a death in the family, loss of a job, and the like.

We've all seen cases of people who've undergone terrible ordeals, who've narrowly escaped death . . . only they haven't quite escaped. Some part of them never returns to life.

Just the year before, a man in our apartment building at Quogue, Dick Hirsch, had come out for the summer after having suffered a massive heart attack and undergone a triple bypass. He was, as one might expect, wan, dazed, gray. More haunting, and baffling, however, was his state of mind. When we congratulated him and his wife on his return to life, she smiled happily while he barely nodded, said little. Once a jolly, pear-shaped man, who made dill pickles, flew kites, and told jokes, Dick was now a specter who sidled along the wall, avoiding contact. He grew ashen as everyone else turned tan, took shambling walks by himself, talked little, and when he did, it was in barely audible tones and with morose self-absorption. It became increasingly clear that in some profound way he wasn't among us, wasn't alive; he had never gotten up from the operating table. It was like those ghost movies in which a body remains on the table while the outline of the person arises and walks about invisible. Dick died that autumn—officially—but we all knew he had died in the spring. Elsie, his wife, the charmer, the life force who had kept him going, died a year later.

Was it possible that Andrew had been saved against his will, or had been rescued in violation of some even larger design, the will of nature? Was his one of those lives that wasn't "meant" to be saved?

No, not for a minute could I imagine Andrew in that sort of living death. He wasn't an equivocator. He'd go one way or the other.

Yet he was bound to have some sort of depression, despondency. Mightn't the brush with mortality leave one with a longing to return, some residue of the death wish?

In any case, it was reasonable to expect he would be "different" from what he had been. The doctors were always alluding to somebody's mind being "altered," as if it were being cosmetically reshaped or repainted. A little "adjustment" and we might get a new and improved Andrew—quieter, thinner, a little "off" perhaps, but in a perfectly harmless way.

Andrew being tough-minded, I suspected that the boundaries of his personality and the structure of his mind were too firmly in place for the interior redecorators to get a toehold. Also, as Jeffrey constantly reiterated, the brain has amazing recuperative powers. Depression, however, was another matter; and since Andrew himself seemed anxious for reassurance, I began researching the problem, inquiring about psychiatrists who would be particularly helpful in this situation and collecting names and numbers.

I'd gotten some names and on Monday, August 27—Andrew had been on F7 a week—I decided it was time to break down and call Sam. Break down, for I was a little hurt that he hadn't called me. He had been away three weeks, Andrew near death more than once, and I'd heard nothing. I had to assume he was keeping abreast of the medical situation through the hospital, but who knew? I made the call. A panting son answered the phone, called his father, and a no-less-breathless Sam got on, obviously fresh from a tennis game.

"Did you win?" I asked. Tennis was a bond between us, the initial one, in fact—we had met at a tennis party. So, during my hospitalizations over the years and sometimes to my annoyance, Sam would stop by the room for my nightly checkup and "cheer me up" with blow-by-blow accounts of his weekend tennis games with his sons. As I lay there in varying degrees of agony and discomfort, slobbering over my nasogastric tube or clutching my abdomen, I was treated to proud progress reports of the boys' improving games from one month, one year, to the next, as Sam, with a suspicious lack of ambivalence, looked forward to the day when each son would overtake him. (No Oedipal struggle there. Indeed, Sam and his happy family were so *normal* they seemed abnormal.)

When he realized who it was, Sam's voice immediately switched gears from happy exhaustion to sincere concern. To my surprise, he hadn't known that Andrew had been transferred from the ICU to F7, and didn't even know about the paralysis of the legs! He rallied now, all eagerness to help me track down the best psychiatrist. He talked to several knowledgeable people, and within a day or so he came up with the same name I'd gotten from my own sources: Dr. Myron Westerman, the universally admired chief of medical-psychiatric liaison between New York Hospital and Payne Whitney. When I called him, he at first demurred—he would be leaving on an extended trip to Europe in two weeks to research a monograph he was doing on Magritte. Naturally, this only whetted my appetite—a cultivated and artistically inclined psychiatrist—and I told him I was sure that Andrew, though depressed, wouldn't need regular or continued therapy. We made the appointment.

He came and saw Andrew in an interview that seemed highly satisfactory to them both.

"He's in amazing shape, considering what he's gone through," said Westerman. "It's astonishing. He's not really depressed."

"Well, maybe not clinically," I said, proud of Andrew for his good showing, and a little abashed at my misdiagnosis. In fact, it was I who was feeling depressed, and left out. Especially when I went in to join Andrew.

"At last I have somebody who's on my side," he said, a jab that could only have been intended for me. It felt very strange to be shut out of Andrew's life this way—more than shut out, explicitly excluded. Andrew and I had shared our thoughts for so long that for one of us to turn them over to someone else, however extreme the circumstances, was to reject the other, to put up a No Trespassing sign. And I felt a little envious: I wanted to lie on the couch and have someone worry about *me*.

Meanwhile, Ramir was insisting, no doubt on the basis of reflex tests and spinal taps, that Andrew was "neurologically unchanged," which seemed to me patently absurd, like meteorologists who say there's a 30 percent chance of rain when it is pouring outside. Andrew's clearheadedness and bright moods did come and go, but he was more alert, more cognizant of his condition than he'd been since he entered the hospital. He would want to read the paper one minute, then the next he would say, "Why isn't there anything about Frank Sinatra's murder in here?"

One persistent fantasy had to do with Sinatra: he had been killed in a Mafia gang hit in the room adjacent to Andrew's, and now the killers were after Andrew, as the only witness. One day I brought him the *Post*. It happened to have a photograph of Sinatra and Dean Martin on the front page. Andrew saw it and, finally convinced that Sinatra was alive, breathed a huge sigh of relief.

I had called in Dr. Donovan, the head of Infectious Diseases, as consultant; he was making tests and more tests. The problem, he said to me, is that with a viral disease, there are so many possibilities, we have to narrow it down just to know what to test for—and how do you narrow it down without having something to go on?—a Catch-22 situation. We still didn't know what we were looking for, and whatever we found wouldn't help with treatment, only as a prognosis for recovery. I think one of the things that bothered me most was the doubt the doctors expressed about a "complete" recovery. There was, as Donovan pointed out, still the chance that the disease hadn't finished its rampage, that some fresh disaster might still occur. After all, who would have expected him to suffer mental derangement, a perforated colon, pneumonia, a partial paralysis (or paresis) of the legs. Both Donovan and Seltzman felt that one of the most troubling signs was how poor Andrew's memory was, which Andrew himself confirmed.

"It is bad," he said. "It's terrible."

Andrew was still weak, thin, exhausted. He had the Foley tube, and complained bitterly of it, but the doctors were unwilling to take it out yet. Seltzman had gotten back the results of the blood tests from the CDC in Atlanta and none showed increased antibodies, meaning we could definitely eliminate the five types of mosquito-transmitted viral encephalitis for which they'd been checking. Even mumps and chicken pox were being considered, but Andrew and his mother, al-though always vague on such factual matters, seemed to think he'd had them.

It was the week after Labor Day and Sam had returned. When I talked to him about Andrew's mood swings, distant and sweet one minute, aggressively present and grumpy the next, he said it could still be illness doing its work, "the process."

I felt as if I were living in a daguerreotype in which the positive view—Andrew well and better each day—and the negative view—Andrew poor and declining rapidly—continually coexisted, one turn-ing into the other and back again with a flick of the finger. I was still coming in twice a day, once in the morning, then just before dinner, and my journal during this period reads like the jottings of a frantic child, hysterical with panic one minute, pumped up with optimism the next. One bright image of Andrew—tender, mentally acute—would set me up for the day. "Here I am full of self-pity," he said one morning, "after getting through that ridiculous operation, when I should be jumping for joy." And the rest of the day I would find joyous confirmation of his improvement. Conversely, he would be weak and pale and drawn and my hopes would spiral downward and I would almost seek evidence to support the negative prognosis. Because he was bedridden, his only movement being to sit in the chair for an hour each day, his paralysis seemed remote, unreal. Since he was still so exhausted he could barely move his arms—he still wasn't eating, but was being nourished with a feeding tube—his legs seemed almost an afterthought. I was simply blotting out the paralysis and the prognosis for the future. (There would be rehabilitation, something we had been waiting to discuss until Sam returned, and the reversal of the colostomy either before or after.)

Back on the nursing front, trouble was brewing. Andrew complained bitterly that certain of the private-duty nurses were mistreating him and demanded that I get rid of them. Given his unreliability, the odd choice of words in which he framed his charges (Augusta was "cruel," while George, a night nurse, was "insincere"), and my own priorities of concern, I tended—unfortunately, but perhaps understandably—to ignore these complaints. Although there were surely lapses, moments of inattention or roughness, I couldn't imagine there being deliberate cruelty. Yet, why not? These were people who were tired and overworked, often moonlighting on the side, who often had families for whom they were the sole support at home, and who weren't as carefully selected and supervised as the regular nursing staff. They were not given any psychiatric training and were often insensitive. In some strange, illogical reaction of their own, watching their patients lying there day after day and "taking it easy," they might become angry and exasperated, convincing themselves that their charges were malingering, and treat them accordingly. Or, out of ignorance or resentment, they would assume that a disoriented or delusional patient was stupid, insensitive, and treat him abusively.

And then, it was also possible that Andrew was helping to turn the tide in that direction. There was the fact that Andrew could drive people crazy without even trying.

It was his imperviousness, a mantle he had acquired as a child, he told me, as a strategy for coping with fear. When he was in trouble with one of his parents, he had gotten into the habit of "disappearing," willing himself into invisibility. Actions that would provoke another person into fight or flight would make him withdraw inward, like a turtle.

The good part of it was his easy disposition where I was concerned: he never rose to the bait when I attacked him, or nagged, but instead let it roll off so that battles rarely erupted.

The obliviousness was part of what I saw as his lack of narcissism, the fact that he wasn't aware of the impression he made and did little to create a favorable one. He was a B type let loose in a world of As, a slowpoke who would hold people up on line and not notice, bump into people on the sidewalk and make no apology. He had his own agenda. For instance, Andrew emerging from a taxi was grotesque, a comic opera in slow motion. He had an *idée fixe* that we would leave some important part of ourselves behind in a taxi. (We were always losing things, but never in taxis.) To avoid such a disaster, he spent long moments scouring the taxi at the end of each ride. While people stood on the curb waiting, freezing or sighing (and there is no more aggressive form of impatience than New Yorkers waiting for a taxicab), Andrew would rub his hands along the cushions, examine the floor, and finally emerge, like a caterpillar nibbling its way across a leaf. He was unbelievably and embarrassingly slow, as fussy and infuriating as four old ladies arguing about the fare, and yet I took secret delight in (and envied) his ability not to be intimidated by withering New York scorn.

But others didn't always understand. I could see from the expressions on their faces, those who knew him and those who didn't, that this imperviousness was often misconstrued as stupidity. People would assume he was obtuse, unobservant, whereas he had radarlike intuitions. Ask him a question about someone he'd seemed hardly to notice and he'd size them up in a sentence, or intuit a person's entire personality from a written paragraph. In the early eighties, he reviewed a book by Richard Schickel, a colleague we knew only slightly at the time, though he was to become a friend. Schickel called.

"Andy," he said, his voice still awestruck, "you could have saved me thousands of dollars in shrink fees."

Since it took some of our friends a while to grasp Andrew's aware-ness, it stood to reason that the nurses, tending a sick Andrew, had little occasion to see any of it, and had no doubt responded in kind.

Still, I was shocked when I was told that Augusta, the night nurse, had turned on him. Augusta was a big, capable drill sergeant of a woman who'd been with us on day duty back on the neurology floor, for the week leading up to surgery, and I'd made a special effort to get her back. She'd been tough with Andrew, but kind, bullying him into action, forcing him to move when the rest of the nurses had allowed him to lie still. She'd agreed to come, although there were problems at home, but now it seemed those problems had gotten the upper hand in her treatment of Andrew and she'd gone slightly crazy. The hall nurse took me aside—it was a day or so after Andrew had made his complaint—and told me Augusta was verbally abusing Andrew. (Who knew what villain at home he had come to stand in for?) She yelled at him during the night, treated him like a child, and left him alone for long periods. I was horrified. How could this woman who had been my ally, who had taken Andrew's interests to heart, who had pushed him to turn and sit up and move when he wanted to lie there, suddenly turn on him?

She and I had written each other missives, hers long and en-couraging, full of information, hope, discussing Andrew's condition. I got rid of her, as I was obliged to do, but my confidence in my power of judgment was shaken, as was my convenient assumption of Andrew's unreliability.

Then came Miriam. Miriam, who replaced Augusta as the eve-ning nurse, was a bossy, self-important woman with the besetting sin of practical nurses—a compulsion to render nonstop homage to her-self, mostly in the form of accolades from past patients. I put up with this litany because 1) she came in the evening and I saw little of her, and 2) she brought me Barbara. Barbara, the Mutt to her Jeff, was everything Miriam wasn't. If Miriam was horsey and overbearing, Barbara was tiny, a frisky colt, smart, tender, and full of ingenious strategies for prying Andrew out of his cocoon of lethargy. The sun shone the day she became the day nurse, for she liked Andrew im-mediately, drew out his sweetness and humor with her own, but also saw she'd have to light a fire under him to get him to do *anything*. She was my ally, too, intuitive about both of us to an uncanny degree.

"Molly," she said to me one day, "you're always up when he's up and down when he's down. It ought to be the other way around —you should lift him up when he's down, and vice versa."

And she was right. There was a crazy inversion in the relationship of my states of mind to Andrew's physical and mental condition, the cart pulling the horse. That is, I had a way of finding details to comply with my moods rather than the other way around, and the moods were extreme and uncontrollable. In the black mood, I'd seize on a symptom—his heavy sweating, his forgetfulness—and from then on I would find further symptoms to corroborate, and when I was "up" I'd find only signs of recovery in Andrew. When Jeffrey didn't call for a day, I was sure it was because he was concerned, and would spiral into a down mood. Of course, there was enough in the illness itself to make mental seesawing inevitable, as Andrew changed almost literally from one minute to the next. His mind would be clear all morning, and then he'd have lunch, and two minutes afterward he couldn't remember what he'd eaten.

He'd begun eating by now and was pleased to announce that he'd gained a pound. His legs and arms were emaciated, but, curiously, not his face, which seemed to belong to a different body. Barbara and I both remarked on it. It was not only extraordinarily healthy-looking, smooth rather than gaunt, but the dark circles had disappeared from under his eyes; his hair, formerly curly and on the oily side, had gone completely straight and was as soft as a baby's; and his expression, his face, when he wasn't agitated and unhappy, had a beatific look I'd never seen before.

There were tiny signs of progress. He moved his legs ever so slightly. Barbara coaxed him into the chair more often and for longer periods, teased him and prodded him, humoring him as she did so.

"Don't worry, he's going to come back," she would say, confirming my view but counterpointing the doctors. Whereas back in July, it was I who had been reluctant to accept their almost universal optimism, now it was the other way around. They seemed dubious, and what bothered me most was their skepticism regarding his "complete" recovery. That, and the possibility hinted at by Dr. Donovan that something else could still occur. There were, and had always been, so many *different* problems that it was difficult to know what anything meant.

That night I dreamed that Andrew had called, and in that whispery voice he had acquired from the irritation of the feeding tube, said they'd found something in the throat or upper chest and had to operate. When he told me, I knew at once that it meant death. In fact, he still did have a slight fever, and if anything else had happened, I felt sure it would have meant the end.

The next day, he looked pale and sickly again, so I called Jeffrey. He hadn't been returning my calls, which usually meant he had nothing reassuring to say, and sure enough, he didn't sound sanguine. (Or did he? Perhaps I was looking for a "downer" and I heard it in his voice.) He noticed the sweating particularly, and talked about Andrew trembling a good deal, and said he'd meet me in his room the next day. He felt the sweating could be a neurological problem with the same origin as the trembling (a virus, dormant or semi-active in the nerves). In contrast to Seltzman, he felt that a European rather than a local origin of the virus was possible. This was a very speculative diagnosis, Jeffrey told me later, but everyone was speculating at that time.

We were still coasting along, not ready to declare Andrew on firm ground, but he seemed a little more normal each day. He was like someone coming out of a fog, coming a little farther out each day. I was consumed once again—or still—by money worries and when I wasn't at the hospital, I camped out at the Blue Cross/Blue Shield office trying to get reimbursement for the nursing bills.

There were little victories for me as well, little gasps of relief. I went to my office for the first time, my sanctuary on the West Side, and though my efforts to get back into the novel I'd been struggling with before Andrew fell ill were unsuccessful—I wasn't able to disconnect the part of my mind that was attached to Andrew—it felt like a triumph to be there at all.

Joan Alexander had been trying to persuade me to go out to Quogue—she and her husband, Artie, would drive me out—and on Thursday, September 6, I accepted their invitation. I felt my chest expand as we drove across the Fifty-ninth Street Bridge, my shoulders relax over a festive dinner, with Long Island wine, at the Inn at Quogue. I gratefully accepted being pampered. But it wasn't until I walked into our apartment, opened the blinds, and saw the moon shimmering on the ocean, creating a lapping phosphorescent silver path to heaven, that I surrendered to a relief so overwhelming that it seemed like a natural wonder. I looked around. Everything was just as we had left it on June 24, things not quite put away, waiting for us to return the following weekend. There was Andrew's mug in the rack beside the sink as if it were still drying, radiant with a sense of expectancy, as was the sugar crusting in his sugar bowl, his water glass leaning on the brown puckered place in the work surface that he had burned two summers ago with the teakettle.

I spent the following day walking the beach, swimming, rejoicing in Andrew's progress, but my sense of peace was short-lived. That night I was sleeping soundly when the phone rang. It was 12:30 A.M. and Andrew was calling collect. It seemed that the call for a relief nurse had been answered by, of all people, Soopie, and Andrew was out of his head with fear and fury.

"Of all people!" he cried. "You know she's my enemy."

By this time, I was ready to believe him, or at least believe in his emotional state and accept it. I asked him to put her on the phone. Reacting with complete poise, she said Andrew was seriously upset, that she'd leave and I didn't have to pay. But when faced with the option of Soopie or no one, Andrew agreed to have her stay the night. She said she would stay only until someone else could be found to relieve her.

Unable to stay away from him for long, I thus had an excuse to come in early Saturday morning, which I'd planned to do anyway as it was the penultimate day of the U.S. Open at Flushing Meadows— the tennis orgy day of the year—and we were going to watch it together.

I turned on the tiny television, pulled my chair up close to the bed, and we both put on our earplugs for what was always the high point of the tournament, the men's semi-finals and the women's finals. We didn't know it, but this would be one of those days that went down in tennis history.

We watched Ivan Lendl play the new Aussie flash, Pat Cash, and pull it out in a match that had streaks of brilliance and those hideous misses that the commentators politely call lapses but that we hackers recognize as choking. Everyone was rooting for Pat Cash, the obstreperous crowd-pleaser, but Andrew and I liked Lendl, the dour Czech racehorse. He was unpopular—because he lacked the self-deprecating charm to make his machine-like perfection palatable. Andrew was a believer in form, was more interested in the actual spectacle of form playing itself out than in the suspense of a match, which is why, when we taped a match, he didn't mind knowing in advance who won. I always thought there was something extremely grown-up in this: to Andrew suspense was a false value, a distraction. I think he actually preferred to know the plot of a movie or the outcome of a match before he saw it. Advance knowledge would free him from the reflex anxiety of wondering what happened next and allow him to devote himself to the pure contemplation of the drama, to *see* more because his nerve ends weren't being manipulated. Unlike me, he didn't like uncertainty, got no titillation from sitting on the edge of his chair. He looked for form to be confirmed—in directors, in sports figures—which, in the latter category, often drew him to the great, unpopular athletes, people like Wilt Chamberlain and Ted Williams, those slightly superior human beings who accomplished their feats without the energetic panting and puffing that pleased the crowds.

Martina Navratilova, bursting now with the perfection of a mind at last in tune with a powerful body, was another athlete whose excellence raised her too far above the ordinary herd for people to identify easily with her, for this amazing, candid, smart woman never won the hearts of the American people she so longingly courted. To watch her and Chris Evert engage in one of their mighty struggles was to want them to go on forever, in close matches, the two titans of the women's game, showing what women could do if they ever overcame the block against winning. What separated these two from everyone else in women's tennis was their ability not to choke, not to succumb to the "feminine" impulse to beat oneself, to defer, even things out. To be loved.

After that emotionally draining match—Andrew's head was by now sloping downward, but his eyes were glued to the set—on came Jimmy Connors and John McEnroe in a match that went well into the night and became an overnight classic, in many ways a replay of the women's: like Chris, Connors was a veteran, a ground-stroker with more fire and determination than any man in the game, played his best, and still couldn't beat the brilliantly talented serve-and-volleyer McEnroe, playing at slightly less than top form.

They were inspiring: Connors, who would go on, beat players half his age, and in refusing to say die, win over fans who'd been put off by his crudeness and ungraciousness in years past. And McEnroe, who had more natural grace than anyone else in the game. The glory of competition itself which separates human beings into winners and losers and for one brief moment rescues life from ambiguity.

The vicarious tension in watching such a match is enormous, and we paid for it the next day. Both of us were exhausted and Andrew could hardly talk. He had just been raised for a pill feeding and he was slumped over when in walked the Williamses. Visitors! Andrew was so far from being able to receive any that we hadn't even given instructions at the information desk not to let anyone up. The Williamses, Southern friends, were theatrically madcap, hosts in their ramshackle Park Avenue apartment to poker players, transcendental meditationalists, born-again mystics, defrocked Southern aristocrats, and Yankee entrepreneurs. I didn't really want anyone to see Andrew in his present condition, and particularly not them. I wasn't quite sure why. It had never occurred to us—or rather, to me, as Andrew didn't have any say in the matter—not to tell people about Andrew's illness, though I was beginning to find out how many people do just that: I heard stories of men having everything from heart attacks to minor surgery in strictest secrecy. It was a horrifying glimpse of our dog-eat-dog society to realize that men are afraid that their weakness will be counted against them, that somehow their competitors will sniff out vulnerability like sharks smelling blood and move in for the kill. I heard about men who had gone to out-of-town hospitals, signed in under false names, all testifying to the need to conceal frailty in a society in which illness isn't admissible, isn't a normal human occurrence but something one has to be ashamed of.

Although, as I say, such secrecy would never have occurred to me, Andrew's illness had gone on too long for disclosure to be avoidable. Still, his brain, his meal ticket, had been affected, and I didn't want the Williamses spreading the word through their various circles of friends that Andrew could hardly talk. They sensed instantly that we weren't ready for visitors, and apologized for coming without calling, or stopping to inquire, trying to cover up the awkwardness with chatter—we all had postgraduate degrees in cover-up chatter—but they were obviously shocked by Andrew's appearance. I could see it in their eyes, and in their hurried leavetaking.

"It was too soon for us to come," Sadie said apologetically as they left. "We didn't realize how sick he was."

They don't think he's going to make it, I thought to myself. Or if he does, they think he'll never be his old self. How could I explain to them, or anyone, why, though he was "out of the woods," he was still too sick to see people. I wouldn't have understood it myself if I hadn't gone through it, hadn't watched him crawling back, like Lazarus, from the dead. He just wasn't "normal" the way somebody who's just had kidney stones removed or had open-heart surgery is "normal"—weak but capable of carrying on a conversation, even of talking about his experiences. Andrew had no operation stories because he hadn't known about it before and hadn't been conscious of it afterward; even now, more than a month later, he hadn't rejoined the world of the living. Tennis, to which he reacted on some primal level, had awakened his interest; I could get his attention, but only in the most basic way. Beyond that, he simply hadn't the mental or physical energy to be *interested*.

Yet physically, he was improving every day. His fever had finally gone down and stayed down; he was sitting for longer and longer in the chair. I was still going to the hospital twice a day, but thought I might cut back to once. He could call me on the phone now, and didn't get as tired from talking. His improvements—he was also eating better—improved me. I was finally beginning to sleep through the night. In my journal I recorded on Monday that I slept till 7:30, and it was the first time since June 27. Sam had returned and was amazed at how well Andrew looked, and we both agreed that at the end of the week we would terminate the private-duty nurses. The nurses on the hall would dress the wound, which was still very infected. When I broached the subject of the nurses with Andrew, he was furious. He felt as if he were going to be abandoned, which I could understand, but at the same time, why didn't *he* understand that we were $19,000 out of pocket, eating away at our medical policy, and the staff felt he was ready to be on his own. I told him what he knew already, that the nurses on F7 were the best, but he refused to be reassured. He also maintained he didn't want to go to a rehabilitation clinic; he wanted to come home. I, in turn, was becoming increasingly exasperated. During his crazy period, I was always able to imagine him as the lovable, haloed Andrew of his good moments. Now, I was forced to deal with this cantankerous person as a real, rather than a demented, Andrew.

It was mid-September and we now had to decide where Andrew should go for rehabilitation—Rusk in the city or Burke in White Plains—and whether or not he should have the colostomy reversed before he went. This was not a small operation, and no one except Sam felt it should be done now. Sam's reasoning was that removing the colostomy would make Andrew a better candidate for Burke— Sam's preference—because it would reduce the amount of nursing care he needed. Burke was tougher to get into (does one ever get off the competitive treadmill?) and probably wouldn't even accept him. Among all the other tubes and dependencies, Andrew still had a Foley tube, and the infected wound with its requirements would be a major handicap in the runoff.

The arguments for Burke, mostly advanced by Sam, were that it was beautiful and bucolic, an estate with extensive grounds and a rolling countryside; that his father-in-law, a doctor, was on the board; and that I would be able to visit Andrew only on weekends, which (Sam felt) might be a good thing for me. For all of these reasons, except the father-in-law, Andrew was opposed. He maintained that he'd rather not go to a rehabilitation clinic at all, but come home. Rusk, once the great pioneering establishment of its kind, was said to have slipped in the last decade or so, but it was still good. Jeffrey thought it was actually better than Burke. In its favor the fact that Andrew wanted desperately to be in the city and that he would be able to help me with a large lecture project I was preparing to deliver in his place. Some months before, he had accepted an offer to give the annual Seposnikow lectures at City College, a series of two lectures and a panel on French cinema. Andrew had already suggested his titles: "Iconography in French Cinema" for the first and, for the second, "French Cinema and Structuralism in the Other Arts." And there would be a panel with Alain Resnais, Jeanne Moreau, Vincent Canby, and, if I accepted, me.

I would follow the lines Andrew had indicated—for $5,000, a much larger fee than usual for such an engagement, how could I not accept?—but it would require a good deal of work. I lectured frequently myself, usually on my specialty, the image of women in movies, but I had a thorough grounding in French cinema. Still, this would demand considerable research, even if Andrew could help me, and that was a big if.

There was another problem. Andrew and I felt that he was much too weak to undergo that second operation now, the closing of the colostomy, and Ramir and most of the other doctors seemed to agree. Even without another operation, it would be at least three weeks before he would be ready to go for rehabilitation—by then we hoped that at least the Foley tube would be out. Now that I saw lengthy recovery stretching out before us, I was more nervous than ever about expense. If there was any sizable difference between the two clinics, which Sam indicated there wasn't, that would have been a deciding factor. Meanwhile, I was anxious to see if the hospital would begin to assume responsibility for the private-duty nurses, something they will occasionally do in cases of long illnesses. Just after Labor Day, I had gone to the patient ombudsman and in the course of the conversation asked to see the hospital bill to date. (It is only submitted at the end of the stay, not at intervals, but I wanted to know the worst.)

"Are you sure?" she asked me wryly as she pulled it out of a file drawer. The amount, for just over two months, or about sixty-five days—an amount that did not include any doctors' bills, which were flooding in, four or five a day, like greeting cards at Christmas—was $72,000. This was a staggering sum (it would be at least twice that now), and there would be another month probably, then the rehabilitation. She promised to discuss the nursing situation with the staff, and it was decided that Andrew could be switched to the floor nurses at the end of the week.

I tried to soothe Andrew regarding the departure of the private-duty nurses, but I was having a harder and harder time finding and expressing the sympathy I knew he needed. The crises were occurring less frequently but so were the spurts of adrenaline that kept me going. No longer did I enjoy the mile and a half walk to Sixty-eighth Street and York Avenue or feel even a twinge of exaltation as I trod the well-worn path to the hospital door, though the grounds, with their late summer plantings, were beautiful. The linden trees were now a lustrous dark green, and the border of caladium and impatiens, within the evergreen hedge, created color-coordinated tiers of pink, purple, white, and green. Yet I couldn't respond; found myself overreacting with irritation at things that shouldn't have bothered me, or that I should have gotten used to: the slow people hogging the sidewalk in front of me; the contrast between the handsome first impression of New York Hospital's cathedral elegance and the old-world grunginess inside the rooms and corridors. Worst, I now found I practically had to shut my eyes to get past the burn patients.

New York Hospital had one of the best burn centers in the state, and it was located just off the hall that led into F7. Though sealed off to visitors, patients beyond the danger stage could come out into the alcove, where they would sit and smoke. Although many were those who'd suffered from freak accidents—electrical and industrial fires— the largest proportion, according to the staff, were people whose wounds might have been termed self-inflicted: violent and rough types, drinkers or abusers, and they were a scary lot. You could feel the antisocial fires still burning as they sat on the benches for hours at a time, hunched over and smoking, not talking, their smocks and pajamas sliding insolently off their shoulders to expose their raw, blistered skin. The anger of their wounds seemed to echo the fury in their breasts, and just walking by them made me shiver.

Most familiar of all, like a part of myself I could never get rid of, were the smells, different on each floor. I could have recognized Payson 6 or Whitney 6 without opening my eyes. There were the warm stuffy wet smells of the orthopedic floor, the terrifying nonhuman odor of the ICU seeping out of the closed doors to assault you as you got off the elevator. There were, on F7, the cool rubbing-alcohol smells, food trays in various stages of decomposition, dying flowers, urine, and somehow, most of all, the smell of adhesive tape, white adhesive tape on skin: IVs taped to inner arms, Foley tubes taped to lower bellies, bandages on wounds, NG tubes taped to noses, Baker tubes to abdomens, the various antiseptics in between, tapes ripped off, skin swabbed in antiseptic, new tapes applied.

These were the well-worn paths—now almost pleasurable—of my nostrils.

Things were going from bad to worse with the overbearing Miriam. She was like some horror-film monster who had gradually taken over our lives, making Andrew eat when it was convenient to her, shoving food down him, slacking off and doing nothing while inflicting her endless stories and self-aggrandizing anecdotes on us as we sat in helpless silence. She was guaranteed to bring out my own squirmy inability to be "firm"—as my mother would have said—with employees. Members of my generation had winced at the imperiousness of our mothers, at the overt distinctions between employer and employee. Yet now we had a world in which nobody knew the rules, and nobody was quite comfortable, and I was stuck in that quandary into which false egalitarianism had plunged me. I was a pusillanimous wreck, not only unable to fire anyone I had hired but hardly daring to criticize them. I was hoping things wouldn't get any worse, and I could wait until the end of the week, when Miriam and the other night nurse would be discontinued anyway.

Things were decided for me when the psychiatrist, Dr. Westerman, came in for his second session with Andrew, entering just as Miriam had started helping him with his dinner. Instead of retiring instantly as was the custom when a doctor entered, she blew up, telling Dr. Westerman he had no business interrupting the dinner. Westerman quite rightly gasped, let her have it in no uncertain terms, and told her to leave.

She did, disappearing down the hall, while I sat nervously on the bench in the alcove, waiting for the session to end. In due time, Westerman came and sat down. A passing word on Andrew's remarkable attitude, then, "You ought to get rid of that nurse. That was outrageous what she said to me just now."

"Yes," I said, meekly, "I am getting rid of her." I was red with shame, my ineptitude and cowardice exposed. And angry. Yes, it was remiss of me—more than remiss, weak and inept—not to have fired the woman. Yes, it had been inexcusable, her act of insubordination, and what it implied about her contempt for both doctor and patient. But at that moment, Westerman's criticism was more than I could bear, and tears of anger and self-pity filled my eyes. I fought them back.

All I wanted, at that moment, was for someone to pat me on the head and tell me what a great job I was doing, or at least see how difficult things were for me. Andrew "seemed" more normal, more well, yet he wasn't himself, and I wasn't coping very well. I wanted someone on my side, yet here was this sage who with his psychiatrist's radar had seen through me to the incompetent I was. I tried to explain: yes, she was insufferable, and protocol had been breached, but she hadn't started out that way; and besides, she was leaving by the end of the week anyway. Yet the words sounded hollow, even to me.

Yet I felt the attack so keenly that I wondered if there wasn't something more, some message from Andrew, behind it: perhaps he had been airing resentments, with Westerman's encouragement. For doesn't therapy begin, like the French judicial system, with the presumption of the spouse's guilt? If Andrew now had somebody "on his side," it was by definition adversarial and on the *other* side from me.

When I went in and told Andrew I was letting Miriam go, he breathed a dramatic sigh of relief and extolled Dr. Westerman, his savior.

"If you think the way she treated him was bad, that was gentle compared to the way she treated me."

I didn't argue; I fired Miriam, but not with the relish or ease I would like to have brought to the task. She had emerged in the full flower of her impertinence, yet I had trouble doing the dirty work. It wasn't merely that I was uneasy with authority, but that I half identified with Miriam as a woman with professional ambitions in a world that was constantly sending mixed signals. We no longer knew where we stood or where we belonged. I was too close to it, to her, to the tasks involved. It was easy for Westerman and Andrew to dispatch Miriam with a wave of the hand because they were far removed from her and dissociated from the role she served, a role they didn't want to think too much about or feel too seriously indebted to. It was something "anyone" could do: interchangeably female and subservient.

In my helpless anger, I felt isolated from both sides, and felt

Andrew and Westerman's detachment as a sort of male conspiracy in which they sustained each other and the illusion of their own power by turning an indifferent shoulder to the peonage. As I watched Andrew, I became increasingly aware of a dramatic difference between his "public" behavior—toward the doctors, male doctors—and his "private" behavior, toward the nurses and me. The class/gender demarcation was definite and striking. What Westerman referred to as Andrew's "remarkable" attitude was a sham, or at least a fairly elaborate masquerade mounted for the benefit of his doctors, just as their bonhomie was a show for him.

Andrew was improving, talking more fluently, looking at television a bit, eating, sitting up for longer periods of time, but his "normalcy" was inconsistent and selective. He would be fussy, querulous, thoroughly impossible with me and the nurses, behind the scenes so to speak, but let a doctor walk in the door and an instant transformation would occur: his personality took a bath, spruced itself up in coat and tie; he would smile, crack jokes, indulge in gallows humor so the doctors would murmur to themselves, "What a guy!" Nor was it a one-way street. For the doctors, in return, all signs of fatigue, irritation, short-temperedness that might have been apparent moments before— say, while the nurses were bringing them up to date with the charts of the day—would fade when they walked in the door for the evening social call. They were all smiles, manly charm, and casual know-how, flattering Andrew's vanity, in a mutual admiration act that was worthy of an Oscar. Then, vanish the doctors and enter the nurses, and Andrew would immediately retreat into his Mr. Hyde persona, complaining, sulking, refusing to obey.

No wonder the hospitals were beginning to have difficulty holding nurses. As I watched this extraordinary group on F7, I wondered how long any of them would be here. Intelligent, attractive, conscientious, constantly on the move, it was they who tracked the patient's ups and downs, and really got to know their individual bodies and needs, understood the changing status of one or another organ, blood pressure, temperature, who made important decisions, knew when to call a doctor or an IV specialist, who were often better at inserting IVs than the specialists and the interns, who were *there* . . . and who were underappreciated and underpaid. And it was the doctors, who breezed in for their evening curtain call, who got the credit, the status, and the paychecks.

Not only was it for the doctors that Andrew would perform, but for friends. I had been so looking forward to Andrew's recovery, to the long conversations, or even short conversations, we would have, but now that he was able to talk, we seemed to have nothing to say to each other. I was, and had been, so consumed by him that I'd become a virtual numbskull, all my "news" being news of him, as if the entire content of my mind had been emptied and replaced by the vicissitudes of his condition at any given moment.

"I need stimulation," he told me frankly, meaning from the outside world, something beyond the meager fare I provided. His words stung unbelievably. He needed something more and I couldn't give it to him, and I resented him for turning me into the person who couldn't give it to him. Our marriage was based on our being interesting to each other, and I was failing to uphold my side of the bargain.

Hurt, I nevertheless encouraged friends to call: the late Tom Allen, film scholar and Andrew's invaluable aide-de-camp at the *Voice*, came in for an hour here and there, catching him up on the news. Now there were occasional visitors, mostly good friends, who would either come by or call on the phone. Vincent Canby, Tim Clinton, Andrew's very knowledgeable teaching assistant from Columbia, and Roger Greenspun, all of whom had been faithful allies to me while Andrew was too sick to talk, now talked directly to Andrew. He would regale friends with comic horror stories, playing the rueful war veteran, displaying himself as the gallant invalid, bravado mingling with self-mockery, in the role that played so well with the doctors.

One evening Richard Roud and his friend Harvey Gram came by before taking me out to dinner. I could see they were apprehensive before they entered the room, since no one knew quite what to expect with Andrew. But both relaxed as soon as they saw him, and he was in unusually good form.

"In this situation," he proclaimed, "the possibilities for pathos are unlimited."

They came away stunned by his alertness and humor.

"He's easier to understand now," Harvey said, "he talks more slowly."

Other visitors would drop in, still a relative few, but he always managed to rise to the occasion. Ross Wetszteon came with a huge red tomato from his vegetable patch, the Blumenthals with champagne and cavier. (Andrew enjoyed the callers, I the edibles.) Georges Borchardt, my agent, and his wife, Anne, dear friends, had sent flowers and had telephoned me regularly, but when Georges dropped by to see Andrew, it was a visit I especially appreciated, knowing he was one of those people for whom merely walking into a hospital is an ordeal (how many others were there?), and therefore what it cost him to make the gesture. It was a hopeful period. All of us, the doctors and nurses, were looking forward now; he was on the road to rehabilitation, a change of scenery, new surroundings.

Yet I kept feeling depleted and depressed.

Sam agreed that this was a particularly difficult time, but when I complained that he turned on for the doctors and collapsed for me, he seemed to think that quite normal.

"Would you want him to fake it?" he asked. Naturally, I replied no, but in my heart, I thought yes, dammit, just once in a while, why couldn't he fake it for me, too? If acting was what he was doing with doctors and visitors, couldn't he extend the run a little longer for me? I acknowledged and rejoiced in his improvements, but why wasn't I ever the beneficiary? The more he "improved," the lonelier and more left out I felt.

We still had only the most limited conversations. I would sit in the visitor's chair as he talked on the telephone, and the livelier his conversation, the more rejected I felt. I remembered the words of Barbara, that wise little nurse, who'd said, "You're doing it all wrong, Molly. You're down when he's down. Instead, you should be lifting his spirits when he's down. And he should be raising yours when he's doing well." Now I should have allowed these displays of vigor to encourage me, but instead I felt excluded, let down, especially since he refused to take an interest in my activities. My writing projects, or my limited social life—things he normally would have been curious about—he felt understandably jealous of, as they reminded him of what he didn't and couldn't do and share. The closeness of our lives had turned into a negative parallel: instead of supporting each other, we felt each other as a mutual rejection.

*   *   *

The days went slowly, with improvements and setbacks. The Foley tube was removed once again . . . and reinserted. Andrew had gained 12 pounds now, and was up to 142. But the weariness was mind-boggling: he couldn't read at all, to watch television was an effort, and sitting in the chair remained an inhuman ordeal. It was also one to which he did not submit with grace. As usual, he was not responding enthusiastically to physical therapy. His laziness was by now legendary, and his evasions had become a sore point with the nurses.

Even here, however, he was capable of heroic effort when necessary, and in one particular case the effort was heartbreaking. It was the day that a doctor/examiner from Burke was coming down for an official planned visit to interview the various candidates being considered for admission at the rehabilitation institute. There was great agitation on the floor, and Andrew had been primed and coached like an infant for a preschool interview. He was shaved and clean and sitting up, and because we had no idea when the man would come, had been sitting up all day, an enormous ordeal, trying to look in command. Finally, a call came to the nurses' station at four, saying the doctor would be there soon. Four went by, and five, and six. He never came. Andrew was so let down by the end of the day there were tears in his eyes. Sam, whose pet project it was to get Andrew into Burke, was mystified, as were the nurses on the floor. What could have happened to the doctor? Several days later, Sam found out through colleagues at Burke that the doctor had actually filed a report on Andrew—without ever seeing him.

Sam was surprised, but tried to brush it off.

"Haven't you ever reviewed a movie without seeing it?" he asked.

"No," I said, furiously.

Then Rusk called, saying Andrew had been accepted, and though they wouldn't have a bed for several weeks, this was a great moment that gave the rest of our time at New York Hospital the shape of a leave-taking.

On Tuesday, September 27, Andrew stood with a walker for the first time, and his feeding tube came out. They had planned to remove it Friday, but it just fell out, as if the time was right. *Voice* editor

David Schneiderman visited and he and Andrew had a long discussion of the upcoming election. David was astonished at the clarity of his mind and how in touch he was with things politically. When Tom Allen came, Andrew would do a little work, dictate some capsule movie reviews for the "Revivals in Focus" column, feel as if he were getting back into harness.

That same day, a day like any other, I was walking into the lobby for my second visit when I ran into Jeffrey leaving the hospital.

"Have you heard?" he asked. I shook my head.

"They got a positive identification."

"You mean a diagnosis?" He nodded. I waited breathlessly.

"CMV: cytomegalovirus." I'd never heard of it. He explained it was a monolike virus that most of us have as teenagers, and to which we develop an immunity without getting the disease itself. Either Andrew had never developed an immunity or the virus had lain dormant and been reactivated.

What did that mean?

"You get it from kissing," Jeffrey said, only half jokingly. "Maybe Andrew didn't kiss enough." Andrew's case was wildly atypical. But how and why did he get it? I wanted to know. Had a bookish, sexually backward adolescence resulted in this? Had it caused the septicemia, the perforated colon, the paralysis?

Jeffrey shrugged. Whatever, it was an extraordinarily unusual manifestation of a relatively common virus; either that, or it was piggybacking with another virus.

Where did that leave us? Nowhere, since no one had ever seen such a case, and therefore no one could predict the course of recovery—i.e., would he be able to walk again? How well?

"If this was a virus reactivated, could it happen again?" I asked Jeffrey.

"It could, but it's extremely unlikely," he said.

"Jeffrey, is this what you expected? Back when you said, 'He's not going to die, he's not going to die'?"

Jeffrey shook his head and smiled. "I believed it: call it prayer, self-delusion, an expectation of miracles, also a lot of medical arrogance."

Then came the news that Rusk was going to be ready for him

earlier than expected, either Saturday or soon after. Sam sat me down for a preparatory talk, warning me that at Rusk I would have to maintain my "vigilance." Vigilance? I hadn't known Sam thought I'd been vigilant. I was pleased, shamefully pleased, at this "compliment"—indirect and ambiguous as it was. Finally, the pat on the head I'd been yearning for, and how good it felt, and how sad to realize how childishly hungry and in need of praise I'd been.

I was exhausted and had a cold but decided to indulge myself: I went to the "Van Gogh at Arles" show at the Met, and, like everyone who saw it, was transported. My mother's favorite painters were van Gogh and Matisse, and I'd grown up with reproductions, and books, of both of them, before they, and van Gogh particularly, became a megabuck commodity, postcards of his work dotting drugstores and train stations. It was stunning to realize how those weird, mixed marriages of objects and colors, the yellow roads, the violet grass, had come to look completely normal. It's not so much the colors themselves—arguably splashier and less subtle than those of the other Impressionists—but the obsessional eccentricity behind them, the ferocious brushstrokes, that speak to us nowadays. For me, he had been a disturbing but exhilarating household presence: in our living room in the country, where we lived from the time I was eight until I was thirteen, there hung a reproduction of *Starry Night*. With its vibrating cedars, its fiery whorls of celestial anguish, this was one of the "crazy" paintings. Yet now it seems that what we call van Gogh's madness was really the last heroic vestiges of sanity, the artist bridging the gap between self and world by seeing that reality is what we make of it, envisioned, illuminated, given shape by the inner mind and consciousness. When I got older, it seemed incongruous that my mother so loved a painter whose style was the antithesis of her own—paintings in which nature was as precise and benign as the abstracted figures whose faces it framed. The reserve was part of my mother, her very essence, impossible to imagine her breaking through it, yet perhaps there lurked within her a raging van Gogh, an artist greedy to burst through the veil of politesse by seizing and possessing nature with wild brushstrokes.

I talked to Mother on the phone and couldn't stop crying.

The Talbots—Toby, who had phoned the hospital almost every

day, been my ally for eight weeks, and her husband, Dan—came to see Andrew before taking me out to dinner. Toby marveled at the sight of him and thought, as I did, that he had changed, grown beautiful. There was a serenity to his face. He was tired now, but no longer agitated.

At a restaurant in Chinatown we drank and ate joyfully.

"You know how I always remember Andrew?" Toby said. "Sort of half sitting, half lying on our sofa and the two little girls playing with him. He would have dropped by after a movie, or to talk over some project with Dan, and suddenly there they'd be, Nina and Sarah, crawling on top of him. It was so funny, so sweet."

I could imagine it vividly, the two little girls clambering all over Andrew as if he were a jungle gym, or a giant panda, an animal that Andrew, with his doleful eyes, his gentle, sedentary manner, and his indifference to the imperatives of procreation, resembled to a remarkable degree. Andrew would notice them, receive them, but without focusing on them, without making a fuss, and on they would go, playing on and around him as he talked. He had a quality that children instinctively responded to.

Like the grandmother in Proust, Marcel's loving guardian, Andrew was blessedly unselfconscious. One of the most lovable characters in literature, she's the slightly dowdy woman who embarrasses her grandson in the chic hotel lobby at Balbec, and then, hours later, when her little pigeon is feeling poorly, engulfs him with love. She has no idea of fashion at all or of the figure she cuts, never notices the hotelier's disdainful glances in her direction, but when it comes to sensing appeals for love from her little one, she can hear through walls.

With what energy we had left, and with a new spurt of adrenaline, we began looking forward to Rusk, to a change of scenery and of Andrew's status. We'd work together, have long conversations. On Monday Rusk called at 11:00 A.M. and said they had a bed and for us to be there by four. In a mad rush, I packed up Andrew's belongings, took some home, and came back in time to get him ready for the trip. When it came time to say good-bye to the nurses, I felt once more that wrench of separation; once again, I was leaving my "family" for the unknown.

It was pouring, just as it had been when we arrived three months before. We boarded Andrew, looking pale but excited, into the ambulette from the Emergency Room entrance. The driver lurched out the familiar cobblestone courtyard, which we were seeing for the first time in daylight, and headed for the East River Drive and south to Thirty-fourth Street.

"There it goes," I said, looking back at Andrew, and beyond at the Emergency Entrance. "For the last time! Right?"

Andrew nodded wearily. "For the last time."

8

The Rusk Institute, an architecturally undistinguished modern building at Thirty-fourth Street and First Avenue, was newer and shinier than New York Hospital. It was also drearier, a diesel engine gone slightly to seed. An affiliate of the New York University Medical Center, it had been built in 1951 as a pioneering effort in rehabilitation under the founding genius of Dr. Howard Rusk. Rusk was a World War II figure, a doctor from St. Louis, whose great innovation was to combine physical and mental therapy. But he had been the charismatic source of motivation, and his semi-retirement had created a certain vacuum. Besides, it was a different world now. One look down the corridors, where old people hobbled on walkers or sat slumbering in wheelchairs, and you knew the nature of the beast had changed. These weren't the returning war veterans, men with shrapnel wounds, missing arms, leg injuries, on whom Rusk had developed his techniques— young men with good prospects of recovery, and the gratitude of society to sustain them. These were people with grimmer prognoses: elderly stroke victims, young men with spinal-cord injuries, patients with injuries and afflictions ranging from neuromuscular diseases to rare and atypical diseases like Andrew's. I had heard testimonials from former inpatients as well as outpatients (friends with back or knee injuries) on both sides: Rusk was the greatest, or it was in sad decline. Whatever, it was the only game in town, and in town was where Andrew wanted to be.

212

After hustling to get down there, we were made to wait for an hour, and when Andrew was finally settled into Room 110 D, I looked around. Although the room was much larger and brighter than the rooms at New York Hospital, and its equipment more modern, it struck me as cold, metallic. It was just below ground level, its wide window looking onto a cement yard with a few scrubby bushes and trees, and just beyond, buttresses of the East Side Drive. The East River was itself visible only to someone standing at the window, a position in which none of the four men I saw was likely to be. Andrew's roommates were a young man in his late teens or early twenties with both legs in a sling, an old man who could talk only haltingly, apparently a stroke victim, and, in the bed next to him, a man on a respirator, who couldn't talk at all (a seeming contradiction of the rule of not admitting patients requiring acute nursing care).

It was still pouring outside, a cold, forbidding September day, as we waited for the nurse. And waited. Andrew was lying on the bed in his street clothes, weak from exhaustion and worried about his colostomy. When the nurse finally came, she didn't stop to get Andrew undressed, only to tell me the name of the doctor we'd been assigned. To my disappointment, it was none of the three doctors I'd requested on our application, names I'd been given by friends.

She disappeared, promising to return, and in the interval, Andrew's colostomy bag burst. The fecal odor rose and filled the room, flies swarmed. That had never happened at New York Hospital; indeed, I'd almost forgotten the colostomy existed. There had been a "colostomy lady"—a lovely white-haired charmer we both adored, whose mere presence seemed to tame the bowels and soothe the nerves. She was an unusual woman, elegant, supremely capable, but above all a proselytizer whose mission it was to help people adjust to colostomies and, if they were permanent, enable them to envision a normal future. She was so matter of fact, had such authority, that she instilled calm in her patients and their systems had responded. Two hours at Rusk, though, and Andrew's insides had had an anxiety attack.

When the nurse came back, it was to give us pointers.

"That's your husband's locker," she announced, showing me to a standard metal upright locker. "He should have two complete outfits of clothes suitable for therapy: warm-up or sweat-suit pants and tops,

T-shirts, jockey shorts, sneakers, several pairs of socks, and then pajamas and robe. You'll be responsible for the laundry. There are machines on the fourth floor."

"Laundry?" I gasped. By now she was already out the door. With those two syllables something in *me* burst. I simply couldn't, wouldn't do it. The idea of coming all the way down here each day to see him and *then* traipsing up to the fourth floor and running (perhaps waiting for) the washer and the dryer was . . . unthinkable. A task I normally would have accepted, if not relished, was the proverbial straw that broke the camel's back, the apparently trivial chore that, precisely because of its triviality—pure drudgery without moral recompense—overwhelms.

I went to the locker, put Andrew's few little belongings on the shelf and on hangers, his one T-shirt, his clean, sweet-smelling pajamas, his scruffy bedroom slippers, and a sports jacket, then I buried my head in one of his T-shirts and cried. I was miserable—for Andrew, for myself, homesick for New York Hospital. It was like going to camp for the first time, or going away to school, that moment when the parents leave. A minute before you were arguing with them, annoyed at the sight of their faces. Then, as they recede into the distance, they become precious. With a terrible pang, your heart remembers every detail—the inside of the car, the dashboard, the map folded up wrong, the tear in the upholstery, everything worn and familiar. They wave back at you, smile. You wave, more and more frantically as their hands and faces get smaller and smaller until you can see only the car and finally not even that. And now you're all alone in this strange unfriendly environment and you can't remember for the life of you what it was you'd been so looking forward to.

I emerged from the locker refreshed and managed to pull myself together in time for the arrival of Dr. Ming Wu. The roster at Rusk, as I knew from my own preliminary selection, was filled with Asians, no doubt because they had entered the field of physiotherapy earlier and in far greater numbers than we had, and were using techniques that were still considered unorthodox by our medical establishment. The preliminary examination was brisk, the questions basic: Why was Andrew here? What had happened? Did Wu really have no idea, or was this an instance of the teacher wanting to hear why the student is in his class in his "own words"? It wasn't that I expected Andrew's fame as a medical phenomenon to have preceded him, but I thought some information might have been sent down from New York Hospital, and that Rusk, in turn, might have shown some sense of welcome and foreknowledge. The impression conveyed was that we were starting from scratch. Since Andrew was too tired to talk, and in any case didn't really know what had brought him here, I replied.

"High fever; CMV encephalitis; septicemia; pneumonia; perforated colon; surgery for perforated colon; colostomy; peritonitis; paralysis of the legs; bed sores."

Wu looked at me dubiously but said nothing. Did he resent my doing the talking? Did he not believe me? He continued to play the inscrutable Oriental when he concluded by saying he suspected the leg problem was not a genuine paralysis but the result of lying in bed. He planned to have Andrew examined by a neurologist, then perform an electromyogram (EMG). At least, that was what I thought he said because his English, whether by design or lack of linguistic felicity, was almost unintelligible. Perhaps he felt he wasn't sufficiently on top of the case to comment, but it was clear that he didn't feel it was his job to talk to me.

Suddenly I felt deserted, without family support (Themis could no longer make the trip in and Mother and Chevey had gone home), and attacked by spasms of homesickness—for Barbara, for the nurses on F7, for Sam, even for the doctors who were always running in the opposite direction. Andrew, tired and preoccupied with his paraphernalia, wasn't reacting. It was, as Sam had warned, a different atmosphere: I had become persona non grata, a member of a category called "the family," whose relationship to the institution was that of a potential enemy. If at New York Hospital the family had been regarded with a mixture of support and veiled impatience, here they regarded you through suspiciously narrowed eyes, as someone who might advance but was more likely to impede the therapy process.

On Tuesday, before stopping in to see Andrew, I decided to attend an "orientation" meeting for families of new patients. In a small classroom I found about eight people, sitting in stiff-backed chairs and looking as if they hadn't slept for weeks. Most of them were women, most middle-aged or older, and most were wives of stroke victims.

Numb from shock and exhaustion, they began talking of horrors in weary, deadpan voices. One had had to bring her husband back on the plane from Spain and, on arriving at the hospital, had slept for three hours in his bed while he sat in the wheelchair. I knew that feeling: I'd often looked longingly at Andrew's bed, wanting to crawl in while he served time in the chair. The social worker gave a brief lecture on Rusk's goals and *modus operandi*, but the women were bursting with their own agonies and questions.

One complained that her husband didn't recognize her, or thought she was somebody else: did she have to come and visit him? That would be up to her, of course, said the instructor, but one never knew when he might come out of it, or how much her being there might help subliminally.

Another, in a voice tense with control, asked how long she should stay for her evening visit. We all sensed that what she was really asking was how short a visit she could get away with and not feel like a heel. The lecturer suggested an hour and a half at dinner, whereupon the woman exploded.

"He's always harping at me," she said, fury finally overcoming her self-possession, "asking me to do this, do that. My nerves can't take it."

I could barely stand to look at these women's faces, haggard with sleeplessness, their eyes tormented by too many conflicting emotions in too short a time. In the space of an hour or a day, the marriages of twenty or thirty years had become grotesque caricatures of themselves. The husbands they had relied on had become helpless, children going backward instead of forward; aliens who—if they could talk at all—were cranky and unloving. And where did they go from here? They hoped, of course, however overwhelming the odds. But they were also being asked to face the prospect of a journey to a place they would never have chosen, a journey they would have given their lives not to make. They were used to going to Spain with their husbands, to Italy, the Caribbean, or to the Jersey shore, to a movie, not to rehab centers and the various sideline accommodations for the handicapped, not into the shadow world of permanently benched players, to lying down at night with someone who would need attending to rather than someone who attended to them and thought they looked great even in hair curlers. To living off insurance instead of salary, to being looked at without longing and loved without heat, if at all; to the death of one kind of marriage, the only one they'd ever had, perhaps the only one they'd ever wanted.

They were being asked to make an adjustment—to keep up their spirits (there was always hope) but to lower their sights downward to the possibility of hopelessness. They were being asked to *adjust*, and it was too soon, and perhaps it would always be too soon, and they would never be ready.

After the bleak atmosphere of the orientation, I was looking forward to seeing Andrew, but when I got to his room, there had been an accident with the colostomy. In fact, in a chorus of excremental effusions, there had been accidents all around, one man having urinated . . . well, not to go into details, except to say that the whole place smelled like a stable. It's not that I'm abnormally squeamish, I even grew up in and around stables—though Andrew, with reference to my acute olfactory sense, occasionally called me the Princess and the Poo. But this was too much. Andrew was lying in pants, sweatshirt, and sneakers, unshaven, too tired to notice or talk. The laundry was looming like Mount Everest, and I was no mountain climber. I decided to go and unburden myself to the social worker assigned to us, and made an appointment for the next day with June Narayama.

At a half hour past the appointed time, there appeared a trim, businesslike Asian in a red suit.

"Mrs. Sarris?" she said. (No Ms. Haskell here.)

I nodded and followed her into her office.

"Yes?" she said, without preliminary. "What can we do for you?"

I might have been alerted by the institutional "we," but I was too angry and unhappy to shut up now. I reeled off a litany of complaints—we hadn't gotten the doctor we wanted, the room smelled, the nurses were never there, and I couldn't do the laundry —which she heard with dragon-lady impassivity. Her manner, like Dr. Wu's, seemed designed to discourage the personal or the confessional, and to convey the feeling that the Family was tolerated only out of necessity. Then, as happens in a completely one-sided conversation, when the person you are talking to fails to nod, blink, make any of those tiny responses of sympathy we are used to, I began to falter, hear my voice go shrill. Into the vacuum of June Narayama's blankness, I lurched, rising to a note of theatrical self-pity that was far from the effect I'd wanted to create.

"I've been through a three-month ordeal," I shouted in desperation, "during which my husband almost died not once but several times. I went to the hospital twice a day, twice a day for three months, I'm worn to a frazzle and I can't, *can't* do the laundry."

Then, to my shame, I broke down and cried.

She didn't bat an eyelash. "We're not like New York Hospital," she said impassively, "not warm and attentive. That's part of our policy, to get people on their own. His doctor is very good and cares a lot about his patients." She paused. "We expect the Family to support our program, not put pressure on the patient."

This was a reference to our joint work project, I felt sure. Andrew had apparently told her that we were planning to work together on the French lecture project, and indeed, the next thing she said was that she thought our plan to collaborate might be too much for him.

She probed further. Did we have children? she wanted to know. When I said no, I saw for the first time a glimmer of an expression on her face, a look of curiosity. She paused expectantly, waiting for me to provide an explanation. It was, I realized, not personal but professional curiosity, as if this aberration of ours (whether from choice or biological incapacity) would have some bearing on Andrew's prospects for recovery according to how it affected our lives. Perhaps our childlessness was further proof of my Career-Woman selfishness and would alert her as to how much of a problem I would be. (Presumably, if I had children to distract me, I would put less pressure on Andrew.) Or perhaps she saw it as some genetic or psychological defect on my part—a tragedy I'd overcompensated for, or merely a choice of self-fulfillment over unselfish procreation—that had better be placed on the table right away. We-the-Family were there, her manner seemed to say, to oblige Andrew and the hospital and not the other way around. My desires and disappointments were simply irrelevant. She listened to me through a kind of filter to find out not what I needed or felt but how much of a problem I was going to be.

I wanted to ask her if *she* had children, but contented myself with not supplying the information she so obviously wanted. It's surprising how hard it is, at least for a compulsively ingratiating person like myself, to simply not answer a question, even an unstated question, when the person is sitting straight across from you and looking into your eyes. In the tacit struggle between us, between her perception of what was right for Andrew and therefore for me, and mine, I had won a tiny victory.

There was something . . . if not admirable, then impressive in that facade of casual despotism. Because it was institutional, impersonal, nothing could touch it, her. There was no room in this system for my needs or ours as a unit. She reiterated several times how tired Andrew was, as if I were too stupid or insensitive to realize it. Then, probing further, she asked if I was repelled by the colostomy.

"Well, yes," I said (no point in lying now), "when it bursts." Who wouldn't be! Now that she had me pegged I'd go ahead and play the enemy, live up to her conception of me as the bitch-wife who is squeamish, repelled by bodily functions or menial chores.

"I just can't do the laundry," I said, in conclusion. "There must be some other way."

"I'm afraid that's your responsibility," she said. "You'll have to do it. Or make other arrangements."

I tried to see it from their point of view. They weren't there to hold our hands. One sweet word, one look of compassion, and we would have dissolved into puddles at their feet. There were other people to give us "caring." This was professional dispassion, compassion bracingly "withheld" for our own good. Still, what had "the Family" done to warrant armed opposition? Did it arise from experience or from some bad Hollywood movie where wives swooped down on ailing husbands like vultures, or went on spending sprees or had affairs while their husbands were bedridden, or nagged them to throw down their crutches and walk.

Thinking about the experience later, I realized that it went further than that: June Narayama and I were staring at each other across one of those cultural divides in which hospital life abounded. She and Wu were the "Other," repressed, stoical, self-subordinating, while I was no less an "Other" to them: the emotional and individualistic Westerner. Although we discussed matters of common interest, we did so with feelings and attitudes so different we might have been speaking a different language. English only gave us a false sense of communication.

Perhaps that's all she was saying, that Andrew came first, but the hospital's idea of how that priority might best be realized and mine were two different things, and our *feelings*—his and mine—entered into it in ways they weren't prepared to accommodate.

Now the scenario should have called for me to break down again, or throw myself on her mercy. To wave the white flag by asking her what I should expect of Andrew and when I might hope to begin work with him. In other words, to sign over my claims on Andrew to them, to surrender him to the Rusk time frame, to the Rusk regime. And she, refraining even from the tiny smile of victory, would have answered by telling me not to expect anything from Andrew. Anything at all.

But I didn't ask. I dug in my heels, refusing to give any sign that I valued her opinion or deferred to her in this matter. Because I didn't. What did she know of Andrew? What did she know of CMV encephalitis? (In fact, what did anyone know of its effect on Andrew? CMV was itself little known at the time except to infectious-disease experts. It wasn't until much later that it began appearing with some frequency as an opportunistic disease affecting AIDS patients.) And most important, what did she know of *us*? Of our relationship, of how beneficial working would be for Andrew, and the astonishing things we could do in collaboration with each other.

To what extent are the people who become our enemies demons of our own creation? I suppose there was an appalling amount of childishness in my attitude toward June Narayama, and toward Rusk, yet there was enormous gratification as well, and, possibly, an energizing force that might just as easily be healthy rather than unhealthy where Andrew was concerned.

In fact, we did make other arrangements for the laundry: Andrew found a nurse's aide who would do it for a small fee. And we began to talk about the French lectures, which proved to be just the sort of stimulation Andrew needed.

In a strange way, the interview with June Narayama, with its edge of unpleasantness, was a sort of release, a turning point for me. Henceforth, the boundaries were clearly drawn: I would expect nothing from

Rusk in the way of emotional support; in return, I would grant them no authority. They were a way station, a place for Andrew to recover, with none of the paternalistic allure of New York Hospital.

At the moment, they felt that Andrew was too weak and anemic for physical therapy, and were trying to improve his stamina with food, blood tranfusions, rest, a regime that was perfectly agreeable to Andrew. Dr. Wu kept telling Andrew it wouldn't be long, apparently in an effort to reassure him, having formed the erroneous impression that Andrew, no doubt like most Ruskees, was impatient to get started. How soon, and sadly, he would be disabused. They gave Andrew the electromyogram—a horrid examination in which electrodes are placed in the muscles to record electrical activity. Andrew hated it, and it apparently did little to advance their knowledge. Wu admitted he was even more puzzled than he'd been before.

"In ninety-seven percent of the cases I see," he said, "I can tell what's wrong by using an EMG. In the other two, I have an idea. But then there's that one percent that is completely baffling."

Andrew was still extraordinarily weak, barely eating, unable to watch television, and little given to conversation. I felt oppressed by his condition, with its continued ups and downs. I couldn't seem to get the hang of it, couldn't remember to expect the bad days and couldn't accustom myself to his endless self-absorption. He was lost in his illness and its details, the colostomy, the wound, the all-pervasive fatigue.

I missed his lovingness, and felt the loss less keenly when I was physically away from him and could imagine him as his old self instead of this relentlessly indifferent presence. I knew from my own surgery what it felt like to reside in a twilight world, to never quite have the energy for eating, or reading, or talking, for days on end. I remembered the way you begin to look upon your body in the third person—it's an object, out there, with which you're fascinated, transfixed. You treat yourself as if you were a wounded bird, listening to your own breathing, stroking your feathers, taking your pulse hourly. A kind of fetishism occurs in which your whole life is gathered into your body and the obsessional contemplation of it; your symptoms absorb you utterly, screening out the robust emotions and appetites of the well.

We were like two people in opposite time zones, China versus

New York; or different seasons, Brazil and New York. Andrew was in body time, and I was in mind time, and in a struggle that seemed to prove the power of entropy, his lethargy was stronger than gravity, pulling us both down.

Now that we were away from New York Hospital, I began to have strange dreams of Andrew dying, always in preposterous ways. In one, horrible yet slyly comical, a chicken bone got caught in his throat and he died. It fell to Sam to break the news to me. I went through all the familiar emotions: agony, fear, disbelief, despair. Then Sam implied that there had been negligence: there was supposed to be someone with him at all times, and there had been no one. There was a sort of time-lapse effect in the dream, following which Sam said that there had been a successful lawsuit and Lloyd's of London was going to pay me four million dollars. Like so many of my dreams, it was deceptively transparent. There was the obvious impulse of both wishing for and fearing Andrew's death, for a fear as intense and prolonged as mine usually contains an element of wish. Hating someone for making you love them so much. There was the unpredictability, the sense that it would come not in the obvious and expected way, through the disease toward which all energies had been marshaled, but through some fluke. And wasn't CMV, that homely little virus, a fluke? But primarily, as in Freud's famous Irma Injection dream (the face-saving—and Fleiss-saving—interpretation of a dream that referred to his friend Fleiss's disastrous nasal surgery on Emma Eckstein), the strategy seemed to be to allow me to emerge untarnished from a situation loaded with unacknowledged misgivings and guilt: i.e., my negligence regarding Andrew and my wish not to be present; Sam's negligence exonerated by his honesty and his appearing to side with me rather than the hospital; his part in the lawsuit, which simply "happens" without my knowledge, thus freeing me from the taint of desiring to profit from my husband's death, but which nevertheless leaves me secure for life.

Dreams, so many more, testified to an abiding insecurity. I didn't trust Andrew to stay alive. The ground had given way and would never be solid again.

After I told him my dream, he confessed that he had had hostile fantasies about me until very late in his illness. He remembered his hallucinations with remarkable clarity, and was describing them.

"You were always Gloria Steinem," he said, "or you were with her. I was terrified of you."

Though I had suspected his hostility at the time, it was still unsettling to hear it. When he told me this, I was lying by his side, having seized a rare opportunity—there was no one in the room—to get in his bed with him. It was a Saturday. Saturdays were always quiet, the nursing staff reduced, patients out riding or walking with families. It was the first time I had lain alongside him, the first time in three months that I had felt his body next to mine. It was a strange body, inert, passive, letting me love it rather than turning toward me. I became once again the loving one, he the object, as I luxuriated in the smell and feel of his soft skin, and the smell of adhesive tape with which his skin had become forever associated. We began piecing together our memories: how he felt when I came and went, the apparent image of health; how I felt when he glowered at me, or held a knife in my face. We were like two lovers when they first acknowledge their love and begin talking of the moment when it began, only ours was a negative image of lovers, for we were chronicling spasms of hate, fury, hostility.

"One day Vincent came to see me," he said. "It was in September, when I was no longer even hallucinating. But when he told me how much you had done to pull me through, I got furious. I didn't let him see it, because he was obviously in collusion with you. I'd been thinking all along the whole illness was a plot on your part to use my ideas and become famous, and Vincent's words somehow proved it." This, too, took me aback, coming as it did so late in the illness.

This idea that I could have been plotting against him: was it part of some anger lurking beneath the surface that our intense intimacy had prevented from emerging? In the early days of our marriage, there had been fights, and explosions—I'd even gotten to the point where I could yell back at Andrew, decibel for decibel, and had rather enjoyed it—but somehow the altercations had grown less frequent, to be replaced by a sort of ritualistic fight, a pattern of indirection: I'd deliberately, if unconsciously, provoke Andrew by complaining about something at precisely the "wrong" moment, when he was tired and disgruntled, but just as he was on the point of blowing up, I'd deliver a preemptive defense.

"No, don't do it. I shouldn't have said that. I was wrong, I was wrong, I was wrong," I'd say, backing down, and he'd weaken, and deflate, and we'd look at each other conciliatorily, "making up" as if we'd actually had the fight. In that split second, our imaginations resurrected the archetypal fights of the past and we fought them by reference, so to speak. We were like members of the joke-telling club who had only to call out the number of a joke for everyone to burst out laughing. We had three or four stock conflicts whose permutations were so well known to us that we could escape all the agony by a quick, pantomimed exchange: evil accusatory glances, shameful glances, then the making up. We had gotten to the point where we couldn't stand tension between us, even for the fifteen minutes of a fight. Unlike other couples, who manage to inject suspense into the stalest of chronic disagreements, we knew how it would end, how our parts had gradually gotten enmeshed and entangled so that nobody ever really "won" or "lost."

"Don't you see?" Andrew said about his hallucinations. "You're so central to my life that anything that happens is bound to revolve around you. If people are trying to kill me, you must be there, masterminding the effort!"

How was it possible, once joined, to pull back. "To hold my soul suspended above" Andrew's in the words of Rilke's "Love Song"

> *so that it does not touch on yours? How shall*
> *I succeed in concentrating on other things? . . .*
>
> *But everything that touches you and me*
> *takes us together, like the player's bow*
> *who out of two strings creates one melody.*

After a dramatic fall in blood pressure Andrew had been diagnosed as having anemia, and had been given transfusions, but he was beginning physical therapy.

The world was pressing in now: visitors, books, television, and news of friends struck down by illness and death. First, two friends were diagnosed as having cancer: one a breast malignancy, the other Hodgkin's disease. Illness seemed contagious, a plague, hitting ruthlessly and at random. We were on tenterhooks throughout their surgeries, within days of each other, but both came through with excellent prognoses.

Then François Truffaut, who'd been hovering near death with a brain tumor, died. Truffaut was exactly Andrew's age, a friend and a kindred spirit. They had met back in the sixties, when Andrew had taken up the *Cahiers* line, elucidating the beauties of such overlooked or underrated *auteurs* as Otto Preminger, Howard Hawks, Nicholas Ray, Edgar G. Ulmer against the officially recognized masters—in Britain, David Lean, in France, the old-guard directors of "quality films" like Claude Autant-Lara and Jean Delannoy. As a polemical warrior, Truffaut was a holy terror, far more savage and personal in his attacks than his *Cahiers du Cinéma* colleagues Jean-Luc Godard, Eric Rohmer, or Jacques Rivette. A far cry from the sweet and endearing personality he became when he turned director, Truffaut wielded the *politique des auteurs* like a samurai's sword, slicing up reputations at will, and there were stalled or ruined careers in the French cinema to prove it. I was surprised to discover, in my researches into the French cinema and the old copies of *Cahiers*, just how brutal Truffaut had been. I didn't meet him until several years after he made his first film, *The 400 Blows*, when he was well on his way to becoming the French director Americans loved best. But somehow I would always think of him as the child on the beach at the end of the film, whose face—woebegone yet full of a fierce curiosity—haunts us in freeze frame. We know now what became of that lonely and rebellious child, played by Jean-Pierre Léaud and resembling Truffaut himself: he grew and developed and adapted (sometimes too charmingly) to bourgeois society in the movies Truffaut made of him, just as Truffaut had been reclaimed by the cinema, loving it, writing about it, making it.

Truffaut's movies were full of a love of movies . . . and of women. He was a womanizer of the most ingratiating sort, shy, self-deprecating, funny, projecting a vulnerability, a need to be taken care of, that no woman could resist. I got to know him when he came to New York for the opening of *The Wild Child* and I was working at the French Film Office. The late Helen Scott, his official escort, interpreter, and devoted friend, saw herself as his buffer against the world and generally let no one near, but she'd had to stay behind this time and he was in my charge. To know Helen was to feel an intense, and simultaneous, love and annoyance, and she was never more Helen than when she was plowing her way through New York restaurants or presiding over hotel rooms with Truffaut in tow. Large, overbearing, hilariously funny—about others, about herself—she lived on diet pills and Gauloises (the doctors finally gave up on persuading her to drop either). She'd arrive at some restaurant for an interview, cheeks puffing, huge breasts heaving, the wind in her sails like a flagship with her one tiny vessel—Truffaut—by her side. The assumption, to which Truffaut charmingly deferred, was that he couldn't take a step or have a conversation without her. He pretended to be just as helpless as she claimed he was, but I soon realized, when it came my turn to mediate, that his inability to speak or understand English—that justification for Helen's, and my, presence—was a charade. When I was supposedly interpreting for him, his face responded to a journalist's statement or question before I'd translated a word. His razor-sharp mind took in everything, but he enjoyed the drama of being shielded, the intimacy of having a private semi-secret relationship within a larger professional one.

Truffaut was a complex mixture of calculation and obsession. One felt that never, in his films or in his relations with women, would he completely lose himself, and perhaps there was something almost reassuring in that. He loved women, in the repressed manner of the American movies he'd grown up on, romantically and delicately, rather than in the more uninhibitedly carnal style of the French. I say this from firsthand experience. Andrew, whom I'd begun seeing fairly steadily, was away at the Berlin film festival, so in the three or four days we spent together, Truffaut and I had a chaste romance. We went to see 2001 and held hands while watching spaceships gliding to Strauss, went home and later necked with sweet passion on my sofa, and in between stolen kisses—which was as far as it went—talked of movies and France and political ferment (this was 1968, just before the "événements de mai" and the closing of the Cannes Film Festival by Truffaut and his fellow directors); we talked of Andrew, whom François had christened "le roi du Village," in honor of his role as trailblazer and keeper of the flame of serious film criticism in America.

As at the funeral of Charles Denner in Truffaut's The Man Who

Loved Women, I imagined there would be a great many female mourn-ers for François. One could picture them lined up around the block, and down to the Seine, like a queue at the Trocadero Cinémathèque for an American movie, the famous and not-so-famous, Catherine Deneuve, Jeanne Moreau, Isabelle Adjani, his devoted wife, Made-leine, and the others, the "nobodies," tall, short, old, young, former lovers who still loved him, joined, without jealousy, to honor his passing and smile at the memories he'd left behind.

Andrew was getting more intense physical therapy now, and was more exhausted than ever when I came in. He was being very close-mouthed about exactly what he did, but I gathered it was a combination of strenuous muscle work on machines, games, and coordination ex-ercises (largely for stroke victims), and "occupational therapy" (in a room with typewriters and computers). When I arrived, he would be fast asleep from his exertions, and I was always feeling immensely sorry for him until one evening Dr. Wu dropped by while I was there.

"Mr. Sarris," he said sternly, "where were you today? I was told you left occupational therapy class. Was anything wrong?"

Andrew, lamely but uncontritely, said he was tired. It was then I found out from one of the nurses that he had been skipping class regularly. He would arrive in his wheelchair for the afternoon session, remain at the back of the room and slip out, return downstairs on the elevator, wheel himself to his bed, and climb in. Or in the morning, he would simply pretend not to hear the bell for class and remain where he was.

An hour later, the nurse would come in to attend to something and find him there.

"Mr. Sarris," Cindy, one of his favorite nurses, would scream, "are you still in bed!" And she would hustle him up to class, but he had already had a blissful hour of reprieve.

I began to get a fuller picture of Andrew's hooky-playing from the nurses. Once so fond of him, they were looking increasingly angry and disappointed and made cracks to the effect that he needed help to get into his wheelchair in the morning, but somehow he managed to get out of it and back into bed unassisted. Wu seemed dumbfounded at Andrew's behavior. Where was the team spirit, the desire to show his stuff? He formed a plan: he would wait until Andrew had company, then he would come in and chastise him before his friends, thinking, in the venerable Asian tradition, that public exposure would humiliate him into action. But Andrew had no face to lose, and was beyond shame. If the disappointment of the nurses, whom he adored, couldn't spur him on, Wu's stratagem certainly wouldn't.

Andrew's resistance to exercise of any sort was monolithic. He resisted it chronically and temperamentally, and long before CMV got to him. "Greek men," his mother had said one day, in an exasperated generalization that took in even her beloved Andrew. "They don't do anything. They just sit in the café and talk." Most of the stories you hear are of patients "overdoing" it and having relapses, straining muscles and joints, even breaking limbs in crazy competition to beat some record known only to themselves. Doctors, familiar with the New York overachiever syndrome, routinely warn patients to "take it easy" rather than the opposite. But "overdoing" it was not a word in Andrew's vocabulary.

He was certainly not what a doctor or physical therapist would have desired at the Rusk Institute for Rehabilitation. His face would never grace one of the institute's inspirational brochures on which were pictured gung-ho patients, smiling bravely, struggling gallantly to walk. Andrew was surrounded by go-getters and overachievers, by people who were either truly courageous or at least tried to get brownie points by seeming so, and his lack of camp spirit stuck out like a sore thumb. He was shameless, and it was the shamelessness, the refusal to acknowledge wrongdoing, that violated the Rusk spirit, and, more than the actual derelictions, got Wu's goat. Even so, Wu seemed to take an especially harsh approach with his lethargic patient, and we wondered if there might be some irritation at Andrew's being a "professor," a title that carries more weight in other countries, or with our not displaying sufficient fealty to the doctor and what he did. There were always undercurrents of tension, sensations of unease that one could never quite get hold of. They had less to do with the strict patient-doctor relationship than with the general atmosphere in which it took place.

Just as I'd often been on the nurses' side at New York Hospital,

I wasn't entirely without sympathy for Andrew's castigators here, because his slacking off was an amplified version, and a reminder, of Andrew's irritating inertness around the house. The eternally nap-taking, TV-watching Andrew now had an excuse for what he always considered was his birthright—a much-needed and well-deserved rest.

On Monday, October 29, I headed up to City College in the Bronx to deliver the first of the two lectures on French cinema. The collaboration had been therapy for both of us, a sort of collective reminiscence, in which we refined our views not only on the individual films and general movements of French cinema but on the glories of French criticism that had so influenced us both.

Lecturing for me was always an existential adventure. First, would anyone come? Then, why would they come and who were they? Unless you were Henry Kissinger, or were addressing a self-defined group, there was little way of knowing who your audience was, and why they would brave boredom, the elements, or just inertia to come to hear *you* speak. Then, the better I did, the worse I felt afterward, as if I had vamped the audience instead of edifying them. Both my Monday and Wednesday lectures, talking from notes, went well, but after the initial high, I fell into that downward spiral that all performers know and that sends many of them into drugs and alcohol, or into the arms of flunkies and groupies who will hover round, buoying them up, soothing them into sleep.

For women, or some women—those of us with a rigidly dichotomized sense of our "male" and "female" selves—the problem is particularly acute. Lecturing—"showing off" and exerting authority, assuming one should be listened to—is a traditionally male prerogative (therefore both taboo and infinitely desirable), which we take up with an inevitable conflict: we want to be applauded for our brains, our "masculine" half, but then we fear retribution for having forsaken our femininity. Psychoanalysts, noting the assumed and constructed character of this image, call it the "feminine masquerade." A friend of mine, the psychoanalyst Louise Kaplan, has written interestingly on what she defines as "perversity," seeing the whole charade of exaggeratedly feminine behavior as a mask that both reassures the world and screens earlier longings and conflicts, a woman's desire to identify with her father and compete for male trophies, while needing to appease and identify with the rival, her mother.

I myself always needed reassurance after a lecture—that I was both incisive and *still* a woman—and Andrew gave it to me. He was my audience, my cheerleader, my peer and lover. It was Andrew who held and approved, desired and comforted me—by phone, by his presence, or, if I couldn't see or talk to him, by the continuous sense of him surrounding and justifying me.

I may have needed such reassurance more than most: my father, a confirmed traditionalist, had had narrow ideas on the roles of women. He believed they shouldn't have careers, or pursue higher education, or, in fact, do much of anything for themselves. We had locked horns over my desire to be an actress, but then he became ill, and the struggle, and my sense of self, were frozen in time. Since he died the day after I went to college, it was hard to escape the symbolic weight of the fact that my first steps into the world as an independent woman were forever linked with the last struggling moments of my father's life.

In some way Andrew assuaged this guilt, allowed me to be both mind and body, male and female.

But now we had the Rusk Andrew who was unable to share my —"our"—triumph, or do more than squeeze out a little smile of pleasure when I gave my abbreviated report. He hadn't the energy to feel curiosity, even to listen to details, much less involve himself emotionally in the experience.

"I told you you'd be fine," he said, and that had to satisfy.

Wednesday was Andrew's birthday and the Bentons and Corlisses came by for a birthday cake and ice cream. It was a joyous moment, everyone crowing over Andrew, swapping movie gossip, Andrew beaming.

The panel on Friday, the concluding event of the French week, brought comic relief, which in my experience is the best one can hope for from a panel. Those who plan panels talk in high-flown terms of debate, secretly hoping for fireworks, while the goal of panelists is merely to avert disaster, usually by dissociating themselves from the subject of the panel and their fellow panelists.

Jeanne Moreau had raised this strategy to an art form, as I knew from previous experience. She had upstaged—and been upstaged by —the best of them, and in today's civilized lineup, there would be no contest. Nothing threatening in Alain Resnais, courtly and diffident; Vincent Canby, ironic and self-deprecating; Danielle Thompson, a smart and articulate producer but, like me, not one to hog the mike; and Fred Tuten, our knowledgeable host and a fine writer himself, playing the awestruck yokel. The incomparably gracious Mlle. Moreau simply took over. Before the group of culture vultures, Francophiles, and who knew what drifters in from the street, she might have been in her own living room, so at ease was la Moreau in making the audience feel they were part of her charmed circle. She made it clear, saying she would prefer to have them express their ideas and feelings rather than ask questions of the panel, that this was a democratic forum; we were not there as some sort of elite, to imperialistically impart information to our ignorant subjects; no, we were there to learn from *them*. This was the impulse that I understood—being feminine meant being nonauthoritarian, "reducing" oneself to the same level as one's audience—but artfully twisted into a star turn, in which the rest of the panelists were excluded, as Moreau's fans were treated like preferred houseguests at her Provençal home in a tête-à-tête with the Star-as-Real-Person. The moment one of us on the panel talked for more than thirty seconds, Moreau, in a diversionary maneuver, turned to Vincent, on her right, and began whispering noisily.

Actually, I have a feeling that Moreau picked her panels carefully now: I was probably the only person there to have seen Moreau outclassed. And I mean *outclassed*. It had happened in 1971, in a West Side high-school auditorium, at a panel that I moderated on the occasion of the Second Annual (and as it happened, final) Women's Film Festival. A huge audience of mostly angry women had turned up to see Jeanne Moreau, Arthur Penn, and Warren Beatty, no less, discuss the subject "Where Has Love Gone (in the Movies)?" How had they gotten such an all-star lineup? This was during the brief period when men were feeling defensive and paying their dues to the women's movement (and Beatty, having just released *Shampoo*, had a good deal to feel defensive about). Moreau had come with her film

Lumière. One scheduled panelist, Dyan Cannon, had suddenly discovered she had a "prior beauty parlor appointment," and had withdrawn.

I'd agreed to moderate before I knew who was going to be on the panel, and once I found out, nothing would have induced me to listen to the voice of wisdom and stay home. Every critic who has ever shared a podium with an Artist (a director, a writer, and so on) knows it is a losing proposition: however bad the artist and good the critic, the former wears the wreath of Creativity, the latter the furrowed brow of negativism. When placed alongside the soulful and stumbling artist, even the critic's articulateness is a strike against him. Still, there is some satisfaction in knowing that even the "artiste" must lose ground before the movie star, and a lesser movie star before a greater.

I looked at the audience: women, frizzy-haired, smart, jean jackets, gigantic black bags full of scripts, projects, letters, lunch, their faces tense with a sense of aggrieved purposefulness. I introduced the panel and Warren Beatty leaned over and wiped his aviator spectacles on my jacket. I shrugged it off with a nervous giggle and then, in a misplaced spirit of conscientiousness, Arthur Penn and I launched into the topic, discussing why and how and when romance, as in male-female love stories, had disappeared from the screen. We had talked a few minutes only when Jeanne Moreau broke in.

"I don't want to talk about that. It's too intellectual. I want to talk about *life*," she said. The word *life* burst forth theatrically, and she immediately won the hearts of the crowd, for life was one thing they knew about.

Then, when Beatty's turn came, an astonishing thing happened: without any effort at all, he simply seduced them away from her. As he gazed at the "Women's Libbers" whom he'd come (possibly nudged by sister Shirley MacLaine) to propitiate, he saw a bevy of would-be screenwriters carrying unread and unproduced manuscripts in their carryalls, and records of unreturned phone calls.

Would he placate them, woo them? Not on your life. "I've read some of your screenplays," he said in a brilliant maneuver, "and they're no good. Show me some good ones, and I'll give you names and numbers." Aghast silence, then bedlam. They began talking and shouting, one after the other, one on top of the other, and as I watched, hardly believing my eyes, this raggle-taggle audience of supposed sisters turned into a chorus of careerist Eumenides. Angry epithets came out of their mouths, but their eyes were moist with lust. "I hate you, you gorgeous son-of-a-bitch!" they were saying. The tension mounted, the rest of us were ignored, the air grew thick as pleas and accusations flew, and three hundred women could hardly keep from rushing to the stage en masse and throwing themselves on Beatty in a final orgiastic surge of collective ambivalence. If Emmeline Pankhurst could have seen us now! In fact, there was perhaps no moment more symbolic of the conflicts within the women's movement, and within the breasts of women, than the love-hate spectacle playing itself out that day on the West Side. At one point, a woman, coming retroactively to my defense, said, "I didn't like the way Warren Beatty wiped his glasses on Molly Haskell's jacket," thus not only reminding everyone of my initial humiliation but compounding it with a further one in implying I wasn't able to defend myself. (I got my revenge, the writer's revenge, by reporting the event in *The Village Voice*.)

By now Beatty had them in the palm of his hand, and it took Moreau only a fraction of her famous intuition to know she would never get them back. Taking stock of the situation, she abruptly rose from her seat, made some reference to a previous engagement, and in grand *Comédie Française* style (no low-key *nouvelle vague* here), flung her black cape behind her, stalked off the stage, and strode up the aisle and out of the theater. Beatty the male principle, Animus personified, had come and taken the daughters from Moreau the Earth Mother.

The panel wound down, ended, and then there was a stampede onto the stage as feminists rushed to express their high emotions, give their screenplays and phone numbers to Beatty. Just before the crunch, Beatty leaned over and asked me to have a drink afterward (ah, I thought, the opportunity to get my own back at the legendary womanizer by *resisting* seduction!), and I was about to accept when I looked into the audience and there, forcing his way through the growling horde, was my husband. Andrew had been in Washington at an all-day meeting, but had somehow managed to get back to New York, to the West Side, into the auditorium and up the aisle, as fascinated by Beatty as everyone else, and just in time to prevent my being whisked away and soft-talked into not writing the article that Beatty's shrewd intuition told him I was planning to write. In the final bit of grotesquerie, Andrew, too, became part of the throng, angry women shoving him out of the way as they all surged up the aisle from which Moreau had just made her exit.

Here at City College there was no one to eclipse Moreau and no need for extreme tactics. The pouty mouth, hushed voice, rich with memories of decadence, was enough.

There followed a spirited cocktail and dinner party at the Lotos Club, one of the few "events" of my life these days. Fred Tuten had rounded up some of his artist friends, including Claes and Katia Oldenburg. Old friends Leslie and David Newman, back from a *Superman IV* or V deal-making power trip to London, were there.

Assorted nobs and non-nobs. Most pleasurable of all, it gave me the chance to talk to Resnais's wife, Florence Malraux, one of the world's extraordinary women.

I had met Florence some years before after an interview I'd done with Resnais had appeared in the *Voice*. She'd liked the interview, thought I'd caught her husband as well as anyone ever had, and the more I got to know this woman, the more of a compliment this seemed. Florence was the daughter of France's late and eminent minister of culture, the writer and *philosophe* André Malraux, and like him she had the best qualities of the French intellectual—openness, a gleaming intelligence. Florence, like no other woman I've ever known, gave a sense of *completeness*, of being great of heart and mind without any apparent conflict between the two.

Resnais and Florence were people, to paraphrase Malraux, whose lives were shaped by ideas, yet they took a passionate interest in Americans and things American. Resnais, director of such classics as *Hiroshima mon amour* and *Night and Fog*, was an otherworldly sort, yet was a well-known fan of the New York subway system, comic books, and American hotels.

Florence was a great listener, an active, imaginative one—the sort who made people she talked to feel brighter, more intellectually adventurous, in her presence. She heard not only what you said, but what you had wanted to say and hoped to say. Whenever we saw each other, which was once every four years at most, she remembered exactly where our last conversation had left off, and took up the thread, getting down to essentials right away. Thus it was that I found myself telling her not only of Andrew's illness, but suddenly—had I just thought of it, had she sent out some subliminal suggestion to which I responded?—that I might write a book about it. Her reaction was instantaneous. Of course I should do it, she said, her eyes alight with enthusiasm as if the book were already between us, she was taking it in her hands, eager to read it. I hadn't told anyone, hadn't even formulated the idea, yet there it was, almost as if Florence had thought of it herself, and it was Florence who saw and believed in it before I did. She became my talisman, the affirmative voice within, this woman whom I hardly knew but who, without realizing it, gave me some measure of the strength I would need to counter the taboos which would rise up like dragons in the night. Sometimes all it takes is the words of one person—the right words, the right person—to provide us with a key that opens a door we hadn't even known was there.

Andrew responded listlessly to my reports of the panel and party, but became instantly, almost comically alert when Annie and Catherine walked in one day. We had met Annie's friend Catherine, a willowy blond beauty from Memphis with a sly sense of humor, in the Bahamas when we spent a wonderful, silly week as guests in Annie's rented house. Annie, the catalyst of our lazy Southern group, had hustled us here and there, gotten up tennis games, introduced us to people (within three days she was on first-name terms with everyone on the island, native and tourist), had the locals taking us on their boats, inviting us into their tiny cabins, feeding us strange papaya potions, and telling us sinister island stories.

Annie, the perennial charmer who turned life into a continuous talk show, was a child of the sixties as she went flying fearlessly into new terrain. The less charming side of her enterprising spirit was a ferocious need to control ("I'm a control freak, I know it, I know it," she admitted, as she invaded your life on her terms, or disappeared, leaving you high and dry), and as Catherine, more passive by nature, needed to be cajoled, energized, they were a perfect duo, with Annie cooking up schemes and dragging Catherine into them. In hilarious fashion, Annie would recount her version of their latest scheme, beneath which there might be only a paper-thin wafer of truth. The point of the project—their current one involved getting paintings and artwork from obscure Southern troves and selling the stuff to New York galleries—was never to make money, really, but to furnish Annie with entertaining material. Annie was always going to the latest group-therapy hangouts.

"On my way home from Tennessee, I went to Halcyon Farm" —that's the retreat in North Carolina where you Gestalt your unhappiness away—"and guess who I met. T., the Mafioso boss, you've heard of him! He said he'd do *anything* for me! And Andrew, I met a Greek porno publisher who said he knew you."

Not to be outdone by Annie's performance, Andrew launched into his own comic routine—a wildly funny rundown of a day in the life of Rusk, beginning with the 8:30 morning bell. As patients went careening into the corridor, rushing to get on the elevator, a traffic jam would ensue, a sort of marathon of the handicapped. It was New York gridlock, as wheelchairs collided, wheels got caught in wheels, and everybody (except Andrew, who I hardly need say was watching from a distant and more leisurely perspective) shook their canes at each other like taxi drivers.

I hadn't seen any of this, either because I hadn't wanted to come down or because I hadn't been asked. It had never occurred to me to come, actually, though I discovered that a great many, perhaps most, of the wives would spend the whole morning here, assisting in getting their husbands cleaned and shaved and attending therapy classes. Andrew now issued me an official invitation, and so the day after the election, which Reagan won in a depressing landslide, I paid my first visit to the ambulation room, a kind of mini-gym with an oval track. Round and round they went, pale and spectral, like the condemned in one of the circles of Dante's Inferno, the halting and the infirm, doing laps, with walkers or crutches, their faces strained with effort. Andrew had watched the election on television the night before, and I knew he would be more tired than usual. I sat on the side while he started round, his walker clumping in front of him. It was a shock. Until that moment, I had had no need or desire to face up to the possibility that he might never walk normally again. I hadn't even seen him standing other than when he was balanced between the wheelchair and bed, going from one to the other. He had been just a sick person lying in bed, but now he became one of *them*, the handicapped. The body that had looked rested and normal in bed now looked weak, drawn, helpless. He was trying so hard. He would take a few steps, then look over at me, an eager-for-approval smile on his face, while I would try to smile back before turning away so he wouldn't see the tears streaming down my face. I wanted to run across and take him in my arms. The experience was so wrenching that when, panting, he announced apologetically he could only do two laps instead of his usual three, I breathed a sigh of relief. I couldn't have watched another.

Yet as I rode the bus, I thought how lucky we were: what of the ones who couldn't walk, who couldn't bring their hands to their mouths, who couldn't talk. The halls and exercise rooms were filled with old and middle-aged people who might not walk or work again, and the emphasis was not on recovery but on facing hard facts.

Yet oh, how they tried, the old people, the mute, the incapacitated. The gains were measured not in remarkable improvements but in the tiny movement of a finger, the articulation of a need. In this atmosphere, so lacking in the larger and more dramatic forms of hope, it was a wonder how good the therapists were. Most were young, and might not be around for long. They would come, work their miniature marvels, and move on, into private practice where the pay was better and the progress more noticeable and gratifying.

Whatever rough road we had, at least Andrew had his mind and his speech, unlike other patients around us, and in his room. For some time, in the bed across from Andrew, there had been a lean, handsome man in his late fifties who had suffered a stroke and because of aphasia could say only one thing, "This is the paper."

He used the phrase for everything, desires great and small, commands, complaints, varying the tone not according to actual meaning but because he grew baffled when no one understood. "This is the *paper*," he would say in a loud voice, furious at the blank faces that greeted him; then he would say it again, his voice growing raspy, his face gnarled with frustration.

There were two women visiting him, never at the same time, which gave rise to speculation—later confirmed by one of the nurses—that one was his wife, the other his mistress. He was tall, weatherbeaten, Scandinavian, an extremely attractive man who, rumor had it, was a seafarer. His two women were also striking in different ways. They would come and talk quietly to him, managing, no doubt by some civilized prearrangement, never to overlap. How did they feel, I would wonder, when this once-dashing man would look at them, perhaps with love, perhaps desire, and say, "This is the paper"? What could Rusk's forward-looking philosophy do for them to initiate them into this private language?

And what of all the women in the halls, waiting while their husbands were examined yet again, or walking beside them in their wheelchairs while their heads lolled or their minds wandered? One hears of celebrity cases and inspirational tales. There was the true-life story, dramatized on a television show, of the English conductor who had lost recent memory—he couldn't remember what had been said five minutes previously—but retained all the scores he'd ever memorized and could conduct as beautifully as ever. The wife, with her brisk, brave, best-of-the-British-Empire attitude, was as memorable and inspirational as the husband, but she seems to have been blessed with both supernatural courage and the luck of being greeted, each time she entered her husband's presence, like a long-lost love. He didn't remember he'd seen her only minutes before. But what of wives of lesser mettle; what of wives who didn't feel their husbands' love so strongly? Or whose husbands are beyond communicating it? What of the wife whose husband mistook her for a hat? In Oliver Sacks's charming tale of the musician whose perceptions had gone haywire, we are invited to feel, and do feel, tremendous sympathy for the confused but fanciful man, but what about his wife, the poor woman who traded in her humanity to become an object? He could listen happily to the music of the spheres, but she, who had perhaps lived for him and the music of his words and love, would hear them no more. She would be asked to care for him, while seeking to satisfy her own needs elsewhere, as if emotional needs were college applications that could be sent first to one institution, then another. As if love were eggs in a basket that could be redistributed. And where? Which baskets? Children? Friends? Would they rub her feet at night? Would they listen to some slight that had wounded but would become funny, lighter, in the telling? Would they cushion the endless little blows of life too minor to tell anyone but a husband? Would they be there to consecrate the banalities of life, turn them into little miracles of joy? Or as a sounding board for the exchange of ideas, a reference point for the funny ways in which men and women, this man and this woman, are different? Who would fill the vacuum left by those seeing eyes, those hearing ears, that embracing personality?

What about the women who remembered the way two minds and spirits had interacted when their handsome sea captain had said something more than "This is the paper"? When anger had been furious and reciprocal, not this dead weight, unanswerable. Who, in such a situation, wouldn't prefer memory to reality, the past of the imagination to the future they were being asked to face?

Because there was a serious shortage of nurses, particularly on weekends, families, mostly the distaff side, were roped into service. Everyone up and down the hallways complained bitterly. One woman told me she had to come down every morning at ten to dress and shave her husband and described a situation in which patients were left lying for hours in their beds, unshaved and unattended to. Her daughter, a reporter for *Newsweek*, came with her husband every night and we exchanged stories and compared notes. He was amazed, he said, by the difference in the way nurses treated male and female visitors, with men being deferred to like royalty, their every request answered, while the women were either ignored or expected to fall to and help.

It was clear that there were too many critically ill and incapacitated patients, and not enough staff, trained or otherwise. Yet I was both too tired, and too sure that Andrew would improve on his own, to get overly anxious about the quality of the nursing care. So what if Andrew went without a shave once in a while—he adored the nurses, and they'd made peace with him. There was also the fact that, in different ways, Andrew and I both felt detached from Rusk. Andrew never signed up for any of the group outings or recreational programs, never got to know any of the other inmates, while I kept my distance emotionally, which may be why I felt an occasional edge of resentment from the staff and once outright hostility. I was meeting Andrew's therapist, Peter, for the first time, to discuss the equipment I should buy or rent for Andrew's homecoming. There was a list of about twenty items designed for the handicapped—special chairs, utensils, shower equipment, and railings, railings that were meant to be installed throughout the apartment like a ballet barre. I was appalled, and said so.

"He won't need these things, and I won't buy them."

"If he improves," Peter said crossly, "he can do without the handles for—"

"*If* he improves?"

"I'm not a prophet," he said brusquely. "I can't tell about the future." Prepare for the worst, in other words—this was always the implicit advice of doctors and therapists, a safe philosophy, since it protected them if the worst did indeed occur and freed them from having to speculate on the whole range of intermediate possibilities. But why the edge in his voice? Was it simply that I had asked, or implied, the unanswerable question: Will he get better? How much better?

And perhaps they resented us because more and more we drew our sustenance from being together. Andrew was beginning to hear me, respond to my needs, which in turn lifted me out of my depression and made me come alive. He was receiving visitors, presents. People would come bearing books and saying "Aren't you bored?" not realizing that he hadn't the strength to be bored, the energy to feel curiosity. Not only was he unable to read, it was all he could do to watch a half hour of television a night, and that half hour wasn't even the news but that mélange of showbiz Pablum, *Entertainment Tonight.* The actual attraction of the program, he later confessed, wasn't movie gossip but Mary Hart's legs; the only lechery of which he was capable or which seemed likely to be satisfied was that of looking up host Ms. Hart's very short skirt as her crossed legs took up the whole screen. "Lust is part of my therapy," he explained to nurses and visitors. On a slightly higher plane, I had given him a cassette player, and he would listen for hours to the tapes people brought him. Leslie and David Newman spliced together a tape of great movie songs and music they thought Andrew would like. It started with "Good Morning" from *Singin' in the Rain,* and included *Top Hat, Bandwagon,* Renoir's *French Can-Can,* the Nino Rota theme from 8 ½; Jeanne Moreau singing "Tourbillon" and a good deal of the score from *Jules and Jim;*

Vertigo, and, from *Swing Time* (our favorite Astaire-Rogers musical), "Pick Yourself Up," "Never Gonna Dance," and "Just the Way You Look Tonight" (Andrew's favorite song). Roger Greenspun brought Schubert, Mozart, Liszt, and Joan Morris and William Balcolm doing Jerome Kern, which I stole and replaced with Puccini. I would walk in and there would be Andrew, earphones on, with goose pimples or smiling from ear to ear ("Never Gonna Dance"), tears streaming down his face (*La Bohème; Jules and Jim*), laughing and crying at the same time ("The Way You Look Tonight"). We were so in tune with each other's taste that I could almost tell from his expression what he was listening to.

I had been living so much in the present tense, responding to the incremental leaps forward in Andrew's status and my blind faith in his recovery, denying that the disease would have any residual effects, that I hadn't thought to put friends into the broader picture, or wonder what they might be thinking. As no one dared pose a question directly, it wasn't until people began coming in and making indirect comments that I came to realize what sorts of apprehensions had been circulating.

"He's as sharp as ever," someone would say, unable to keep the surprise out of his voice. Or, after Andrew had made some joke at his, or Rusk's, expense, "What a sense of humor he has." They had all suspected he would be brain-damaged, and I, worrying about his death but not his mind, hadn't thought to reassure them. Now I was surprised by their surprise.

Proof of his mental recovery was that he was now ruminating on his past experience, trying to make sense of it, particularly the hallucinations, which he seemed to remember vividly. In occupational therapy, he finally got hold of a typewriter, and wrote the following sinister account of what he'd felt during a certain period in New York Hospital:

"Molly, in her absence, gave rise to many shadowy conspiracy fantasies. Her sexual infidelity was taken for granted, but with whom and to what purpose? My 'information' was perforce secondhand. . . . I was apparently the last to know. My fellow patients in intensive care had infinitely more knowledge of Molly's notorious affairs than I did. Much of her treachery seemed to be politically motivated. Before my

illness she had cunningly feigned boredom over my long, boring dis-
quisitions on politics and economics."

I don't know what the vocational guidance instructor thought of
this, but it struck me as deeply funny. By a twist of his still paranoid
logic, Andrew had found an ingenious method for explaining a heretofore inexplicable anomaly: my lack of interest in his pronouncements
on economics. I wasn't really bored (how *could* I be!), I was feigning
boredom in order to obtain his insights and relay them to an enemy
agent. The style was Andrew, yet not Andrew. There were remnants
of the crazy Andrew in the stuffy, self-important tone and archaic
locutions—"perforce"—and in the formal distance from which he
regarded his plight. Also, he had conflated two settings: Intensive
Care—where there were no "fellow patients" in the plural, only one
poor dying woman with whom he never spoke—and his previous stay
on the neurology floor where the hallucinations started.

He continued: "But the minute I was incapacitated, she began
hobnobbing with political luminaries. The question of whom among
our mutual friends I could trust to tell me the truth began to perplex
me. No one ever came forward to tell me anything helpful. Even the
illness itself was the product of a conspiracy. I had been in the way,
and a great number of people had combined to give me a fever by
slipping worms into my brain. My bloodstream was repeatedly infected.

"My past had been repeatedly embellished with bizarre involve-
ments. I had been an airline pilot in Canada."

This has a startling ring now, as it foreshadowed the report, several
years later, that a promiscuous AIDS-infected Canadian steward had
transmitted AIDS from the Caribbean to California whence it had
spread throughout the United States.

"Frank Sinatra, Greta Garbo, garbled stories about Molly's affairs.
The Foley tube may have been source of nightmares about my having
been castrated, not once but twice. That castration and decapitation
figured so prominently in my hallucinations expresses in a narrative
form what was happening to my body from some unknown virus.
Indeed, my hallucinations were a way of making sense out of this
otherwise senseless catastrophe."

We were both coming to theorize that, indeed, his hallucinations
had formed a sort of protective cover, shielding him from the true

horrors of his medical situation. If he had known that all around him family and friends were baffled, sick with worry, he might have died from fear himself.

We were too close to events to have gained any real perspective on the horrors, or to see whether the changes we both felt were permanent or temporary. Was this one of those cataclysms that alters the map of one's life, or simply a tornado that had dashed us to the ground, picked us up, and was about to deposit us on a distant shore in the direction we were already traveling? There was no doubt that Andrew was "altered." Gone was the look of wariness, gone the dark circles under his eyes. He seemed genuinely transformed by the generosity that had come his way, could still hardly believe the expressions of love and hope, the devotion of his nurses, the visits and presents and calls of friends. Several people had told us that, thanks to a friend's request, the Madison Avenue Presbyterian Church had included Andrew's name among those for whom prayers were given at the end of the service.

"I didn't know I had so many friends," said he, the face of a once-melancholy grouch and disbeliever wreathed in serenity. Like certain unusual physical changes—his hair having gone from curly to silky and straight, for example—some of the kinks in his psyche appeared to have smoothed themselves out. Would such a miracle be so unthinkable: that the simple and astonishing fact of his survival, in addition to the endless manifestations of love and support, had exorcised his old paranoia once and for all? But would it last?

9

The holiday season was coming up, those thirty-odd days between Thanksgiving and Christmas that were a horror to be gotten through, a time in which religion had been routed by the gods of commerce, who in turn had prolonged the season unbearably. The short days and the long hours leading up to Christmas were an emotional minefield, a time of suicides, sadness, dread, when even those of sound mind and healthy body became unhinged. For me, it was a time when loss came suddenly and in spasms, and memories of a perfect childhood hung over me like mistletoe just out of reach—too bright for the present to compete with, too bright to have been quite real. Andrew and I had always tried to get through Christmas by ignoring it. Now at least there was a compelling distraction: Andrew's illness and simply being at Rusk took both of us away from the seasonal rites, from shopping, parties, the thirty-day hangover.

And there were projects. After Thanksgiving, we had two "trial runs" planned for Andrew (a "furlough" day at home, and an outing at the movies), so to get some rest in advance, I went down to visit Mother in Florida.

To me, Florida was the past, my childhood when the family was all together, my father off from work, Chevey and I taking an extra week from school (he had bad ears and needed the tropical air). Sometimes we'd come by train and rent a car, more often we'd drive down from Richmond, stopping along the way. There were no motel chains then, no interchangeable Holiday-Howard-Ramada inns, so off the road we would go to some little hotel, a step above a rooming house, with a fire escape across the front and a front porch where people sat in rocking chairs in the early March sun. And a good restaurant, which was the most important thing.

"Your father is a *gourmet*," Mother would say, half proudly, half ironically, suddenly making palpable the culture and language I was struggling with in school and that would become so important to me. My father, Southern-sybaritic when it came to food, could always sniff out the great eating places, where there would be homemade biscuits or hushpuppies, fried oysters or specially cured ham or sausage spiced just right. Rich fat greasy wonderful Southern food that was better for the soul than the blood count.

I loved the moment when we left I-95 and went east, over to the coastal route, A1A, at Vero Beach, and it suddenly became Southern Florida. It was magical: the first fat coconut palms, the smell of the sea, the exotic flowers—bougainvillea, sea grape, hibiscus, oleander —it was another country, the country of eternal summer. You stripped off sweaters, sniffed, smiled, stretched. We'd drive on down the coastline to wherever we were staying that year, usually an efficiency apartment at some modest motel on the other, nonocean side of A1A, with a sandy little passage through the dunes to the beach. To the ocean.

And that was where I would head early the next morning, as excited as a child at Christmas, pulling everyone with me, in order to plunge into the ocean with my father. I think there is in all of us a single childhood memory that colors the rest of our lives. Perhaps it is a whole period of life squeezed into an image, perhaps an event repeated only once or twice but remembered as happening over and over again, casting a spell of enchantment, even a prison of enchantment, over one's whole life. Mine was learning to swim in my father's arms. How old was I? Three, four, five, seven? Nine? Surely I was very young—I took to the ocean at once and loved swimming—yet in my memory, it seems to have gone on over a period of time, at one beach or another, one summer, or one spring vacation; up and down the Eastern Seaboard—Fort Lauderdale, Delray, Gulfstream, Daytona, Wrightsville, Virginia Beach, Cape May, all flowing together in one ecstatic moment. Having been told to play by myself, I would do so for as long as I could stand it—looking for shells, drawing in the sand, glancing longingly at the grown-ups. Finally—my bathing suit would have just begun to dry from the last swim, the water to have turned to salt on my skin—I would dash up the beach to where he was sitting on a towel alongside Mother, and whatever other aunts and uncles were gathered, grab his hand, he pretending to resist, drag him into the ocean; then he would lift me, float me into the waves. He would extend his arms in a wide circle around but away from my body, while I would spew and struggle, dog-paddle and grab on, free within our little harbor to develop my strokes and confidence. He would leave an escape hatch, releasing me into the open sea when I was ready. I would launch forth like a porpoise, then I would let a wave throw me back into his arms. Going and returning, going and returning, I could never get enough of it, moving away, exhilarated by my freedom, then giggling and sputtering back into his arms. I was a good swimmer, but did I delay the process by which I would be on my own, independent of his arms; and did he unconsciously collude in prolonging it? That exquisite balancing act of ambivalence: I longing to go free, yet pulled irresistibly back into the magic circle; he delighted at my independence, yet sensing that with each stroke I was moving farther away, away from needing and adoring him absolutely. In the gaze between a father and daughter there are strings attached, soft as silk and as strong as steel wire, and every moment of happiness weaves them tighter and tighter. He grins at me, I at him, the ocean shoving and pushing us together and apart, spewing foam like laughter. How can I not want to prolong that moment . . . and seek its equivalent ever after?

Now I walked on the beach, and saw a little girl and her father at the water's edge. She held his hand—this man who looked so young and vulnerable to me, so old and powerful to her—gazed into his eyes and jumped up and down, screaming with the anticipation whose shrillness I recognized. And I knew, from the light in the father's eyes as he swung her into the air and into the ocean—this very ordinary man made suddenly godlike—how my father had loved that moment almost as much as I did, and had felt an unconscious reluctance to have it end.

Even now I'll be swimming in the ocean, leaping in giant waves, proud of my fearlessness, and I'll suddenly feel that just beyond the horizon, just out of sight are my father's arms. He is somewhere in the clouds, looking down and calling me "Squeedunk." I am no bigger than a goldfish in a goldfish bowl, and he is breathing fearlessness into me.

Andrew had done the same. I seemed to be free, acting under my own power, but wasn't I still swimming within the wide circle of his arms?

I talked to Andrew on the phone: he made reassuring noises, but I couldn't trust the sound of his voice, the report he gave. At every turn, life would seem to be returning to normal, and then some crisis would occur. I was scared to put my foot down heavily, with my full weight on it. It was like walking on the beach when a northwester had eroded the sand and brought rocks from the old highway, once buried three or four feet under, closer to the surface. I'd be walking along at the water's edge, not paying attention, and suddenly hit something sharp, stub my toe on that camouflaged rock. It was like that with Andrew, only I never had the luxury of being absentminded. I was always on guard.

Sure enough, the day after I got back, his temperature suddenly shot up to 104°. I had talked to Dr. Gaines, Andrew's surgeon at New York Hospital, before I left, and we were going ahead with plans for him to go back in a month, on January 5, for the final surgery, the closure (in effect, the removal) of the colostomy.

Without Andrew to guide and support me, I found myself reaching out more and more to my female friends. Ever since adolescence, I'd always had good friends, many of them, but without quite realizing when it had happened, or why, Andrew had come to play not only the central role of husband/lover but that of confidant, "best friend," as well. I talked to him about everything—or rather, it seemed like everything because I'd simply eliminated or forgotten a whole area of my life, shied away from those depths and shallows that one shares only with female friends. What had happened?

A subtle disillusionment with the promise of the women's movement, perhaps? A realization of the competitiveness that lay beneath our proud claims of solidarity? The seventies, when we were riding the crest of feminism, had been a grand, if somewhat unreal, moment in history. To borrow from Wordsworth, in his eulogy to himself and his fellow Romantics in the aftermath of the French Revolution, "Bliss was it in that dawn to be alive." Hope was everywhere, contagious as spring fever; barriers were crumbling. We met in twos, threes, groups, talked feverishly, explored our history, saw and examined films and books in radical new ways. There was no line between writing and reading: we were all published or about to be, all bursting with ideas that were finding their way into print, and we read each other's books, articles, generously and excitedly. We were rejecting the past, rejecting being circumscribed, rejecting the ways of our mothers. It was as if an entire landlocked race had climbed up a cliff and seen the vast wide sea for the first time. Women marched; I wrote. I came out with a book on the image of women in film, and when I lectured at colleges and universities the spirit was tremendous. The feminist and counterculture fever was at its peak. *Everybody* was turned on, angry and exhilarated by turns. Sometimes it got uncomfortable—too angry, militant, uncivil—ideologues propelled more by hate than by curiosity, but it was a pre-eighties anger, before the counterreaction had set in.

Everything was possible. Even complete and total trust among women. It seemed, at first, like a glorious reliving of the camaraderie of adolescence, but on a higher plane.

As a teenager, my freest and most liberated moments were with my girlfriends. This was the era, the mid-fifties, when as teenagers we were separating from the mainland and forming our own culture, with music, cars, jokes that were by definition unintelligible to adults. We were loose, full of laughter, at ease with each other, cruising around town in Babs's secondhand Chevy, listening to Elvis, buying bagfuls of hot doughnuts from the drive-in Dunkin' Donut, making jokes, planning ridiculous escapades to ambush boys in "accidental" encounters which were never as much fun as the planning before and the hilarity afterward, in which our laughing was orgasmic, nonstop. Boys and food were the pretext. No stand-up comic was ever as funny as we, as cruel and generous, warm and aggressive, as happy. Our rivalries were real enough: we stole boyfriends from each other every two weeks, but no boy ever broke up a friendship. Girlfriends were real, underlying and abiding; boys came and went. There was a manic quality to our tribal rites, our sleep-overs, our hilarity—or there was for me. The more time I spent with my friends, the less time I spent at home, where my father was slowly dying, and where my mother was bearing up stoically, perhaps needing me to stand by, behave well, be there for her in ways I could never quite measure up to.

Unlike the girls a year ahead of us, who at thirteen or fourteen were already acting like ladies, disgustingly mature, our group was fiercely tomboyish, forestalling the day when we would have to wear makeup, a bra, lying about the arrival of menarche. The careless intensity of our bond was based on an awakening to boys that was not yet a surrender. I knew nothing would ever equal it again, I would never laugh with quite such unguarded gusto, yet there was, in the early days of the women's movement, a camaraderie that came close to catching that rarity, a uniquely female esprit de corps. But then the drive for self-realization seemed to consume all our energy. Instead of closing off competition, the women's movement had simply opened up new areas in which rivalry could grow and flourish, had upped the ante. Men were no longer the battleground, marriage the arena in which we turned in our assets for a husband who would provide security for life. In some ways feminism had acted the part of Hades, dividing mother and daughter. Now the pressure was on to achieve, and the attendant insecurity: we hadn't *time* for each other. We turned our backs on the traditional roles of our mothers and suddenly found ourselves feeling high and dry, cut off at the roots, since without meaning to, we'd rejected a huge portion of our identity as well. We were "too busy" for each other and we were edgy; our relations, like our lives, were going up and down like an overactive stock market.

Rather than risk the fallout of competition and envy, I retreated into my cocoon with Andrew.

For me, the eighties had brought a sadder and wiser appreciation of the difficult road to independence, of the inner as well as outer obstacles. There was a sense of getting our bearings anew, of seeking the lost continuity between mother and daughter, if not in our real mothers, who were often far away, at least in our female friends. I eagerly sought them out now, needing the grounding that their companionship gave me because I had become frightened by the degree to which my moods, my very sense of self, depended on Andrew. I had dinner with two writer friends, Kay Larson, art critic for New York magazine, and Francine Gray, the essayist and novelist. Our husbands had all been in peril that summer; we commiserated, discussed our fears, and from there launched into more private matters, talked of writing struggles, and then one of us told of an old childhood wound, evoking anger and bitterness, and that gift of self-revelation became a catalyst, drawing the other two in, exchanging similar stories (glimpses of the separations, the spiritual dissonances, that had driven us to become writers in the first place), until our conversation became a river of confession and empathy that left us feeling cleansed of resentment, and closer to each other than we'd ever been.

Overwhelmed by paperwork and plagued by nightmares, I told someone I was desperate, but didn't know whether I needed an accountant or a psychiatrist. Along with all the staggering and numerous medical bills, there were the routine monthly bills: how *many* there were! Andrew had always paid them, and I'd had no idea how much work was involved. Still, there was a certain momentum to our lives now; each day contained some new plan or sign of progress. On Friday, November 30, I walked with Andrew—now on crutches—down the hall, and for the first time he was able to put one leg in front of the other instead of moving one, then bringing the other up alongside it for balance. They moved differently, though; the right moved naturally forward, while the left was like a prosthetic limb—Andrew swung his hip out and around in an applied motion.

December 15 was the day of the furlough, and it was a triumph in the sense that nothing went awry: we got taxis, Andrew's colostomy behaved itself, and as a dry run for the future, it allowed us a moment of communal joy while showing us that it would be a very long time before life returned to normal. Andrew, exhausted by the effort and tension, collapsed on the living-room sofa as soon as he walked in, and never got up. I rested in the bedroom, listened to tapes, and relished the sense of his presence in the apartment. It had been twenty-four weeks exactly since I had guided him, stumbling and delirious, over the threshold and on to New York Hospital. But I felt all the lonelier after his return to Rusk.

On the following Saturday we had our most triumphant and

carefully planned outing: Andrew's first movie, and lunch at a hamburger joint in the neighborhood. We had been anxious about the weather, but it was a lovely warm day in the high fifties, and we were nervous and exhilarated negotiating the two crosstown blocks, Andrew in his wheelchair, to the Trans-Lux 34th Street, to see *The Cotton Club*, Francis Coppola's new movie about the famed Harlem night spot. We entered the theater and took an elevator up to the mezzanine, where we sat in the back, I in the aisle seat, Andrew beside me in his wheelchair. Coppola's homage to the heyday of Harlem nightclubs wasn't a classic, wasn't even one of his best, but it was good enough, and in terms beyond the aesthetic ones, it was certainly the most glorious moviegoing experience of Andrew's career. It represented the return to life in the dark that to Andrew was light; it meant puzzling out the idiosyncrasies of casting, of style, it meant penetrating the obsessions that pushed Coppola closer and closer to the edge of self-destruction. Entering the dark of a movie theater was for Andrew like pushing aside the stone of the grave and emerging into daylight. He sat there rapt, the illness forgotten, the colostomy forgotten.

Afterward we went to Mumbles, a pub around the corner that welcomed diners in wheelchairs, and though Andrew had never been one to get excited about food, when he sank his teeth into that first cheeseburger, an expression came to his face that was no less ecstatic than his smile while watching the movie.

"Nothing ever tasted so good!" he said. He was a child eating his first banana split, he was an ex-con having his first meal on the outside. It was the context that made it so delicious, the headiness of freedom and choice. The exquisite ordinariness of it. Even if Rusk could have produced an identical cheeseburger—unlikely on the face of it—it wouldn't have tasted the same.

Not long after, Andrew wrote his first movie column, another marker of his reentry into the world. The *Voice*, which had been tremendously supportive through the whole ordeal, not only financially but with visits, calls, flowers from editors, had been printing regular notices of his illness and progress to answer the huge number of letters and queries they were getting from his fans. Now finally, he was appearing in print. He had caught a rerun on television of *Bedtime for Bonzo* and wrote a witty appreciation of our new president as the natural and charming actor he would prove to be in the White House. He concluded the piece: "In the end, Bonzo's trainer has made monkeys of us all."

His mind was clear now, but he could remember very little of what had happened. He had no memory of my taking him to Sam's office that Wednesday in June or of going into the hospital early that Saturday morning, though he could remember some of the more lurid episodes of what came after—the medical-history questions about his sexual activities, mistreatment by the nurses, the day he hit his mother.

On Christmas Eve I spent the day hunched over my typewriter trying to finish two writing assignments, but that night we had a surprise feast from *The Village Voice*: a basket of pâté, wonderful breads, marinated vegetables, lace cookies, and champagne. The next day, we were going to celebrate with Themis—a car would bring her in for lunch, then take her home. She had been getting along reasonably well. Her legs were too weak, and perhaps her spirit too tired, for her to make the trip in to see Andrew, but they were in touch daily by phone. As long as she could hear his voice, nothing else mattered. I looked forward to seeing her, and to stopping off and making some of the social rounds Andrew and I usually made together.

My first stop, before going to Rusk, was at the Hamiltons', the only "family" I had in New York. Jeanne was my oldest friend in the city. Her mother, whom I had christened "Mother Bounds" when she used to bake pies and cookies for me, take me on trips, was up for the holiday. Jeanne, with her brood of four and her handsome four-square Wall Street husband, was like someone from another era. We'd gone through twelve years of school together and three of college, and among our mutual friends and fellow alumnae, spread throughout the South with their 1.8 children and some form of job or money-making project, this woman, who was so happily devoted to her children (three of whom she'd had at ages thirty-nine, forty-one, and forty-three respectively), was the one to whom people pointed in amazement, as they'd have pointed to Amelia Earhart or Margaret Bourke-White in earlier decades. This was no Earth Mother. She was an ace mathematician, and IBM had begged her to stay on, but Jeanne, who'd been an only child, wanted children, as many as she could have and she went through miscarriages, fertility drugs, surgical procedures, to get them.

She was of the old school, a selfless volunteer, who devoted herself energetically to charitable and neighborhood causes, but I suspected she was never happier than when she was sitting on a stool in her kitchen, making peanut butter and jelly sandwiches, surrounded by the din and clamor and love of children. And children's friends. To me, her apartment was a foreign country, a nursery rhyme, with Jeanne as an eternally young Mother Hubbard. Ross junior, Jeanne's oldest, was my godchild, and Jeanne, who went as far back as anyone except family, was all I had of the past in New York. We had taken different roads—though our both leaving Richmond was a bond we never discussed but knew was powerful—yet she and I remained close in the way that only relatives are. She was the one, for instance, whom I would have called at three in the morning in an emergency, she was the one to whom I never had to explain anything, because our mutual acceptance was irrevocable and made explanations unnecessary. She knew my family and my past firsthand, I hers; indeed, my family was part of her past, hers of mine.

Hearing the din of Christmas outside the door, I entered and submerged myself in the free-for-all, embraced everybody, bathed in the Yuletide spirit and the glow of happy bodies, and left, with a pang of longing. It wasn't precisely children I yearned for; I didn't envy Jeanne's life. What I envied, I think, was the simplicity of her nature and her being in the world, what appeared to be the undividedness of her spirit.

At the other end of the spectrum, and the day, was Harriet Coleman. Harriet was another old Southern friend, a sort of intellectual role model at one time, who had come apart at the seams, and who I couldn't think of without pangs of guilt. Which is how I found myself trudging to her open house after having had lunch (turkey in the Rusk cafeteria) with Themis and Andrew.

Such were the paradoxes of Christmas day, and of women: Jeanne, the mother by vocation, light of heart; Harriet, the "liberated" woman, beaten by life. It was after dark by now, and I was beginning to feel ill. I'd been overeating for a week—the usual Christmas binge to which I was prone—plus the stress of meeting deadlines, and of getting through this particular Christmas. There were parties I'd rather have gone to—Judy Rossner's annual bash on the West Side and Patti

Bosworth's on the Upper East Side—but out of a sense of duty, or perhaps not having the energy to be "on" for my more with-it friends, it was to Harriet's that my reluctant feet led me.

Small, intellectual, and interesting-looking in the manner of a librarian or a Victorian diarist, Harriet was unlike any other Southern woman I'd known, an idol whose "escape" to New York and the literary world had blazed a trail that I had followed. She was three or four years older than I and was writing a novel and working as a magazine editor when I came to the city. She gave me job-hunting advice, coached me on interviews, introduced me to single men, invited me to her parties. She was an example of just how brilliant, and *different*, a Southern woman could be.

But gradually it seemed that our interests, or maybe it was just our emphases, diverged. She became more and more obsessed with men and marriage, and less and less interested in literary pursuits.

Her cocktail parties, which she presided over like a dance mistress, took on a utilitarian aspect. If one or more of us women friends arrived before a quorum of men had been reached, Harriet would hustle us into the adjoining bedroom and ask us to remain there until she gave the signal to come out. We would look at each other in astonishment, and giggle. She was Scarlett O'Hara at Twelve Oaks, she was Blanche DuBois, trying to keep up the fiction of gracious days, of gentlemen and ladies in equal numbers, courting, mating, marrying.

Up to this point, Harriet's voice—the voice of big sister, the voice of reason—had been hard to resist. But at a certain point, Harriet's conversation began to slip away from its commonsense moorings. One moment she was talking about prospective husbands (even that should have been a clue) and equal relationships, the next of wanting to marry a well-heeled Wall Street executive whom she could treat like a king, and before I knew it, she was in Bellevue. Her friends all visited her, gathered around, and we were relieved that they had "stabilized" her condition with lithium. But she came out speaking in that flat, un-inflected voice of the lobotomized, without affect.

Was it the strain of trying to be a writer, and feeling guilt over same? Were Southern women so different from the seventeenth-century women who were constrained by "modestie"—an all-important and embracing concept—from unseemly behavior, of which writing might be considered the most unseemly? Wasn't writing an act so selfishly indecorous, so contrary to the social rule of living through and for others, that to attempt it, even to want it, was to risk either losing society or losing one's mind! When she lost her balance, there were indubitably other genetic factors—an enzyme or chemical imbalance—but it was impossible not to feel that some cautionary tale was being enacted in this chilling drama. My determination to visit her, to "stick by her," faded before the horror of this flattened-out and unreal person. I felt the horror even of her "strength"—the legendary strength of the Southern woman—which, instead of serving to overcome the madness, supports it, gives the delusions their steely resolve.

I hadn't seen Harriet since the Bellevue episode, and, half zonked out myself, I was in a state of voluntary numbness, a sort of novocaine daze, when I walked in. There was suspiciously little noise as I got off the elevator, though it was well into the appointed hour for the party, and there were only four or five coats on the rented rack in the hall. When I walked in, there were about twelve people staggered around in Harriet's lovely, high-ceilinged living room. I thought there must be Christmas parties all over New York that were filled, bursting at the seams because other parties like this one were empty. I wanted to put out a public casting call, get bodies from Judy's and Patti's and bring them here. I didn't see Harriet when I first walked in, but spotted Gerald, Harriet's first cousin, whose arrival in New York the party was meant to celebrate. Gerald looked like Harriet's twin. He was short, with the same freckles and high forehead, the same intelligent look. But where Harriet turned practical, Gerald, a medievalist and poet, turned dreamy.

He was divorced, out of a job, and, like Harriet, on medication. If the more benign, antebellum Old South still existed, or even the ante-inflation Old South, Gerald and Harriet would have found refuge in one family or another, would have lived with relatives and tended the children and been looked upon as "a little different," two sweet people living "in their own world." But the South could no longer take care of its eccentrics, its addled darlings, and certainly there was no place in New York for Harriet's and Gerald's dreams. Instead, Harriet and Gerald were tethered, rather precariously, to doctors, medications, hospitals, and each other. Harriet's ambitions were now centered on Gerald. She would sit with him by the fireplace, bring him his slippers at night, help him with his "job" interviews . . . and launch him socially.

Gerald and I embraced. He was in conversation with two rather large and well-built German women whose sexual availability did not, I suspect, extend to the impecunious and otherworldly Gerald.

"I was just telling these ladies," he said, after welcoming me like an old friend, "that I became psychopathic when I went off lithium."

"I don't like to use labels," one woman announced, and walked away. I looked for Harriet. She was standing by the food table wearing a blue and white dirndl affair, her eyes glittering. We greeted each other warmly, safely bound by the rules of the Christmas party, according to which private and personal woes remained unspoken, time stood still, nothing had changed. She wasn't as blank as she'd been when she got out of Bellevue, but there was a hollowness in the merry act: there had been too many parties and too few results. She was playing Scarlett O'Hara on automatic pilot. Her large old Duncan Phyfe table was laden with silver platters and substantial food—a ham, a turkey—but there was something strangely impersonal and un-Southern about it. The slabs of rye and pumpernickel bread, the sprigs of parsley, the bowls of mayonnaise and mustard, had all come from a delicatessen. The few people who were here had either already eaten or were saving up for the following party, for the food was still pristine and untouched. In the middle of a table was a huge, antique-silver punch bowl, obviously destined for eggnog . . . with no eggnog in it. I drank some wine, made conversation with Harriet—or rather listened as she outlined her plans for Gerald and herself—and then began planning my getaway.

For Harriet, now completely enclosed in her fantasy world, the madwoman in the closet of Southern feminism, was relatively safe. It was those of us on the outside who were still in danger.

When I left, I felt weariness overwhelm me like a dead weight. It had all finally caught up with me, the anxiety of Christmas and the self-loathing of overeating, doing revisions on my movie column, never-ending thoughts of Andrew in general and the encounter with

Harriet in particular. I dragged myself through the next day and then, coming home on the bus from Rusk, I felt it: the pain. The unmistakable abdominal pain, constant and hard, of an obstruction. I tried to convince myself that my stomach was distended from overeating, but I knew the symptoms too well by now.

This would be an obstruction from adhesions from the surgery of February 1982.

I had often thought, during Andrew's illness, that with all the stress, I might be likely to have some recurrence while he was in the hospital. But as so often happens, you manage to hold yourself together (or your body manages to hold out) during the critical period, and then as soon as you've reached a safe shore, the collapse occurs. The collapse that was wanting to happen, destined to happen.

The pain grew—to about a 7.5 on my Richter scale of 0 to 10 and stayed there, on the outer edge of bearability. Nothing was going through. I knew it wouldn't go away, and that it was an emergency. I called Sam's number at about 11:00 P.M. A covering doctor returned my call—Sam was on vacation in the Caribbean for a week—who advised me to take aspirin and see how it went. As the world's reigning expert on my own abdomen, I knew enough to ignore this advice (one doesn't take pain-killers, which mask the pain and inhibit the bowels), and decided to stick it out for the night. Pain took over my body and occluded my brain, allowing in only a fleeting and macabre pleasure in the irony of the situation, and in the morning I called Dr. Gaines. About noon of the following day, I found myself back in New York Hospital, in a bed on the orthopedic floor, waiting to find out whether I would have to have surgery or not.

10

Surgeons must be very careful
When they take the knife!
Underneath their fine incisions
Stirs the Culprit,—Life!
  —EMILY DICKINSON

On the day after Christmas, there I was lying belly up in New York Hospital, with an intestinal blockage, tubes in various orifices, waiting to see if I would have to have surgery. There is an expression that medical students learn (or that you learn as a patient if you've been this way a few times) a holdover from the pre-antibiotic era, but still taught: "The sun never sets on a small bowel obstruction," meaning that if surgery is not performed within twenty-four hours, perforation is certain and with it gangrene and peritonitis . . . and possibly death. This is not true. A nasogastric tube—popularly known as the NG—to draw off all liquids going into the intestine, is inserted immediately, and if the obstruction is partial rather than total, the kink can unkink without surgery.

Thus it was that for the next few days my entire universe would revolve around the single question of THE KINK and whether or not the knife would be necessary. I was writhing in pain and nausea, hardly aware of my fellow patients in slings and braces (I had been housed on the orthopedic floor until a bed on F7 became available), yet I was not entirely unhappy. For one blissful moment, I was no longer worried about Andrew, but was being worried about. It wasn't the Caribbean, but it was a reprieve. For at least ten days, I wouldn't have to cope with bills, screenings, nurses, Andrew; I would be a mound of immobilized flesh. Conflicts and problems receded and my mind bent compassionately toward my swollen abdomen, my baby of anguish. It wasn't so much a love of pain itself, as a sense that pain absolved me of some unnameable inner guilt or anguish. A self-justification: I defined myself by the amount of pain I could tolerate. I'd even prolonged the distress by waiting until morning to call Gaines and hadn't given him any sense of the urgency of the matter, so that it wasn't until seventeen hours after the onset of pain that I was installed in a hospital bed. It seemed quite natural that I should have an obstruction now, that I should wait until Andrew was out of the woods, then fall apart, and this was my physical vulnerability the way others had migraines or back problems. Nor was I prepared to examine my life too closely, perceive the fact that my stoicism masked a complete dissociation from my body that was itself part of the problem. When I finally called Andrew, he was devastated, as I knew he would be, taking all the guilt upon himself. There was a ghostly feeling that our illnesses were interconnected and that we were in the grip of some toxic emotional process we didn't understand.

I insisted it was just my turn to collapse, and indeed, I would have been completely at peace had it not been for one thing—the NG tube, my nemesis. Hospitals have to find ways to discourage potential malingerers, and the NG tube is a torture device that was invented for me. Some hapless person, usually the intern on duty, has the task of shoving this stiff plastic device through your nose, then pushing it gently but firmly (you gagging all the while) down through the throat and into the stomach. Peristaltic action takes it into the intestines, where it lodges, drawing the juices out of the gastric system and into a suction cup attached to the bed. It is used during and after abdominal surgery and for gastrointestinal problems, and it stays in until the bowels resume functioning. There are a great many people who either aren't bothered by the tube, or who, having happy-go-lucky intestines, get it out in several days (President Reagan, of course, was one of the latter; when he had colon surgery, whose progress I followed with great interest, his NG tube came out in three days). For me, a "long tuber" (Sam's expression), the agony began after twenty-four hours and grew worse day by day. First, there would be a burning sensation in the throat; then the inflammation would produce saliva, until after two or three days, I was spewing constantly, couldn't have a phone conversation, could barely sleep or think. For me, the pain of abdominal surgery, which could at least be dulled by morphine, was small potatoes compared to this bane of my hospitalization. Because inserting the thing was excruciating for both doctor and patient, the team of resident and interns responsible would refuse to pull it out until the last possible moment.

Like so many procedures, the tube had always struck me as one of those unalterable facts of medical life, until a doctor friend, a psychiatrist, who'd had multiple surgeries like mine, assured me that it would be the simplest matter in the world to design a more flexible tube but there's no incentive. Few doctors have ever endured the agonies of the NG tube; if the patient has to keep it in longer than is absolutely necessary, what do they care? It would take another tube or two for me to realize that I could pull it out on my own when it became unbearable, when I realized that reinserting it was nothing compared to the continued misery of having it in, and that even if reinsertion was required, a few hours of relief were easily worth the consequences. Besides, by now I could sense when the D day of passing gas (i.e., peristaltic movement) was approaching, and so I would wait until the middle of the night when no one was around and pull it out. I never had to have it reinserted.

At the moment, though, I was only in Day One, with many hours of the tube to go, whether I had surgery or not.

The second day they moved me to F7—Gaines's floor, Andrew's old floor—and there was a rueful reunion with all my old nursing friends, Moira, the two Jeans, Evelyn, Jill, Rita, and Mary, the head of nursing. By the third day, Gaines still wasn't convinced the problem was going to resolve itself without surgery, and, most troubling, he felt that even if it did, the kink was there and would cause complications at some later date and require surgery.

Mother came up once again, to field calls, to be there for me when I came home, and Andrew said he'd try and get one of the Rusk nurses to bring him up over the weekend. On Saturday, I looked up and there in the doorway, with this gorgeous redhead standing beside his wheelchair, was Andrew, with a silly smile on his face. The smile turned to tears. For a long time we just looked at each other, a look of love, but also of horror. What were we doing to each other? Had our mutual embeddedness made us turn on ourselves like an autoimmune disease? Were we secreting "occult infections" instead of releasing this energy into the world where it might have done some good? Of was it something that only came into being between us, and from which there was no escape? Were we perhaps too resigned to our fates? Too ironic?

After all, however statistically improbable our situation, there were illnesses all around us that were worse.

New Year's Eve, 1984: In the bed next to mine, an old woman named Pauline was dying of brain cancer and burns, and screamed all night. The cries, furious and angry at first, gradually smoothed out into a continuous low wail, a narcotic, a lullaby to herself. Across from her, a Yugoslav woman who spoke no English, and had been given sleeping medication instead of the pain-killer she'd asked for, snored in great sheets of noise, like Niagara Falls. In the fourth bed, a German woman with a hip fracture urinated in such quantities that the nurses had to find larger and larger pots, and she groaned with a variety and timbre of noises not to be found on the human vocal chart. The dying Pauline couldn't talk, eat, recognize anyone, would go rigid when the nurses tried to dress her, yet they paid her such tender and constant attention. Rita, the beautiful Trinidadian nurse, crooned to her, saying, "Pauline, Pauline," and to the Yugoslav woman, she would say, "You going to walk again. You just tell your legs. You the boss. You the boss."

On Tuesday, New Year's Day, I finally got the tube out. There would be no surgery this time around. Sam came in that night, gave me a hug, apologized for not having been there, and we discussed Andrew's next move. To my dismay, he said the closing of the colostomy would be more of a major operation than they'd originally thought, largely because the wound had taken longer to heal.

"Well, 1985 has to be better," my friends said, but Andrew and

I both felt, without even saying anything, that destiny hadn't finished with us yet. We were part of some giant cosmic joke and there were plenty of shaggy-dog digressions before the punch line.

Actually, I was lying low as far as friends were concerned, hoping no one would find out. I was downright embarrassed by all the trouble we'd caused. Together, Andrew and I were like the character in *Li'l Abner* who walks around with a dark cloud over his head, and everyone scurries when they see him coming for fear the storm will burst on them. Eventually, people would just stop calling, afraid of some new Sarris calamity. In fact, nothing in my wildest imagination could have prepared me for the grotesque turn of events to follow.

On Wednesday morning, I was having my first "food," the liquid breakfast of broth and Jell-O that tastes unreasonably good after seven days of fasting, when Mother phoned. She'd just had a call from a woman who lived in Themis's apartment building: Themis had fallen during the night, presumably of a stroke, had hit her head, and was lying on the floor, barely conscious.

I couldn't believe it. My voice tinged with hysteria, I called Sam who, hardly believing it himself, dispatched an ambulance to Kew Gardens. Within three hours Themis was at New York Hospital, installed in a room on the neurology floor, the very floor—perhaps the very room—where Andrew had been admitted on June 30, 1984. It seemed she had not suffered a stroke, but at the end of several days and various examinations and history-takings, all anyone could say was that her legs had gotten worse. It was hard even to know what had happened, since Themis, refusing to be pinned down or concede that anything was actually wrong, gave each doctor a different story. Once I realized she wasn't in serious danger, I grew peevish. (Who else but poor Themis could I vent my frustration on?) How could she do this to us? In the name of not being a "burden," obstinately denying her own mortality, she had refused to call us or tell us of her falls (or at least those we wouldn't find out about by the sight of black and blue marks on her face).

Another way of looking at it was that in our little medical melodramas, she and I were unconsciously trying to upstage Andrew and get some of the attention. After all, she'd been out there in Queens, all alone and unneeded, for weeks on end—not only unable to mother us, but starved of our calls and visits, our concern over *her* health. Now, briefly, she occupied center stage. We were like ninepins, Andrew falling, creating air vibrations and a void into which I would fall, then, in the vacuum I created, Themis falling. The whole thing had become surreal.

The problem, to paraphrase Oscar Wilde, was that to have two members of a family in the hospital at once might be regarded as a misfortune, but to have three looked like carelessness. The *appearance* of the thing! This was no longer serious life-and-death drama, it was farce: how could we face anyone and tell them? What would we have done without Mother? Now, truly, we were a one-family disaster area: people would cross the street to avoid us. Andrew, distraught at first, now got caught up in the absurdity of it. We milked the comic possibilities: Themis and I in New York Hospital, Andrew due to be back here in two weeks—they really should dedicate a wing to us, or at the very least give us Frequent Flyer rates.

I would lie in bed and as the loudspeaker called for one doctor after another, running through the entire roster of New York Hospital, I realized that I recognized practically every name. Not only that, I could affix a sum—his bill to us—for each. Dr. Manners—$600; Dr. Justin—$1,300; Peasley—$1,000; Robinson—$500; Seltzman—X amount, and so on. At one point or another, Andrew had been examined by every specialist in New York Hospital and in every field except gynecology.

Even if we hadn't been inclined to the ironic view, self-pity would have been impossible, for there were shadows descending all around us. Sy Peck, a valued friend and editor at the *Times*, was killed by a drunk driver on New Year's Eve. My roommate Pauline finally died during the night. It was strange—I seemed to sense it happening, through the thin curtain surrounding her bed, even though there was nothing to announce it, no abrupt cessation of breathing, no last gasp, nothing to mark off the stillness of life from the stillness of death, yet the stillness felt different. Eventually, a nurse came in and took her pulse; there was a scurrying, and then a doctor came and asked if I wanted my curtains drawn while they performed whatever verifications and ablutions were necessary, wrapped her and wheeled her out. But I said no, wanting to listen, feeling the sense of death in all its immediacy. We are rarely present when the moment comes for someone we love, and it was a chance to know what it had been like, what it would be like.

Themis and I only had a few more days left in the hospital, and Andrew, with his redhead, came up to visit us, going first to one floor, then the other. By now, we had become the stuff of legend. The nurses, his old friends, greeted him with jokes, our story was the talk of the hospital.

Peter, Andrew's therapist at Rusk, told me that Andrew had reached a plateau, that his leg muscles hadn't improved for two or three weeks and therefore mightn't improve further. I didn't take this any more seriously than I had taken his earlier gloomy prognoses, but it did occur to me as strange mounting to uncanny that both Andrew and his mother had this weakness of the legs. I could imagine both of them at Rusk, hobbling down the halls on twin walkers.

On Saturday, when I went home, Mother tucked me into bed and pampered me, bringing back childhood memories of the sickbed, of delicious, voluptuous hours of being helpless and needy when, as a little girl, I would lie in my four-poster bed in a quiet house and have her attention all to myself. She would make a fuss, puff up the pillows, bring juice and water—I'd ask for another glass, and another, for I loved the curved glass straw. And read me stories for hours on end in her precise, musical voice. And she would scratch my back. "Want a scratch-tickley?" she would ask.

"Mm-m-m," I'd murmur. And her fingertips would dance over my back, my arms, my legs, ten little one-legged ballerinas, up and down, over to the side, exciting and soothing me at the same time. In the afternoon, she'd leave me alone for a "nap," which I spent listening to *Sky King* and feeling smug about not being at school. Then she'd come in with some paperwork. Because her love wasn't forthright, but indirect, curved like the glass straw, I think I felt even more comfortable in these moments when I wasn't the immediate object of her attention, but remained in her marginal vision, half on her mind, while she did other things in my presence, when she would sit there answering letters, paying bills, making grocery or party lists, muttering out loud, and occasionally asking my advice or confiding in me. I felt like a spy, a mole in that grown-up world that was at once so alluring and so boring.

Then Mother and I had a fight, our first during this whole period, as if the time had come for us to let go, if only for a while, of whatever was holding us together. It came, as fights so often do, over that fine line between being well and being sick. There was a meeting of my women writers' group and I had casually mentioned I thought I'd go.

Mother was outraged.

"If you're well enough to go out, you don't need me," she replied, "and I might as well go home." She was right, I guess, but I wanted it both ways, wanted her to stay and mother me, but give me my freedom. Then came the fight, one of our rare and terrible fights that was typically not about quite what it seemed to be about. I didn't go to the meeting but got involved in long telephone conversations with friends instead. She would become furious when I wasted my meager supply of energy, and by implication took her for granted. It was very much the irritation I had felt when Andrew had turned to others for diversion.

We can't bear such "betrayals" by those we love because we sense that they are in part an escape from us, from the oppressive intimacy of familial love itself. "I have secrets I can't tell you, friends who understand me better than you," we are saying, in a desperate attempt to escape suffocation by the one who loves and understands us all too well. Mother's fury was at my withholding, and at my promiscuity.

She was seething now. "If you don't get off the phone this minute—" She left the sentence unfinished. We stared at each other for a moment, I magnetized by her hate, terrified but determined not to look away.

The anger was so fierce that I shuddered, remembering how I had felt as a child. It had seemed to come out of nowhere, and her lovely face would grow stone hard. Where was my Mummy in this Medusa, I would wonder, or was the stone woman the real mother, and the charming, mild-mannered one the masquerade?

I held the phone suspended, stricken. I couldn't say anything to my friend, but I couldn't say anything to Mother either. Neither of us would flinch. The anger on the surface stood for feelings so deep and inexpressible they could come out only in this way. We stared a moment longer and then, turning, my mother said, "I'm just disgusted," and again, as she slammed the door, "I'm just disgusted." The emphasis, the repetition, was as chilling as a gunshot.

By the next day, we were friends again, and Mother agreed to stay through Andrew's operation.

Themis went home from New York Hospital, arguing all the way—she didn't want a cane, she didn't want a walker, she didn't want a nurse's aide to come home with her. The hospital insisted on all three. Three days later, on January 17, I picked Andrew up from Rusk in his wheelchair, and took him to New York Hospital, where he would have surgery the following day.

And then, on January 18, the horror all over again, the pacing, the praying with an even greater sense of foreboding than the first time around. Why? Because it would be just like Andrew to have gotten through surgery that should have finished him off and then succumb to this relatively less serious affair. Perhaps somewhere within me I felt Andrew's unlikely survival had all been a mistake, and this time nature would make up for the oversight and recall him. If he died now, after we and the doctors had been through so much, it wouldn't be just a tragedy; it would be bitter, cruel, a hideous joke, and perhaps the ironist in me felt that this was the mode that nature had selected for our story.

It was a long but successful operation, and after an uneventful ten-day recovery (the NG tube hardly bothered him at all), he was home. Both Sam and Gaines had suggested he go back to Rusk for the recovery but we were sure we could handle it ourselves. I had been warned repeatedly about recovery, but nothing quite prepares you. For some time, ecstasy reigned, and I enjoyed playing nursemaid. A physical therapist and a nurse (for the dressing of the wound) came daily, but I took care of the rest, was a regular Florence Nightingale, fixing special foods, bringing him the paper, books, a glass of water, coffee, whatever he asked for. But by the end of two weeks, I was exhausted and my charity was running out.

"In sickness and in health," I wanted to say, "but not in recovery." He could walk, but only with a walker; thus he had no hand free to carry anything anywhere—a paper to the living room, an empty glass back to the kitchen. It was astonishing how many steps this required.

Count the number of times you get up to fetch something for yourself in the space of a morning, and double it. Also, when you're doing things for yourself, you choose your moment; when you're on call, your patient has no sense of time, your time.

This wasn't nursing, it was abject servitude. I had prepared myself not to expect too much. I knew Andrew was just one day, then two days, then a week better than he'd been at the hospital, and because of the surgery, he was a lot weaker than he'd been his last days at Rusk; and far from responding, or even appreciating my loving ministrations, he hadn't the slightest comprehension of what I was doing.

This taking-for-granted attitude was so unlike him that I had to figure it as endemic to men and part of the symptomology of illness. Had he been *aware* enough to appreciate my efforts, I argued on his behalf, he would have been well. The male patient is as unaware as a baby of his own exorbitant needs and the demands he makes; as content to be taken care of as a newborn calf. But then, there is something charming in a baby's groping efforts at self-sufficiency, whereas a grown man in the same situation begins to look like a malingerer. I suspected that Andrew, no great believer in the Protestant work ethic to begin with, was succumbing happily to the lure of regression.

"Do you know the fantasy I keep having?" he said on several occasions. "I want a big strapping man to pick me up in his arms and carry me around." Yeah, you and me, too, I wanted to say. I understood the fantasy of surrender, would have happily given myself over to a Tennessee Williams-ish giant masseur who would knead my muscles and crunch my bones into oblivion.

Also, after showering us with attention, our friends had suddenly abandoned ship. "I wanted to call you," they would say, "but knew you were too tired to talk," when in fact this was the one time (how would they know?) I desperately needed voices from the real world. I understood: we were no longer Problem No. 1, and everyone had turned their attention elsewhere. When callers came, Andrew would hobble in, looking winningly vulnerable and sweet and brave, and hearts would melt. He was funny, aware, heroic, and I was proud of him. Yet I was also baffled. Gone was the one-cell blob on whom I waited hand and foot and in its place the old scintillating Andrew who had somehow acquired a remarkable sense of what was going on in the world and now enthralled his captive audience with his latest observations on movies, politics, the cultural scene. I smiled generously, echoed the praise of our callers, and tried not to resent the fact that as soon as they left he would revert to a gaping mouth and two hands waiting to be filled. It was like one of those forties melodramas in which killers are holding a gun at the housewife's back and she has to pretend before the unexpected callers that everything is "normal." Andrew was holding me hostage but whom could I tell? Who would believe that this magnificent, struggling, articulate creature would revert, in the absence of an audience, to a primitive form of life who could neither give nor receive. Our culture reveres infants and invalids, insists on the image of smiling spouses, parents, caretakers, thus increasing our shame at the ignoble emotions we constantly feel. Our mythology does not allow for hate, resentment, for faces that grow sour with disgruntlement. Love alters—Shakespeare to the contrary notwithstanding—when it alteration finds. And if the alteration is permanent, then permanently. Even knowing Andrew wasn't altered permanently, my love wavered.

There was also the fact that I stopped feeling like a woman. Before, however becalmed our sex life, he had always *wanted* me, made me feel beautiful, desirable, remarkable. Now, he didn't *see* me; so that I not only felt dehumanized by my servant status, but unwomanned. I knew in my mind he couldn't help it, that there was no *energy* to engage in the mutual responsiveness of love, but that didn't help as I discovered in those strained days what a small part reason played in my emotional life and behavior. It was as if I was as sick and as primitive in my thinking as he was, as unable to do *without* love as he was unable to provide it. The future didn't exist. Our life together no longer had a shape I could count on, and in my resentment—never mind the sexual frustration—I would have had an affair in a second if anyone remotely plausible had turned up. This was unlikely, though, since I was housebound, unless it had been Gabor the super or a delivery man.

In fact, I finally had a night out, and a little flirtation, just enough to salvage my feminine ego without plunging me into the imbroglio of an "involvement." It was a professional gathering, and at dinner following the discussion I found myself seated next to our guest from Europe, one of those overcultivated and professionally amatory Continentals—not the sort I was usually drawn to but precisely what one requires for a one-night liaison. We drank a lot of wine, ignored our fellow diners, and, eyes glistening with the magnetism we projected onto each other, talked of Mozart, French movies, Italian cuisine, American women, European men, ourselves. When it was over, he brought me home in a taxi and kissed me passionately before depositing me and driving off. He'll never know how delicious that kiss tasted, or how grateful I was for being turned for one shining hour into a princess.

Not for long. It was back to my pumpkin the next day, scrubbing the figurative hearth with a less than cheerful heart. Then I exploded.

I got angry. Andrew lay there with a mystified expression on his face as I fumed, yelled, screamed, stomped around the apartment, and gave him what for. I accused him of malingering, of not loving me, of being an ungrateful oaf. I knew I had no "right" to get angry and that this display would have been, in Mother's words, "unworthy" of me, but that didn't matter. If anything, it was more exhilarating for the pure, mean, low-down irrationality of it. I was done with understanding.

I was faced with a situation in which my empathy—one of the qualities I prized most in myself—was of no use. Andrew was like a colicky baby who, by not responding to love, to caresses, to the soothing music of the mothering voice, cut the ground out from under me, rendering useless the very qualities on which the womanly/maternal self-image depends. No wonder the mothers of such infants feel an urge to kill.

Andrew was thoroughly unmoved by my anger, which made the whole thing easier. That way I could keep at it, as a sort of daily cathartic and even a source of adrenaline. If he'd been piteous and contrite, I don't know what I would have done, probably fallen apart, but as he remained in his own world of invalidism, I took refuge in my own weather cycle of storms and calms.

And gradually, of course, he improved, took more steps at a time, gained better balance, regained some of the muscle use in his legs. There was still a certain slippage and a sense of being at cross-purposes:

Andrew's illness set the rules for both of us, as the weak and the helpless inevitably dictate terms to the strong, while I in turn put extra pressure on him without meaning to. It seemed, in retrospect, that it would have been the better choice to have him return to Rusk after the colostomy closure. There, he would have been officially classified as sick, and I would have been more detached, less involved in the day-to-day recovery.

Then, as Andrew went from bed to walker and from walker to cane, from indoors to outdoors, from introversion to extroversion, our relationship began to come back as well—if anything, with more intensity than before. It seemed to happen overnight, as if we had willed it back into "normalcy" in order to blot out the memory of what had happened. Together we—or perhaps I, especially—moved on to the phase of euphoria. We were walking on air, unable to believe our good fortune. Andrew was going twice a week to New York Hospital for therapy; had resumed his *Voice* column, and had the summer before him to recuperate before returning to Columbia in the fall.

Oh, I'd have occasional nightmares, terrible ones in which Andrew was dying of strange new diseases. In fact, there had been a flurry of AIDS cases from blood transfusions, the highest proportion contracted in 1984, just before they'd developed the technique to screen blood donations—the very time Andrew had been given numerous transfusions. Then, there was a news report that 10 percent of those who have blood transfusions contract non-A, non-B hepatitis C. Mentioning none of this to Andrew, I tried to convince myself of the small likelihood of either occurrence, but we had already skewed the probability curve to such a degree that statistical reassurances carried little weight.

I began typing up the notes of my journal, but they looked alien, the strange and unbelievable story of someone else. It was still too soon, I was still too close to it, to assimilate the illness in any understandable way. It was like a nightmare I wanted to get behind me. There's a natural tendency after a disaster to suppress it and return to a normal way of life, as if nothing has happened. Or rather, as if what has happened is momentous enough, but over, not meaningful.

Then, disaster once again. On April 5, 1985, I was riding on the First Avenue bus when the familiar pain struck. But this time, it was worse, far worse than any I'd had before. I wound up in New York Hospital with a 9.5 rating on my pain scale, and with what I knew without an X ray was a total obstruction. All I remember is lying in a bright, sunlit room, and Sam asking me if I thought I'd need surgery, and me saying, "God, yes, do anything, cut off my feet if it'll stop the pain."

Gaines performed the surgery again, adding the Baker tube for good measure—this is a sort of rubber hose inserted through six or seven feet of small intestine to make it heal firmly, which is then withdrawn after ten days. Despite the fact that I still felt queasy, the hospital determined that I was well enough to go home after two weeks. But a week after that, barely able to eat, I was back in the hospital with an emergency obstruction. On May 5, a month after the last surgery, I was operated on for what turned out, to everyone's surprise, to be intussusception, an inversion of the intestine that occurs almost exclusively in children. In children, the obstruction, in which the intestine folds in on itself like a telescope, can usually be relieved by a barium enema. Mine had occurred near where the Baker tube had been inserted, this latest yet another "freakish" obstruction requiring surgery. I'd had a few centimeters of intestine removed, but I still wasn't being classified, in that most fatalistic of terms, as a "chronic repeater."

So Mother came up again, only this time Andrew was at home, and though they tried nobly to get along, there were inevitable collisions. The main one was over the telephone, and as Andrew described it, it was low comedy. During Andrew's illness, Mother had taken over phone duty for me and rather enjoyed it, talking to my friends and getting a sidelong glimpse into my life; it was one of the small dividends of the job. Now Andrew was there, eager to talk to people, but Mother refused to cede. The phone would ring, and the two of them would jump up, Mother racing to get there first ("You just stay there and rest, Andrew") while Andrew, handicapped by his cane, struggled after ("But Mary, I want to talk. They're *my* friends").

Andrew would come down every night, thus hobbled, to see me. And every night was a homecoming. No one could believe he was alive and on two feet. The nurses, our old friends, would gather round, and we would swap stories of Andrew's astonishing survival. People would glimpse him in my room and stop in. "Miracle" wasn't a word doctors and nurses used lightly, but it was often used in connection with Andrew.

It was an effort for him to come down, but it would have been unthinkable for him not to. We were twin survivors, responsible for each other's fate. His illness had been "my" illness; my obstruction was his as well.

One night the resident, a large, genial fellow about thirty, happened to come in just as Andrew was leaving.

"Was that Andrew Sarris?" he said. I nodded. He shook his head in disbelief.

"I was on duty when he came in for surgery back in—when was it?—the end of June '84. I watched Gaines operate on him, saw the wound, then I left for vacation. You know, when you go away and come back there are some patients you ask about with, well, hesitation. You hate to ask because you're pretty sure they didn't make it. With Andrew . . . I never even *asked*! It never occurred to me that he would survive."

A friend of mine was seeing Dr. Carrington, the neurologist who had covered for Ramir at various times during Andrew's illness and had kept abreast of the case. When he found out she knew Andrew, he shook his head in amazement. "That was the sickest man who ever walked out of New York Hospital," he said.

One day as I was trudging up and down the corridor with my IV and various other attachments, shuffling past other patients in their gas-promoting constitutionals, I ran into Alan Seltzman, the infectious-disease specialist who had figured so prominently in the drama. He was writing up Andrew's case history and we stopped to chat. His diagnosis, and title, was "Cytomegalovirus Encephalitis in an 'Immunologically Normal' Adult," and he was calling it the first reported case of cytomegalovirus-associated encephalitis and peripheral neuropathy. The virus had been causally implicated in a number of neurologic syndromes, including meningitis, meningoencephalitis, and polyneuritis of the Guillain-Barré type, but only seven cases of CMV encephalitis had been reported in the English literature. Andrew had had not only encephalitis but transverse myelitis (inflammation of the spinal column that resulted in paralysis and the pain in the feet and toes), with involvement of the spine and spinal cord. At first, there seemed to be no connection between CMV and the bowel perforation, but Seltzman had pursued the link, done some more tests, and found evidence of CMV in the form of transmural necrosis (dead cells) in the colon. Andrew hadn't had an immunologic deficiency. His immune system had been consistent with viral infection; he simply had an extremely abnormal reaction to the virus. Jeffrey had told me that some people have weird reactions to diseases like mumps and measles; their bodies overreact and start to produce antibodies and, in an autoimmune reaction, the cells attack healthy cells too. I asked Seltzman if it had been an earlier virus reactivated or a new one, and he said he couldn't tell, because Andrew had always had positive antibodies when tested.

"He had it in a very big way," said Seltzman, who clung to the view that CMV had been the sole culprit. "He had an extremely low antibody reading in the beginning, then over the course of the illness it rose significantly, thus proving the diagnosis."

When I got home from the hospital, Seltzman called. His first draft was rejected for publication, and he felt it was because he hadn't ruled out AIDS. No test had been available at the time, and now one was, so he asked if Andrew would be willing to come in for a blood test. We agreed, but it was something of an ordeal: because of all the blood that had been taken during his seven-month hospitalization, it took half an hour just to find an intact vein from which to draw blood. For several days, I was so nervous about the outcome, I couldn't call Seltzman, but he finally called to report that the test was negative.

After I came home, we were both swept up again in euphoria, the sheer joy of being alive together. We felt blessed, though Andrew's recovery was slow, and often it seemed as if his new failings—the lurching, uneven walk, the lapses in his speech, the tiredness—were not new failings, but accentuations of the old, as if the disease had simply taken up residence in his vulnerabilities and hurried him further along his own particular path of decline. When I complained to Sam that he "walked funny," Sam replied, "Molly, he always walked funny." And he was right.

Then it was Sam's turn. He had seen a note Andrew had written.

"What was Andrew's handwriting like?" he asked me in an obviously tactful manner.

"Oh, it was always terrible," I replied, to Sam's obvious relief.

Doubts about whether CMV could be blamed for the entire horror remained. Jeffrey, for his part, still felt that CMV was a "presumptive diagnosis," perhaps a piggyback to the real cause. No one could give categorical reassurances that it wouldn't recur, but most of the doctors seemed to feel that this was not likely and to be content with the miraculous recovery, however incomplete, that Andrew had made. There were jokes about what to call it: the "Sarris Syndrome" was suggested, but Andrew said he'd prefer other kinds of immortality.

We went to Ramir for a checkup, wanting to know if Andrew could expect total recovery of the damaged nerves. He was walking without a cane by now, and Ramir just shrugged his shoulders. That Andrew was alive and walking at all was so miraculous that nerve damage seemed incidental. He offered to give Andrew an EMG, which would have indicated whether the damage was to the central or peripheral nerves (the latter usually recover, the former don't), but Andrew wasn't interested, and we left it at that.

But it wasn't really *over*, not yet. Despite our euphoria, we became anxious about symptoms, ailments, hypochondriacal in ways neither of us had ever been before. Every time I had a twinge or gas pain in my stomach, I was sure I was on the verge of an obstruction, and in my journal are nervous recordings of friends' illnesses or suspected illnesses as if they might be my own—ovarian cancer, cystitis, bladder infections.

If we were nervous about ourselves, about each other we were even more so, living in a state of perpetual mutual anxiety, each seeing the other as hovering over a precipice about to fall. On a Sunday in June, Andrew left the apartment in Quogue, as he always did, to go for bagels and the *Times*. It had been raining all night, but five minutes after he left, it turned into a torrential rain, with thunder and lightning. Dune Road, which flooded at the slightest precipitation, would be a river. How could I have let him go out? I wondered, clutching myself anxiously. Never the most reliable of drivers, he was still a little shaky behind the wheel. The time crept by and when I could stand it no longer, I called the Quogue Market.

"Lady," the man said, when I asked him if someone fitting Andrew's description was there, "I've got four hundred people in here buying bagels!"

Somehow, the man's blustery echt-New-York nastiness reassured me, and indeed, pokey Andrew finally returned, to an embrace so hysterical with relief that it shocked even him.

If anything, his anxiety on my behalf was even greater. Once, we got our signals crossed about a location for a brunch rendezvous. We were each going to a different movie, then meeting afterward. After a half hour, when I didn't turn up at the restaurant where Andrew was waiting, he called Cinema I.

"Did an ambulance come to take a lady away?" he asked the baffled manager.

One night, after another missed rendezvous, I was late returning to the apartment, only to find the police there when I arrived. Andrew had gone to one theater and, not finding me, had come directly home. I had gone to another theater and, not finding Andrew, had gone inside to see the movie.

Andrew took his role as worrier more seriously than I did; he was like Dowell, the narrator in Ford Madox Ford's *The Good Soldier*, who becomes a perpetual nursemaid, first to his wife, then to the madwoman he loves ("How engrossing such a profession is," he says wryly). Illness and health had enveloped us both as ends in themselves; our worry had become a secret and "engrossing" land of sorrow and relief, a new "field of interest" like movies, books, tennis, that we could share more intensely and exclusively than we had shared anything before. Calamities can bring couples together or drive them apart, and with us, the magnitude of Andrew's illness, compounded with mine, had dwarfed the differences. There was a sense that we had to pull together just to survive. The healthy have room for maneuver and argument, can cling to their own ideals, are less patient with shortcomings, whereas we had come to cherish each other as if our lives depended on it. We gave in, accepted things we mightn't have accepted before. It was as if we had to find some solace, some compensation for the horrors inflicted on us and so had come to exalt and spiritualize the worry. The problem is that worry carried to such lengths creates an appetite for disaster, if only to justify it.

Whatever complicated forms of ambivalence underlay our mutual worry, I obliged by having two more emergency obstructions. The first, just after Thanksgiving in 1985, was resolved without surgery, but it had been the culmination of an extremely frenetic series of professional and personal crises. A violent argument between two close women friends in which I had tried to play mediator. Irritations at *Vogue*. A trip to Tennessee to interview a sexy singer movie star with whom I had stayed up half the night drinking and talking, and it would have probably gone beyond conversation if someone who resembled a plainclothes detective (presumably hired by the sexy movie star's wife) hadn't been hanging around outside the door. Then, back in New York, I had gone to see Part One of *Shoah*, Claude Lanzmann's disturbing film on the Holocaust, before meeting Andrew at the Murray Hill Racket Club for tennis. This was an inhuman schedule, particularly for someone not six months out of the hospital, but like many New Yorkers (why are we here to begin with?), I had come to see as normal what was clearly a manic tempo, riding the emotional roller coaster for the inevitable fall.

But when I went in again, in January 1986, for an obstruction and surgery, I could hardly ignore the fact that these "freak" afflictions were occurring with a frequency that went beyond the coincidental and that if this one hadn't killed me, perhaps the next one would. It wasn't just the surgery, it was the aftermath. As weeks stretched into months, I continued to be wiped out, waking at five in the morning, unable to work for more than an hour or so a day. Even talking to friends was a superhuman effort that left me exhausted. I would be panting after a phone conversation. The doctors could insist that obstructions were unrelated to stress, but I knew that on each occasion I had strained my energy supply to the breaking point, had cried out for someone else to do what I couldn't do myself: beat me, punish me, kill me.

If I didn't examine my life, my past, my marriage, whatever was driving me this way, I was doomed.

I thought a good deal about death, and what Andrew's would have meant to me. I had been fascinated by the double suicide of Arthur and Cynthia Koestler. He was seventy-one and had Parkinson's and leukemia, but she was a perfectly healthy fifty-five-year-old. Feminists had criticized her for throwing herself onto the pyre with her husband, as it were, for not having a sufficient sense of her own importance to remain alive. I found myself bridling, as usual, at judgment passed by a sane and reasonable person, an undepressed person, on an act so steeped in blind sorrow and rage as suicide. Moreover, I'd always felt not only that the tug to suicide was understandable, but that rejecting it each day gave us what little sense of free will we might claim. More than this, though, I felt a terrible bond with Cynthia Koestler, unable to stand apart from a marriage that a friend had described to a reporter as "impossibly close." I had several friends who'd lost husbands and who, though bereaved and suffering, had nevertheless carried on, made something substantial of their lives, but I didn't see myself as one of them. Why? I looked further into the story of Cynthia Koestler, and discovered an interesting fact: her own father had committed suicide when she was ten. Didn't the death and desolation exercise its subterranean pull? I felt sure that the blood in her veins carried the message of his, that her marriage and annexation to Koestler was a way of finding a surrogate god—a god who wouldn't fail—while fending off the morbid pull of the real father, the gravity of the grave that dogged her every footstep. By taking the father when he is young and in his glory, by preserving him in godlike unreality, death itself becomes darkly beautiful, desirable. Certainly no longer shocking, no longer an alien, but a guest at the dinner table, a familiar.

I knew that Andrew's illness had reawakened all the feelings, and fears, surrounding my father's death. Still, Andrew hadn't died, and the miracle of his being alive was enough to sustain me, give me gravity and buoyancy: he simultaneously held me to the earth and filled me with air. The upbeat surface of my life was Andrew-connected, and loving him continued to validate me. He had become even more lustrous in my eyes, more worthy of veneration. After all, getting sick repeatedly was *my* problem and not his. He had slowed down since his illness, but peacefully, it seemed, and with a feeling of contentment. They had cut his column back to biweekly at the *Voice* instead of every week, but with the same pay, and while this was initially a blow to his pride, he seemed relieved at the more relaxed schedule. He had always had a terrible time with deadlines, was happier with less pressure. He had emerged from his ordeal with a kind of inner serenity, magically sheathed from the slings and arrows of the world and his own demons. His journey down into madness and back up again, coupled with the staggering outpouring of attention, gifts, love that had so elated and surprised him, had seemed to exorcise his paranoia once and for all.

"My life has become a gift," Andrew said. "It doesn't belong just to me anymore." He had found a peace that eluded me.

At the end of 1984, the Los Angeles Film Critics Circle had voted on special awards to Truffaut and Andrew (thinking, no doubt, he would die) and a plaque hung in our living room. The New York Film Critics Circle had sent a magnificent basket of food (opposed, for its expense, only by John Simon), and when Andrew attended the meeting the following year, he was applauded. He was the conquering hero, Joe Montana back from the dead; he would go to Disneyland, there would be Andrew T-shirts and panda bears.

He was still a long way from recovered. When he tried to play tennis, he could move only a few steps, and his balance and concentration were extremely weak. But I didn't mind: his sloppy game, being no longer the product of a lousy player but of a handicapped man, was forgivable. He was precious, a revenant who had undergone a kind of catharsis, and just looking at him, touching his reborn flesh was a kind of sensual and religious experience. Far from being embittered by the failure of his body, he hardly seemed to notice it, and for me, this was part of the continuing ecstasy of the miracle.

His lack of narcissism had always been his most appealing trait and now he had less sense than ever of the figure he cut. Once I caught sight of him as I was coming home. He was walking up the sidewalk, not seeing me, bumping and lurching along like a sailboat on rough seas, teetering, grabbing the side of a building, but never falling, as if some gyroscope were at work within, keeping him aloft physically the way his inner grace kept him from toppling to misery or bitterness or self-consciousness as most people in his condition would have done. People would glance at him oddly (I thought of Sam: "But, Molly, he always walked 'funny' ") but he never noticed. He would see me, light up, and we would both be filled with the sense of the miraculous. Yet there was a difference: Andrew's happiness came from within, while my own was somehow more fragile, still tied to his existence. Beneath the surface euphoria was an unnamed untamed fear.

We all know the "consolations" of death, even if we don't utter them aloud. Death's horrible finality brings to the bereaved a certain liberation. Those who survive—and most people do, somehow—discover, in surviving, a self-esteem they didn't know they had, a measure of self-confidence that can't be gotten any other way. We see the effects of independence in widows who, following terrible grief, "blossom" after their husbands' deaths. Andrew's illness had awakened in me the fearful certitude that I couldn't exist on my own, with a gnawing sense of my own inadequacy, without providing me with the countervailing opportunity to prove that I could survive Andrew. There's also the relief of no longer having to fear that the person you love most in the world will die. He has. The worst has happened.

Yet—do I even need to say it?—I would have accepted being engulfed by fear, torn apart by insecurity and a shaky self-image, a dependency that violated my every principle, rather than lose Andrew.

At the same time, I had to know I could stand alone, that as a woman in a changing world, a world defined by choice and productiveness rather than reproduction, I owned my mind and my body was an organism that could run on its own. I had been raised in a gracious and patriarchal corner of the South, where it was expected that men —the kings who sat at the head of the table—would marry and take care of women for life.

Without marriage, who were we as women? Our path of individuation is a thing of stops and starts, a difficult passage through treacherous family waters because unlike men who are, from birth, pushed into the great world by mother and father, our social and psychological heritage is contradictory, we are sucked in and blown out like bellows. I had looked to marriage to resolve my contradictions. There's a French movie in which a beautiful woman, a drifter (played by the brashly sensual Beatrice Dalle), is "rescued" by a stranger whose first act is to command her to throw her journal into the Seine. He has found the diary in a taxi, located her, and he symbolically makes her his by having her discard this record of her life up until that moment. Which she does, gladly, lightly, eager for her meandering self to be taken over and given definition. This is what many of us do, or have done, in marriage, become tabulae rasae, erase the pages of our inner lives in order to present pure white pages for a man to write on.

I had entrusted myself to Andrew and now I wanted myself back. Writing this book, telling the story, finding words was thus a salvaging act, compulsive, necessary, a way of dredging my notebooks up from the Seine. "Everything exists to wind up in a book," Mallarmé wrote. Telling stories, finding meaning, are ways of bearing unhappiness and sorrow by transforming them.

Andrew and I, romantics and fantasizers by nature, had found an enchanted forest but its beauty was deceptive, stifling, and its fruits had become poisonous. We were "everything" to each other, made for each other, and so much of our erotic energy went into sustaining this myth of ourselves—we were larger than life, heroes to each other—that we had nothing left over for anything else. Like the troubadours, we were exalted as much by the expression of love—the pleasing sound of our words of praise, the exaltation of the intense feelings we had invested in each other—as by the object of our adoration; we were in love with our own lovingness.

Over the years we had grown together like two trees. The branches had filled out, the roots spread and entangled, giving us girth, but we had lost our distinctness of outline. Perhaps too much marriage is too much of a good thing and divorce is the antidote, like a pruning, the cutting off of dead branches that enables us to sprout new growth. As an alternative, writing the book was a way of turning the eye inward, applying the surgical knife to a relationship whose beauty was its seamlessness. I did not move from my enchanted world easily or without pain, a pain in whose stead I would gladly have endured a dozen operations, yet in the end Andrew and I began to move more freely, breathe a less rarefied air. Feeling my own wholeness more, I released him to be ordinary, stumbling, depressed, even monotonous without fearing that my own world withered and faltered, risked collapsing, with every misstep of his. The change wasn't earthshaking, not anything you'd notice from outside, yet gradually I began to experience a sense of fullness, of joy welling up from within. I began to relax and accept the previously suppressed parts of myself—my past, my voice, rhythms and inflections of the South that were as much a part of me as the blood in my veins. I don't know exactly what Andrew felt. For me, it was the sensation of planting my feet in the ground, the earth between my toes. Twigs and sand, mud, grass, worms, and on up, beautiful life, all of a piece. Of feeling deeply and continuously and in the marrow of my bones a reason for staying alive.

EPILOGUE

I had written the last chapter, completing the book, or at least what I took to be a first draft of it, when disaster, no respecter of happy endings or man-made patterns of order, struck again. It was Tuesday, August 2, 1988, and I was alone in Quogue when the telephone rang. It was Andrew calling from New York.

"Sit down," he said.

I did. "Your mother . . . ?" Themis had been bedridden since February, diagnosed as having Alzheimer's disease, and her mind had so deteriorated in the last few weeks that she spoke, when she spoke at all, only in Greek and could barely recognize Andrew when he called her on the phone.

"No." He paused. "I've got good news and bad news. The good news is that the New York Hospital Emergency Room is being renovated. You'd never recognize it." My heart sank.

"The bad is that I have to have emergency surgery. A small bowel obstruction. They'll operate in the morning."

Impossible! I'd had ten obstructions, four requiring surgery, and Andrew, not to be outdone, now had one, too. The day before he'd gone into New York on the Jitney, the special Hamptons commuter bus, with an upset stomach—too much good food and drink with friends the night before, we'd thought—and now here he was back at New York Hospital with adhesions from the abdominal surgery he'd had in 1984.

It didn't fit. Andrew's surgery, for a perforated colon, had been long and arduous and had certainly left an ample supply of scar tissue, but Andrew, unlike me, was not a holding-things-inside type. I remember talking to Gaines, Andrew's surgeon and then mine, about the lingering effect of adhesions. When I offered the opinion that Andrew would never have an obstruction, Gaines had, rather surprisingly, agreed, thus confirming my suspicion that stress and psychology played at least a triggering role in these supposedly purely mechanical occurrences. What made it even odder was that all through July, I had felt bloating and stomach pangs, possible precursor of an obstruction, and Andrew had been sick with worry over me. Had he, in that complicated symbiosis that still defined our relationship, taken on my symptoms?

After the shock, my first reaction when I hung up the phone was: We've got to separate, get apartments across town from each other. We were like some blighted figures out of Greek tragedy—a Curse on the House of Andrew.

On the phone, on Monday, when he was still feeling nauseated with what he thought was indigestion or the flu, Andrew had said, "We've got to stop worrying about each other so much." I'd seen other couples who, living in a hothouse of togetherness, went back and forth this way, exchanging colds, back problems, relatively nonlethal ailments. But we were killing each other with overidentification.

For the moment, I wasn't afraid for his life, after all, I knew pretty much what was involved—an operation of several hours, invasive, grueling, debilitating, but not life-threatening. So this left me free to think of his emergency as a retaliatory strike: he had sensed, with his extraordinary antennae, that I had finished a draft of the book, that I was exquisitely happy out there alone with my project. Perhaps this was a consequence of my efforts to put some distance between us. After all, a marriage grows and adapts to imbalances like the human body: it has its own lumps and defects and asymmetries to begin with—one leg longer than the other, one arm stronger, one foot bigger, one shoulder higher—and then, in a natural act of compensation, the opposing muscles and bones bulge or shrink, creating a balance, a working equilibrium. Any attempt to correct the asymmetry, to strengthen one side without addressing every part of the body, is likely to throw the whole system out of whack.

The book in itself was an act of secession. There was also the fact that in writing the book I was turning away from the "real," subjective Andrew, and creating a semi-fictional husband, my version, that might or might not accord with the way he saw himself. Like the natives who refuse to be photographed, convinced that the camera will steal their souls, he was mocking my ending, holding his hand in front of the camera. You think you've got me fixed, our story set in marble, he was saying, well, think again. Here's one more operation, one more wound, one more angry scar to mar the pattern of what you presume to call "our life."

I began pondering this latest event in the ongoing saga of our medical misfortunes, trying to wrest meaning out of absurdity. Meaning, at this point, meant magic. I would do anything in order to avoid feeling completely adrift on a sea of chaos. On an impulse, I checked an old datebook and realized, to my amazement, it had been August of 1981, exactly seven years ago, when our troubles began. More precisely, it was Tuesday, August 4, 1981, at approximately four in the afternoon that Andrew had driven me to Southampton Hospital for what turned out to be emergency surgery. And now, on Tuesday, August 2, 1988—almost the same day, and about the same time— Andrew had gone into New York Hospital. Seven years of hideously bad luck, seven years of playing invalid back and forth; you didn't have to be looking for metaphors or magic to see something biblical in this chain of events.

Then Andrew called again. He'd just been told that the obstruction was so severe they were going to operate that night, about 10:30, instead of waiting until the next morning. I had already made my Jitney reservation for the next day; it was too late to get in that night, which meant I would have to stay in Quogue and wait for the surgeon's call when it was over.

"Guess what else," he said, a note of irony creeping into his voice. "Gaines is away and my surgeon is his partner, James Clarke." Who was James Clarke? The son of the Dr. Clarke who had operated on me in 1982. We had now dropped down to another generation of surgeons!

I called Sam, who confirmed the seriousness of the problem and the need to operate immediately. I didn't have to remind Sam that we'd all been concerned in July that I might have the problem that Andrew now had. In his voice was a faint but unmistakable echo of my own incredulity.

"Sam, I can't believe this," I said. "It's like a curse. It's . . . creepy!"

"Well, use whatever word you want, I won't disagree." A startling admission from a medical man.

You could say that Andrew, having undergone major surgery, was a candidate for adhesions, but so were millions of others who never got them, and the number of these "freakish" occurrences that we shared between us did seem to contravene the laws of probability.

My reflex was to embrace guilt, to turn the slings of outrageous fortune against myself. Sometimes guilt gives us a toehold, a purchase on misfortune, when nothing else will do. Had Andrew's worry over me in July caused this? I began to blame myself, wondering what I could have done differently. Not pushed him to get his mother on Medicaid. Not told him about the pain I'd felt. But far from giving me a distance on the thing, blaming myself was another way of tightening the screws between us, appropriating *his* illness as he had done mine. It's like the ritual of guilt we go through when someone we love dies, as we imagine how we could have prevented it by "doing things differently," and thus abrogate the finality of death. We play it over and over again, going through the litany of "if onlys" (If only I had been there; if only I had gotten there sooner; if only I had spent more time with . . . if only I hadn't put so much pressure on . . .), as if we were watching a videotape of a horserace, seeing where the jockey went wrong, applied too much pressure, or failed to urge his mount onward at the right moment. Don't blame yourself, our comforters say, failing to realize that not only do we keep our dead alive in these "what if" fantasies, but in inserting ourselves importantly into their deaths, we magnify our roles in their lives. We create a new reality along the border between life and death, in which the two of us are running the race together, over and over again in minutely varying ways, always stopping just short of the finish line.

So perhaps the various ingenious ways I found to torture myself gave me some centrality in Andrew's new calamity. We couldn't bear to be left out of, upstaged by, excluded from, each other's misery. In one's transactions with guilt, there is no such thing as the Marquis of Queensberry rules, and I was suddenly hit from behind by the recollection of what I had written earlier in the day, about the "liberating" effects of a husband's death on his wife. It had been written quickly, and half ironically, with the full intention of further refining and modifying the thought, if indeed I included it at all, since, in my conscious mind, there was nothing in the world I wanted less than to be a widow, and no one for whom I felt more sympathy. Perhaps there are some feelings that tact should forbid us to express. Yet widowhood, the loss of Andrew, was the specter that had haunted and obsessed me for four years, the virus to which I hadn't developed an antibody. So much of what I was, thought, wrote, was directed toward coming to terms with that possibility, exorcising that horror. Yet there was now something ghastly about the fact that I had *just* written it. It seemed unavoidably like a "death wish" that nature would now fulfill. I had to talk to someone, some friend who would talk me out of what was fast becoming a hysterical and fatalistic conviction that I had willed Andrew's death.

I called Judy Rossner in Sag Harbor. Not only had we been together that past Sunday, but of all my writer friends, Judy was the most psychoanalytic. If Judy, who was sure that every itch and sniffle proceeded from psychogenic causes, who saw wonderful tapestries of Freudian designs where others saw dull coincidence and happenstance, told me I was off the wall, giving in to superstitious imaginings and "magical" thinking, I would believe her.

Which she did, and I felt better for a while, then went back to my magical thinking, found strange symbols and twists in the roles to which these periodic illnesses reduced us. Was this some kind of displaced desire to have a child? An inversion of the need to nurture into the need to be nurtured? Once a year, one of us got a big belly, went into the hospital, and came out . . . a child! Whom the other then had to nurse.

Both Sam and Andrew had told me that Andrew would go up about 10:30 P.M. One of the most terrible aspects of surgery for those who wait is that we begin watching the clock from the moment we have been told the operation will begin, even though we know the knife may not find its target until considerably later, and there is no one outside the surgical chamber to alert us to the delay. Stated times are about as precise as airline takeoff schedules, but we always plan for accuracy. Thus it was that nervousness set in at 12:15 A.M., and by 12:30 I was in a state of mounting dread.

From 12:30 on, I was convinced Andrew was going to die and no amount of argument from the rational side of my brain could convince me otherwise. I wanted to burn the computer on which I'd written those odious words, erase the whole book to which his (as it now seemed) inevitable death would be the ironic ending. As the seconds stretched into dead-of-the-night terror, the task was to some-how dull my mind or divert it from the path of morbidity. A small quantity of Valium calmed me a little, as did the tapes I put on my headphones, the sprightliest I could find. Rossini overtures and Mozart concertos did their glorious best, but my mind kept returning like a homing pigeon to the death theme. I found myself rehearsing wid-owhood, doing hypothetically what widows are always advised to do and in fact do automatically: I kept busy with details that related to death without actually confronting it in its true horror. I attacked such "practical" matters as the whole tangled mess of Themis and Medicaid and what I would do with her; I stewed over the chaos in which Andrew had left his papers, and how I would sort them out; I assigned tasks to Chevey, Mother, my close friends. I imagined what clothes I would wear to what kind of memorial service. I decided, with relief, on cremation: Themis was too disoriented now to know the difference. She had a family plot at some cemetery in Queens, and it had been one of my great and unadmitted fears during Andrew's illness that if he died, Themis and I would engage in an unseemly fight for his body, she insisting on his rightful place in the Sarris plot, I on cre-mation and the dispersal of the ashes into the air where I could join him. It was one of the differences between us: her strong religious faith and sense of rootedness, mine of belonging only to Andrew, my home-land.

Death. Every once in a while real death—the image of Andrew as no more, a life without Andrew—rather than this hypothetical event would overcome me like nausea; it would leap up through my bowels and stomach almost like a sexual spasm, the hair on my arms would prickle, and I'd push it back, down, away. And resume my "planning." But when it came, I once again felt that I couldn't live without him. "No, I can, I can live without him," I would say, the survivor battling the nonentity.

Finally, about 2:00 A.M., I could wait no longer. I called Sam's answering service and insisted the woman call and wake him. He called moments later, generously undisturbed by my disrupting his sleep, promised to check with the hospital, and call right back.

Surgery was still under way when he called, but had probably begun late.

"Molly," he said, "there's no reason to assume anything has gone wrong."

Somehow these words relieved me enormously. There was no reason to assume that if anything *had* gone wrong, Sam would know about it, but nevertheless his apparent confidence, the completely normal tone of his voice, was like a sedative. I was able to close my eyes until 3:15 when the telephone rang. It was Clarke.

"Well, we're finished and he's okay," he said, his voice calm but relieved. "It was a long operation. Four hours. There was so much scar tissue from the 1984 surgery that it took a very long time to get at the obstruction. In fact, it was the longest and most difficult of this type I've ever seen. That means—"

"A long and difficult recovery," I said.

"Right."

I went back to bed but couldn't get to sleep. I knew Andrew wasn't out of the woods yet. That the postoperative period would be dangerous, particularly with surgery of that scale and on a body that was no longer as resilient as it had once been.

All the way in, high on the adrenaline of Andrew's being alive, I wrote in my journal, thought, examined various symbolisms of this new disaster.

There were ironies: the last week of July I'd gone by New York Hospital for research purposes, to check out my impressions of flora, fauna, and architecture in a last, fond farewell. I could have saved myself the trouble.

And while I was at it, perhaps it was time to stop thinking of New

York Hospital as a way station, a place to which we went from time to time. New York Hospital was home. It was our apartment uptown that was the waiting room, until that great gray labyrinth would beckon, and we would crawl once again into its hideous lifesaving arms.

We had become characters in Jules Romains's *Dr. Knock*, a play (later made into a movie with Louis Jouvet), in which a doctor convinces the whole town that illness is its normal state and good health only an infrequent occurrence. Dr. Knock, the poet laureate of hypochondria, heralded himself as the doctor of the future. We were the future and his descendants at New York Hospital were our guardians.

Andrew was in the recovery room for a nerve-rackingly long time (twelve hours: his blood pressure had gone sky high). Finally, he was moved to a room, and I went to see him. The whole thing should have been a breeze, I thought, as I trudged up the walk. (There was construction of a new building under way: the Sarris wing?) I knew the path, knew the flowers, knew the procedures; I should have floated into the routine with the ease of a veteran star returning to Broadway for a revival of the vehicle that made her famous. Yet it didn't work out that way. First, high-pitched fear. Then depression when he couldn't really talk to me.

Even though Andrew appeared to be doing well, I was reacting as if it were 1984 all over again. Fear, then depression; depression, then fear. Why, when all seemed going peacefully and by the book? It was as if fear had a life of its own, had gotten into the bones and become a habit. It settled in as if it had never left, as if I had won no battles over my old dependency. I had nightmares, anxiety attacks; I could do no work and was wiped out by the tiniest effort. Maybe the response had some sort of chemical base, a variant of the posttraumatic stress syndrome suffered by the Vietnam veterans: perhaps my experience, like theirs, had turned into an enzyme, had invaded my system during the ordeal of 1984, had lain dormant and was now being reactivated. But I felt it only as a terrible and inexplicable weakness, something I had no control over, and I was baffled and ashamed at how pitiful, irrational, and helpless I was. My strength had been an illusion. My "growth" a mirage. My independence a joke. The triumph of the book's "ending" had been spurious.

When I walked down the corridor to Andrew's room, I smelled

the old familiar smell of adhesive tape, but it no longer smelled to me like a hospital. It smelled like Andrew.

I found myself taking buses and taxis, too tired to make the walk to New York Hospital, something I had done easily, twice a day, four years ago, and I couldn't tell whether it had to do with my being four years and several illnesses older or whether it was simply the ghastly heat of this particular August, the most remorseless month in the most oppressive summer the East Coast had ever had to endure. Whether it was just a worse-and-longer-than-usual inversion or the much bal-lyhooed and debated greenhouse effect, it had made July a misery and now locked the city in a thick, unyielding torpor that was unlike any heat I have ever lived through. My brain seemed infused with toxicity. My feet would hardly move, my mind couldn't concentrate. I kept feeling that my paralysis came from an inner weather, from an un-willingness to go through this again, some deep resistance to what was happening that lay beyond words, or at least beyond my power to acknowledge.

This was the worst of it, that I understood nothing. Nothing. I was at the mercy of swirling emotions but had no idea what they were about. If the climatologists with all their charts and computers couldn't decide whether the heat was from a depleting of the ozone layer or the tides in the Pacific Ocean, how could I understand what was going on in me, in my marriage? Where the hurricane was coming from or headed?

Andrew was woozy on morphine a good deal of the time, but when he wasn't hallucinating he was trying, in characteristic mental-macho posturing, to figure out what his "approach" should be. His "decision" (echoes of the power talk of previous dementia) was that "this time" he knew life couldn't go on in a business-as-usual manner (as opposed to what other time?), and so he would accept his fate without opposition. This apparently gave him a necessary sense of controlling his overall destiny by surrendering to this particular calam-ity. It was what he was inclined to do in any case, to let nature take its course while wresting the offensive with laser-beam insight, his "mastery" consisting not in power games and naked assertions of might, but with game plans and considered opinions. His laser beam was a bit clouded now, but as a disaster and doomsday freak, he was in the place he was usually happiest, a situation of Beckettian bleakness out of which he could draw unsentimental conclusions, his own ability to face it down being the redeeming and life-affirming dimension of disaster.

But Andrew was so busy being heroically rueful that I felt shunted to one side, as I had been during the recovery period in 1985.

While he was hatching plots and I was humoring him, we were both holding our breath for fear Themis's nurse would call. We had decided not to let her know Andrew was in the hospital—she had seemed past understanding anyway the last time we'd seen her, mumbling in Greek, thinking she was already on the other side, with her mother, father, sister. She was used to hearing from Andrew every day, but now she didn't know morning from afternoon, day from night. Although she'd been diagnosed as having Alzheimer's by two different hospitals (New York and Queens General), I had my doubts about the diagnosis—she'd never developed paranoia or shown the kind of frenzied hyperactivity one sees in Alzheimer's patients, never suffered a personality alteration. Still her mind and body were deteriorating rapidly, and incontinence and disorientation were signs of organic brain disease. By July this woman who used to love to swim, walk, and especially talk was barely able to get out a sentence. I would feel such a mixture of emotions—exasperation, love, awe, delight, and a wish to see either the old Themis back or this one disappear—as I watched her lying there, her silver head like a moon on the pillow.

She had never seemed more easy for me to love than now, when she was no longer so overwhelmingly physical. Her exuberance no longer filled the room and used up all the oxygen. This woman who, as Andrew once wryly quipped, "outdazzled the son," had subsided into a quieter, more life-sized woman. She still laughed but less raucously, and for once she accepted being on the receiving end. It was *I* who occasionally cheered *her* up, made jokes, brightened her day.

"*Keeta halya!*" Andrew used to say at our Saturday visits, his hands thrown open at his sides, and she would repeat it, a phrase that, roughly translated meant "Look at this mess!" or "Can you beat this!" With these words, members of the family had stared down the effronteries of fate, Andrew as a child in the hospital, the family on its way to the poorhouse. It was a sign of their closeness as a family, a confirmation that if they had each other things could never be so bad that they couldn't also be ridiculous. Or Andrew would hold up five fingers and ask her how many—the mental test they had performed on her, to her amusement, at the hospital—and when she gave the correct answer, we would all laugh, and assure her she wouldn't be carted off to the mental ward in Queens General. As long as she could say "five" in English, and roar with horrified remembrance at the spectacle of Queens General Hospital (where she was in a ward, no one spoke English, and patients would come in bloodied, drugged, and in hand- cuffs, led by the police) we knew she was still with us. But in July she no longer laughed at the jokes, no longer said "five" when Andrew held up his fingers. Nor did she look out of her window, at the changing of the seasons, at her own beloved ocean of pavement and grass.

When Andrew went into the hospital, we decided that telling her—assuming that she was able to comprehend—might alarm her more than not seeing him. I worried that she might not be able to sleep: she'd been taking 2.5 mg of Valium a night for a couple of months, and because nurse's aides are prohibited by law from admin- istering that type of drug directly, we had been leaving the right number of pills for Themis each week. But as each day went by, and we didn't hear anything from the nurses, we breathed a sigh of relief and assumed she was all right.

All of this time, I had been anxious about Themis for Andrew's sake, how her deterioration was tearing him apart, how her death would remove one of the two figures in Andrew's narrow circle of love. But now I realized how I dreaded her death for my own sake, clinging to her more fiercely than Andrew, who had a philosophical resignation much like Themis's own. He had a spiritual preparedness for loss, for he knew that nothing and no one really belongs to us; we are blessed when we are given the gift of another person for a while, a month or a lifetime, but the time must always come when we let go, and pass lightly out of each other's hands and keeping.

Once, almost twenty-two years before, Andrew and I had broken up. We were on a train coming back from Richmond and a tense family gathering. I was sitting by the window, Andrew beside me, Pennsylvania flying past, almost in New Jersey, a sprinkling of people in the car, two black boys giggling, a man reading a paper, an older woman with a nosy grandchild who kept hanging over the back of her seat and looking at us. I had made my decision and I waited, choked, for Andrew to explode, cry, fall at my feet and plead his case, but to my surprise, he hardly reacted at all. He just sat there, as if he'd expected it all along, as if my breaking up with him were a foregone conclusion.

"It's always been your choice to make," he said. "I knew I could never persuade you or force you. You would choose to stay . . . or to leave."

Within twenty-four hours I was rushing back into his arms. It was those words that had won me over. That simple phrase of philosophical acceptance, with its majesty, its nonpossessiveness, with its offer of freedom, chained me more completely to Andrew than the wildest and most lyrical declaration of love, or a pledge of commitment, would have done. The man who tells a woman "You're free" is the man who tells a woman "You're mine," for what woman can resist the man who seems to give her what she can never give herself: independence.

The sense of doom, that Andrew and I had reached some jumping off point from which death might be the only escape, was only fueled by the apocalyptic, climatic horrors of a summer in which hospitals were dumping debris into the oceans and the planet was unloading fossil fuels into the ozone layer. Our home was a city that was unlivable in an atmosphere that was unbreathable.

The world around me confirmed, as it often did with me, my prevailing mood, an inner anxiety, the feeling of being cut off, unloved and undesired. I seemed to have learned nothing from Andrew's earlier illness and recovery: I went through the same sense of annihilation, of feeling that without being able to give and receive Andrew's love, I ceased to exist. I couldn't see that Andrew's love for me—or its *expression*—had merely gone underground for this period and would resurface; it was as if it had disappeared and I along with it.

But gradually, it dawned on me that there was something excessive in my reaction. My fears had no basis in objective reality, and were so far beyond my control that they might have been issuing from another person—my childhood self? In some distant and long-ago region of my mind, a terrified child was crying, and that cry was powering the engine. The early fear—the fear of abandonment—lies in wait, crouched, ready to spring forth. This new crisis, this coda, was like a restaging of the original horror, enabling me to see just what I had been about. I realized also that in some profound way I had split myself off—Andrew was the repository of all that was kind, loving, generous, while all the bad was in me. Now I began to pull back. Surely I wouldn't be as devoid of inner resources, as emptied by loss, as I imagined. After all, I *had* survived my father's death: and it was perhaps my success in transcending that loss for which I was paying now. It was of my strength, not my weakness, that I was afraid. The reflex of weakness is the one with which we are most comfortable as women, for if we acknowledge our strength, we create the conditions for solitude. If I had run from women and identified with men, if I had squirmed under the onslaught of Themis's life force, expunged my mother from my own nativity myth, it was perhaps their strength as women rather than their "inferiority" as females that frightened me. For they were strong . . . and alone. Yet solitude, too, is a condition we guiltily yearn for while protesting otherwise. Annie, who had come rushing pell-mell back into my life, told me that when she broke up with her husband she went north to her little country house, got in bed, and took pills and drank vodka for three days, moaning her aloneness. Then, suddenly, she woke up, realized she was happy. It became her secret, one she would never dare admit to anyone, even herself. The flare-up of guilt that seized me when Andrew called on August 2 with news of his emergency surely had something to do with my previous state of mind—how peaceful I felt out in Quogue without him. Being alone and liking it is, for a woman, an act of treachery, an infidelity far more threatening than mere adultery.

Themis and Mother were not so unlike after all—Greece, like the South, was a matriarchy pretending to be a patriarchy. Only Mother and Themis had stopped pretending long ago.

The myth of our helplessness is part of the myth of male superiority, yet if anyone's lives were a testimonial to overlapping roles, ours were. We had endured everything, the irritations, the separateness, those moments when you look at the other person as if he is a stranger, can't imagine what love felt like, life holds its breath, and the next day or the next hour, you are in love again.

I brought him home from the hospital on a Monday, installed him, and on Wednesday, we decided I had better go out and see Themis. The nurse's aide had called while Andrew was in the hospital, and we'd told her what had happened, but to play it down if Themis asked, just say Andrew had the flu.

When I went out to Queens, it was with some trepidation. Would she know me? Would she be able to talk? I stepped into the living room: her face was to the window. As I walked noiselessly across the rug, she suddenly turned toward me and said, in a voice as clear as a bell,

"Where's Andrew? What happened?"

I was stunned. I explained.

"Thank God," she sighed. She repeated the phrase, over and over, and it made me shudder to realize how on some level she'd sensed Andrew's absence, feared trouble, suffered. How that fear had gripped her, swelled and tortured her without her being able to express it. Yet also how that same fear had—it was the only word for it— miraculously brought her round, for if she wasn't "all there" in the old sense, she was infinitely more "there" than she'd been in ten months. What other explanation was there? Possibly Valium with- drawal; she'd been taking a tiny amount, but older people fail to metabolize tranquilizers the way younger people do, and even a small dosage can cause severe mental problems. But I knew Themis too well not to sense this remarkable focusing of the powers had to do with Andrew. She had played the patient long enough—her decline had angered and terrified him; it was time to be the mother again.

I went out to see her a week later, and the recovery was even more remarkable. Her bedsores had healed, she was eating with relish, talking and laughing. It was becoming increasingly clear she didn't have Alzheimer's, which is irreversible. Tests, though far more reliable than they used to be, are still unable to definitively diagnose the disease, which can be conclusively demonstrated only by brain biopsy, i.e., in postmortem. Americans are in love with diagnoses, but diagnoses are words, handles, categories that tell us very little about the individuals, the variations within, and they are false friends because once we've pronounced the word—Alzheimer's, AIDS, cancer—we think we've said it all, or at least a good deal more than we have. What did cytomegalovirus mean, after all? For most people, a mononucleosis-type illness; for AIDS patients, an opportunistic infection that might kill. For Andrew—an assault that shipwrecked him and in whose symptoms the doctors could find nothing that resembled their previous knowledge of the disease or anything they might meet with again. CMV, the diagnosis, told us nothing, cleared up none of the mystery. Like "love," another all-purpose word that covers too great a diagnostic field without explaining. Is it an addiction, a neurosis, or God's greatest gift to human beings? A neurological or a psychological state, or both? When Death came calling, Andrew hadn't been ready to go, and given a similar opportunity, Themis hadn't gone either. This was a woman mystical beyond imagining, strong as an ox, spiritual in ways that we secular humanists could never understand, and so attuned to her child that any danger to him would bring out the tiger in her immune system.

She was still incontinent and thought she was in Greece a good deal of the time, or in some Other World where her parents and sister were.

"So where are you now, Themis?" I asked her.

"Well, sometimes I'm in this world, sometimes I'm in the other one." She paused. "I can go either way," she said, and we both laughed.

"That sounds like a pretty good arrangement," I said.

"What, dahling?"

"You heard me."

A week or so later, when Andrew was well enough, we both went out. She was thrilled to see him, but she was concerned that I had missed a day she had expected me to come.

"Molly," she said, "are you mad at me?"

"No, Themis," I said startled. She'd never before asked me such a question. "Why would I be mad at you?"

"Because I didn't help you when Andrew was sick."

"You mean in August?"

"No, the other time."

I was stunned. "You mean four years ago? In 1984?"

"Yes." She paused. "I didn't know how sick he was." Another pause. "Forgive me, Molly."

The irony of it: now, finally, the words I had wanted so much to hear during those long hours when I had felt isolated, childishly enraged and furious at her seeming imperviousness. Of course it was clear now that she had been unable to face the seriousness of Andrew's illness: perhaps, in defense or denial, her mind had started to go, to shut down, at precisely that moment. In collaboration, her legs had begun to deteriorate rapidly, too, so that her inability to *be* there at the hospital—mentally, and then physically—had enabled her to fend off the unimaginable horror of Andrew's dying. Now, for reasons that might never be satisfactorily explained, she was coming back. Her mind. Her legs. Her zest. She could sit up a little. She could wiggle her toes.

"It's okay, Themis. Everything turned out all right." And indeed, her Buddha-like presence, her very imperturbability, had provided that massive and unmoving target for the anger I couldn't possibly express toward Andrew, and thus had done more for me than any amount of direct support could have done. I hoped some part of her sensed what she had been to me—a lightning rod for all the tangled emotions, a lifetime of rage, envy, hatred, love, that I had never been able to release on their appropriate targets. Her love was monumental, un-inflected, unchanging; I had felt safe unleashing the poison darts, secret hates, for she would merely deflect them.

"It did, didn't it?" she said happily. "I always knew it would." And she did. "And don't think you're getting rid of me yet," she continued. Andrew was in another room, hunting down some papers. Her voice lowered. "I don't really want to live, Molly," she confided, "but I don't mind. I'm staying alive for Andrew. If I died, it would make him sad."

And me, Themis, I wanted to say, have you any idea how sad it would make me?

How stoically reticent our two mothers were with respect to their feelings, how used to not burdening us with requests for thanks or forgiveness or love. I had visited Mother briefly during the summer and we were having dinner out. Mother, by her own admission, had never supported my writing, believing I would be happier settling down to a more traditional life, since it was what she had chosen over painting and—so she maintained—never lived to regret. Nor, being especially reserved and secretive herself, was she at all enthusiastic about a book that would expose even a corner of her private life. Yet there seemed some subtle granting of permission, if only in a backhand way. She suddenly referred to my first book, about women in film.

"You know, you had that passage about your father. About when you were at Broad Street Station and he bought you the movie magazine with Elizabeth Taylor in *National Velvet*."

She described it in surprising detail.

"You never mentioned me in the book at all."

I was stunned, first at my own omission (I hadn't thought of it as "leaving her out"; after all, it was a film book), then by the bruising she had felt all these years. Here it was she who had cared for me day in, day out during my childhood, driven me here and there, soothed me when I was hurt, worried with me over my problems, and set me an example of poise, courage, and gallantry through the years of her solitude. Yet it was my father who, by dying early, by being a father, had become precious, turning my moments with him into the sacred touchstones of my life.

Andrew was still relatively weak but we were talking now. After two weeks in which all we had discussed was his breathing, his bowel movements, how many feet he'd walked, the suppurating wound, the gradations of redness (during which time my only thrill was the smell of that tape on his skin), we finally had real conversations. Lying in bed, we talked of movies, books, politics, of the just-announced Republican vice-presidential nominee, Dan Quayle, an instant joke and symbol of the mediocrity to which politics had sunk. It was four years later, we'd come full circle: another election, another opportunity for collective breast-beating and national despair. Yet we were glad to be alive to join in even so bleak a world as we now lived in, glad because we had each other, a finger in the dam of a collapsing universe.

I thought, as we talked, of the line Andrew had once written in a review—was it of Dreyer's *Gertrud?*—in which he had seemed to anticipate our life together before it had really begun, pinpointed precisely what it was that drew us to movies, and to each other, suggested exactly what kind of man he was and why I would never find another man I could love as I loved him. "There is no greater spectacle in the cinema," wrote Andrew, in one of those lyrical hyperboles for which he was famous, "than a man and a woman talking away their share of eternity."

It was about nine o'clock and I was describing a movie I had just seen at a screening, "acting it out," a grotesque pseudo-poetic hillbilly epic starring Kelly McGillis and Kurt Russell. We had the windows open—it was the first night in a month we hadn't needed the air conditioner, and there was a breeze coming in. There were faint noises down below, the lonely peaceful noises of August when children and dogs were away, a plane in the distance, a bus wheezing up Carnegie Hill. As we continued to talk, Andrew's hand came to rest on my leg and then to rove, desultorily, along its surface. It was a familiar, involuntary gesture, one that I loved. I held my breath, against the moment when it would stop. The fingers played over my bare skin, stroking lightly and unselfconsciously. If I said anything, called attention to the motion, it would cease to be involuntary. Andrew's fingers, determined to do "even better," would constrict, curl up like snails, or plow forcefully into my leg, and the almost magical spontaneity of the gesture would be lost, the caress that came and disappeared like the touch of a butterfly's wing.

I was better able now to accept our separateness, even the idea that there might be times when Andrew wanted nothing to do with me. Or when I wanted nothing to do with him. I was reclaiming my spiritual territory and absorbing into myself those qualities I had admired in and projected onto Andrew. Idealization is an addiction, harder to kick than drugs or alcohol, and what had made it more difficult was that Andrew's remarkable survival had confirmed his status as hero, that figure in primitive cults who, as Ernest Becker points out in *The Denial of Death,* could go among the spirits, descend into the world of the dead, and return alive. Yet I had descended, too, in my own way, sustained by the very ideals I had attributed to Andrew, the ones that had lifted me, lived within me, made me what I was. The danger of idealization, as psychiatrists point out, is that in suppressing anger, aggression, sexuality, ambivalence, anything that might tarnish the myth, we cease to see the "real person." But what is the "real person" but a living and breathing and changing being, one capable even of rising to the heights in which idealizing love has cast him. The things we learn looking up are the things that make us change: the heartbeats of desire that lead us into new areas, patterns of thoughts, wells of feeling we never knew existed. Because of time and will and an evolving consciousness, we are constantly transforming ourselves —and consequently the magnetic field that is marriage. That is why, as Auden wrote, "any marriage, happy or unhappy, is infinitely more interesting and significant than any romance, however passionate."

Our life redescended to the mundane, the trivial, the domestic, to turf warfare, to dear, terrible arguments over acceptable degrees of messiness, clutter, fingerprints on the walls. Battles redeemed by irony and sanctified by the narrow escape we had had, but no less intense for that. The unvarying aspects of dailiness were as much the context of love as the peaks and valleys, and with it a recognition that the things we love and dislike in a person are hopelessly intertwined.

What most attracted me to Andrew was what also occasionally oppressed me: his thereness. Monumental, physical, pervasive. The people who stick around bear the brunt of the anger and disappointment created by those who've abandoned us. Unlike my father, who had disappeared in his prime, Andrew had served notice: he had no intention of leaving before his time.

And he would render *his* version (he hinted), his memoir of the evolutionary path of his life of which I had given only a glimpse, *my* glimpse, having appropriated him in the way that all writers do. The tenderness I felt for him was a thousand times more than it had been, the love more robust, the appreciation grounded in an accumulation of kindnesses, one of which was that he had allowed me to make of him what I might.

In going through some old albums, I found a photograph of my mother and father taken shortly after they were married, before my brother and I had arrived to divide their attention and confirm them as a family. My mother looks hauntingly elegant in a crisp white blouse and dark tailored suit, my father in his major's uniform and cap, so dignified and aristocratic, so separate and mysterious. I am seized with curiosity but can guess nothing of the feelings that passed between them, the tensions, what they might have said just before or after the camera clicked, or what feelings flickered below their half smiles. Like characters in a play to which I've not been given a script, they belong to a different time and place, live by different rules, in a world in which marriage seemed more preordained. And then I find a wedding picture of me and Andrew. I am laughing, wearing a wedding dress that tells a story of compromise, i.e., it is traditional white yet mini-skirt short, Andrew smiling sheepishly in his morning coat. And I cannot feel my way back into what we were any more than I can understand my mother and father.

I suddenly have a terrible desire to find out, to ask my mother and father, Andrew and me, "What were you thinking. *Then?*" And they look up at me, all four of them, surprised and uncomfortable, and say something to get rid of me as politely as possible. They are living in the moment, young, depending on a benign fate. Their mystery is intact, yet I will tug at it and worry over it anyway, draw lines of connection, find figures in the carpet, for imagination is the only power we have to keep them alive against our own terror of the void.

At one point, I had backed off from the book completely, worried about "using us up" in the act of writing, but I realized we were no longer the same people we had been when I began.

Perhaps a good deal of what kept us going through the ordeals and transformations was sheer luck. We were together not because of any genius or special application, but because we hadn't failed. That was the big difference between happiness and unhappiness, marriages that "worked" and those that fell apart—a thin line on a spectrum, the luck of not having failed. The luck of not having lost a job, the luck of finding the other person's humor more often funny than not, the capacity for surprise, an aptitude for not bumping into each other too often, congenial line readings.

We were free to leave anytime. "Just because we've been married for twenty years," Andrew said disarmingly, on our twentieth anniversary, "that's no reason to stay married." But who would I find more interesting than Andrew? And who would he? We had worn well, our neuroses had meshed and we had shifted to fit: I was heavier now, and less weightless, and Andrew was lighter, less burdened with the need to shore me up and play God.

If I had turned the searchlight inward—obsessionally—it was because I had reached a point where I had nowhere else to go. The shipwreck—Andrew's near dying—had created one of those disturbances in the rhythm of one's life in which we find the illusions and consolations we have lived by suddenly called into question. If we are fortunate, and I was, such crises may contain an element of marvel, lead to a reshuffling of the atoms of self.

It is, perhaps, only after we risk complete separateness that we can accept the emotional indebtedness that underlies all relationships, the degree to which we are always, by implication, part of a couple. We are born into the blissful twosome of mother and child, wrenched away, and seek ever after to recapture that early sensation of oneness with another, and of knowing ourselves through the other's eyes. The process of coupling and uncoupling is the dance of life, and Andrew and I, rickety on our feet perhaps, and shorter of breath, were still dancing.

For some people it is that way: we became part of a couple and before we know it we no longer have the option of seeing life entirely through our own eyes again.

We had found each other, sniffed each other out, become each other's destiny through some bizarre process that went back too far into our pasts for us to completely fathom. It was enmeshed in our fantasies, in the shaping of our lives from the moment of birth onward.

"How did we find each other, Andrew?" It was a question I loved to ask.

He shrugged. "The ball just took a funny bounce."

He was still as full of platitudes as Chairman Mao and I was still hooked, infected, in love. The mystery remained unsolved, the diagnosis incomplete. And I knew that if I had to go through it all again, I would. Again, and again, and again.